ISBN 978-1-334-09114-8
PIBN 10643773

1 MONTH OF
FREE
READING

at
www.ForgottenBooks.com

By purchasing this book you are eligible for one month membership to ForgottenBooks.com, giving you unlimited access to our entire collection of over 700,000 titles via our web site and mobile apps.

To claim your free month visit:
www.forgottenbooks.com/free643773

English
Français
Deutsche
Italiano
Español
Português

www.forgottenbooks.com

Mythology Photography **Fiction**
Fishing Christianity **Art** Cooking
Essays Buddhism Freemasonry
Medicine **Biology** Music **Ancient**
Egypt Evolution Carpentry Physics
Dance Geology **Mathematics** Fitness
Shakespeare **Folklore** Yoga Marketing
Confidence Immortality Biographies
Poetry **Psychology** Witchcraft
Electronics Chemistry History **Law**
Accounting **Philosophy** Anthropology
Alchemy Drama Quantum Mechanics
Atheism Sexual Health **Ancient History**
Entrepreneurship Languages Sport
Paleontology Needlework Islam
Metaphysics Investment Archaeology
Parenting Statistics Criminology
Motivational

6m

MEMORIES AND BASE DETAILS. By Lady Angela Forbes :: :: :: ::

*With Photogravure Frontispiece
and 24 Illustrations*

LONDON: HUTCHINSON & CO.
PATERNOSTER ROW

LIST OF ILLUSTRATIONS

FOREWORD

I FEEL that a word of apology is due to a long-suffering public for having yet another autobiography thrust upon them. The idea was not my own and I must plead guilty to having succumbed to the possible financial advantages which might be the result of the publication of my " Memories and Base Details." I do not believe that anyone, however fond of advertisement, sits down deliberately to lay bare their life for dissection by a ruthless public, unless the consideration of L. S. D. is at all events lurking in the background. The autobiographer's path is beset with pitfalls. For the book to be a seller it has to appeal to all sorts and conditions. A heterogeneous public has to be catered for, and one man's meat may be another man's poison. Some people enjoy the dinner-table intimate conversation, but the diners probably become your enemies for life. The intimacies of every day life may appeal to a certain section of the public, while to another, domestic details are boring.

To plough the furrow of one's memory, to unearth incidents, long grown dim, but which the reader expects to have related in detail, is not an easy matter. Through the mirage of time events lose their proper proportions as one views them on the skyline of recollection, and one is apt to exaggerate or to belittle their relative values. Apart from this, the autobiographer has to be candid without being caustic, and, above all, he or she must know when to be reticent.

Should there be any merit in truthfulness then my memoirs will go out equipped with one virtue, for I have written nothing that I cannot verify.

ANGELA FORBES.

PART I

MEMORIES AND BASE DETAILS

I

THE very first event of importance that I can remember with any clearness is my half-sister Daisy's wedding to Lord Brooke* in Westminster Abbey, the organ pealing forth " O perfect Love," and myself, small and insignificant and rather chilly about the knees in my ultra-short chiffon bridesmaid's frock, hugging to my chest a huge bouquet of Maréchal Niel roses.

I was evidently not so impressed with the importance of the occasion as I should have been, for I spent my time chewing off the heads of the roses, and most inelegantly, though dexterously, blowing them as far and as hard as I could among the congregation. I can still see Evie Pelly (in after years the Duchess of Connaught's lady-in-waiting), who walked with me, looking thoroughly shocked at my bad manners, and Prince Leopold, who was best man, asked me afterwards if I had enjoyed my breakfast !

At the time of Daisy's wedding I was just five years old, so I think I can be forgiven if I do not remember very much about the ceremony ; but I do know that Daisy looked lovely and that the Abbey was crowded with people.

From every point of view it was a most important

* Earl of Warwick.

wedding. The historical memories that clustered round
Warwick would have sufficed alone to arouse public
interest in the event ; but, added to these picturesque
associations, Daisy was also a figure of no small importance. She was a great heiress and beautiful, and these
" virtues " rarely walk hand in hand.

My mother, who was a Miss Fitzroy, was first married
to Colonel Maynard, who died a few weeks before his
father, leaving her with two little girls, Daisy and
Blanchie (my half-sisters). At Lord Maynard's death
Easton and all his possessions, therefore, went automatically to Daisy.

Mother's second marriage took place a year or two
later, and I, Angela Selina Bianca, was born in 1876,
the youngest of seven, and practically an afterthought !
My entrance into this world caused a considerable amount
of excitement, as my mother had been desperately ill in
Edinburgh some weeks before, and the doctors did not
expect me to live. Contrary, however, to their expectations, I turned out to be an extraordinarily healthy
child. Millie,* my eldest real sister, was most consis-
tently snubbed as a child, and used to be called the " Ugly
Duckling." It is amusing now to remember this, and
impossible to believe that at the gawkiest age she could
ever have deserved the epithet !

After her in quick succession came my two brothers,
Harry† and Fitzroy, of whose quarrels as small boys
I have a constant remembrance, and then my sister
Sybil‡ ; in after years people found it difficult to decide
which was the better-looking, she or Millie.

My arrival, five years later, put me into rather an

* Duchess of Sutherland.   † Earl of Rosslyn.
‡ Late Countess of Westmorland.

isolated position, and I looked upon my brothers and sisters, and certainly my half-sisters, as quite elderly relations !

My thoughtful parents provided me with a wonderful pair of godmothers ; even in these days, when every other person is considered a heaven-born product of sorts, the names of the Baroness Burdett-Coutts and Lady Bradford cannot be dismissed with airy grace by people who now only remember them by hoary anecdotes.

Baroness Burdett-Coutts was a sweet-looking woman, who always wore a quaint shawl folded across her shoulders in Early Victorian fashion, and I have a most vivid recollection of the beautiful presents she gave me regularly on my birthday, on which date I dutifully invited her to tea. She was one of the few godmothers that I know of who took their responsibilities in the way of present-giving seriously, and a gift of some sort generally followed my visits to her house in Stratton Street, or to Holly Lodge, Highgate—in those days quite a Sabbath day's journey. Holly Lodge is only a dim memory to me, but I remember the big corner house in Stratton Street well, and the Baroness's yellow and white china parrot, which, according to the way its head was turned, told her callers whether she was at home or not, and which still hangs in the round window in Piccadilly looking for the long-vanished mistress of the house.

Up to his death her husband mourned her loss. A life-size picture of her hung on the wall in the dining-room, and Mr. Burdett-Coutts told someone I knew that he often dined at home alone to feel she was with him once more.

Lord and Lady Bradford were great friends of both my parents and I used often to be taken by them to stay at Weston. Lady B., one of Disraeli's "matchless sisters," was a typical great lady of her day, but my memories of her are vague, and I should probably have looked at her with more interest if I had realized that her despatch-boxes contained Lord Beaconsfield's flowery effusions.

Our real home, Dysart, was in Fife, but father became very attached to Easton, and up to the time of Daisy's marriage we spent a considerably greater part of the year there than in Scotland.

Easton Lodge was a solid grey stone house of no particular period, and the red-brick wing added by my father gave it a somewhat lop-sided appearance from an architectural point of view ; but the wing certainly made luxurious nursery quarters, for we were a fairly large family to accommodate !

My very earliest recollections hail from Easton, but time has dimmed most of them. The wonderful ball given there on the occasion of Daisy's coming out was to me only hearsay, though it is still talked of, and I believe it was then that " Brookie," the Prince Charming of the fairy tale, appeared upon the scene.

I seem to see endless people coming to Easton, but very few are more than shadows. One of the most tangible is the Duchess of Rutland, then Violet Lindsay. She used to come often with her father and Mrs. Mason, who was a sister of Lady Tree. Mrs. M. acted the part of chaperon, and this old connection is probably the origin of the friendship which exists between the Manners and the Trees.

The Duchess has changed less than most people with the passing of time, and to-day she seems very little older than she appeared to me then, when I used to sit still while she did pencil sketches of me. These sittings were great fun ; but I was a most ruthless critic, and always insisted on some alterations being made, generally to my fringe, which had just been cut and of which I was inordinately proud, or to my up-turned nose—a standing joke in the family, but a joke I did not always appreciate !

Count Montgelas, attached to one of the foreign embassies, is another rather hazy memory, chiefly of the fun of childhood. He used to pretend to be a tall giant and chase me up the stairs on my way to bed, and I was always terrified lest the giant should catch me and pinch my legs !

My father was the most vital personality in my life then and later, and through the years his memory, although I was only fourteen when he died, has been the great keynote and influence of my life.

He had an amazing individuality, with many sides to his nature, and though he may have seemed imperious and impetuous, there was a charm and gentleness in his character which made him most lovable.

He was kind-hearted to a degree ; few appealed to him in vain when any instance of sorrow or suffering was in question, and his sense of humour was supreme. Someone has said of him, and I think without exaggeration, that he knew something of everything, and it would have been difficult to broach any subject upon which he was not well posted. He was really more responsible for our education than my mother, who, in a way, appeared as the attractive figure-head of the household. She always maintained, however, that she gave in over little things and got her own way in the big ones, which, on the whole, is an arrangement to be recommended !

Deportment played a distinct part in our curriculum, and to hear of us learning our lessons stretched on a backboard, or sitting with straps and what-nots on our shoulders and our feet in stocks will probably make the children of to-day shudder ; but we survived, and even throve on the treatment.

Intolerant of stupidity, father would far sooner we had done a naughty than a silly thing. Shyness, he called " exaggerated self-consciousness," and he always affirmed that we could not be shy unless we were thinking of ourselves. He liked us to have our own opinions, and encouraged us to express them, and if he asked us at luncheon whether we would like a leg or a wing of chicken and we replied politely that we didn't mind, he used to say, " All right, then you need not have either."

General knowledge and common-sense were early inculcated, and special intelligence received its just reward, my brother Harry being tipped for looking out cross-country journeys in the Bradshaw correctly ! But there was another side to the medal, and I remember once having my ears boxed at luncheon for not knowing the Latin name for maidenhair fern !

I used to be delighted when our governesses came under the fire of father's questions ; though they didn't admit it, they dreaded the ordeal, and I was not in the least sorry for them.

Those dreadful German governesses ! How I grew

to hate them and their horrid language! How many miserable hours, as I grew older, I spent over those Goëthe and Schiller recitations.

French came quite naturally to me. I really think I spoke it before I spoke English. I had an old French nurse whom I adored, and I can well remember now the dreadful agony I went through saying good-bye to her when she left me to go to the Gerards. I saw her a few days afterwards in the Park, and I cried so loudly that she had to bring me home herself; the people who heard me and who didn't know the facts must have thought me a much-injured or very naughty child.

I detested the governess who presided over our destinies at this time, and I didn't like her any better for her treatment of me after this episode, for she in veigled me into her room with the promise of chocolates, and when she got me safely there, gave me a sound smacking. I think this legend shows that even the most careful parents dwell often in a state of blissful ignorance of how their precious offspring are faring upstairs.

*

Daisy's wedding meant our leaving Easton, and it must have been a great wrench for the others. For me there was something rather thrilling in the upheaval which the move involved. Father had sent his brood mares to Burleigh Paddocks, which he had rented from Lord Exeter; he had also taken a small house, known as Lady Anne's House, which stood on the outskirts of the town of Stamford and on the fringe of Burleigh Park.

This he had only intended to use for himself and his stud groom, but mamma was so pleased with it when she saw it, that she insisted on our going to live there, and father, who loved dabbling with bricks and mortar, little by little, not only enlarged the existing house, but also acquired all the other houses in the block and eventually converted them into one.

As I said, the move to me was full of interest : new people, new surroundings, are things of paramount importance at the age of five. After living in the heart of the country, to find oneself in a house in a street was in itself an excitement. Everyone that passed was endowed with a possible history, and half my days were spent hanging out of the window, wondering and inventing, till I had compiled in my own imagination a perfect " Who's Who " of all the passers-by. After daily walks along country roads, a town was brimful of possible adventures. Such a lovely old town, too, full of ancient churches, old curiosity shops and houses, and with ever so many legends attached to it.

The old racecourse was only half a mile away, and was now used as a training ground. Races were held at Stamford from the seventeenth century and only finished in 1873. There were all sorts of delicious customs connected with these races. To begin with, the competitors were first of all inspected by the Mayor of the town at the Nag's Head Inn, and another condition was that " if any of the matched horses or their riders chance to fall in anye of the foure heats the rest of the riders shall staye in theire places where they were at the tyme of the fall until the rider so fallen have his foote into the stirroppe again."

" Burleigh Park by Stamford Town " is almost too

Lady Warwick's Bridesmaids.

Sybil Millicent, Duchess of Sutherland
(now Lady Millicent Hawes).

And Self.

The late Countess of
Westmorland.

[Facing p. 16

well known to need description, with its wonderful associations and history. It was built by William Cecil, Lord Burleigh, when he was Lord High Treasurer of England, about the end of the sixteenth century, and it is crammed full of wonderful pictures and treasures. I was too young to appreciate these fully, and the Grinling Gibbons, I am afraid left me cold. The two treasures that always thrilled me most were a tiny one-button kid glove and a wee parasol which had belonged to Queen Victoria.

The house had gone through many vicissitudes. It had once been besieged and stormed by Oliver Cromwell, and the marks of cannon balls can be seen now beneath the south windows of the banqueting hall.

The greatest Lord Burleigh was, I suppose, that William Cecil who, having survived two previous reigns, was for forty years chief minister to Queen Elizabeth. The Burleigh immortalized by Lord Tennyson lived two centuries later and in 1791 was divorced from his wife. He returned broken-hearted to a small village in Shropshire called Bolus Magna, where he worked as a farm hand for the owner of the mill, and was called by the villagers " Gentleman Harry." He fell in love with the miller's daughter, Sarah, and, marrying her, lived in great content in a cottage near by, until, two years later, he succeeded to Burleigh at the death of his uncle, thus becoming tenth Earl of Exeter. Everyone knows the sad story of how, amidst the grandeur of the castle, his cottage bride pined away.

> " Three fair children first she bore him,
> Then, before her time, she died."

I used to play with the present Lord Exeter and his

cousin, Harry Vane (afterwards married to one of my
nieces), but, being a girl, they did not attach much
importance to me, and I was dreadfully hurt when they
once refused to kiss me. Lord Exeter was an only son
and rather delicate, so terrible care was taken of him.

Of Lady Exeter, his grandmother, I used to stand
in wholesome dread, in company, I may say, with her
own family, my father being one of the few people who
was not afraid of her, and I was much impressed by the
fact that the sons and daughters never called their
parents " Mother," and " Father," but always " My
Lord," and " My Lady." She was a great stickler for
the conventions, and once at Milton the present George
Fitzwilliams' father was just going to take Lady Huntly
in to dinner, when Lady Exeter pushed her firmly aside
and, in an awful voice, said, " I think you are forgetting
the Lord Lieutenant's wife ! "

Once when my governess had been taken ill I was
sent to stay for a few days with the Exeters. The
girls, although they were grown up, were kept as strictly
as children. Not to speak until you were spoken to,
was a doctrine I did not at all appreciate, but one
rigidly enforced at Burleigh ! Prayers were read daily
by Lady Exeter in the beautiful old chapel adjoining the
house, where one can still see the seat Elizabeth is
supposed to have occupied when she visited her Minister.
On one fatal occasion I giggled—and Lady Exeter
stopped dead in the middle of a sentence, looking straight
at me. " When the wicked man turneth away from his
wickedness "—and then there was a horrid pause. No
notice was taken as we went out, but a little later a
message came that " her ladyship would like to see me."

My outward bravado was not in the least indicative

of my feelings as I stood in front of her listening to a severe lecture couched in the most satirical language, whilst her two daughters stood, dragon-like, on either side of her.

I welcomed the day my governess recovered.

The Sunday round of the Paddocks at Stamford was an invariable custom—as invariable as church and learn ing my collect—and generally ended up with a visit to the Home Farm. The Jerseys here were descended from the herd founded by my grandfather in 1840 at Hampton Court.

In the Paddocks lay one of my father's great interests, and in addition, it was a lucrative hobby. A "heaven-born horse dealer " he has been called.

There was a standing joke amongst father's friends that he never let anyone go away from Stamford without selling them something. Going back to London after a day at the Paddocks, Austin Mackenzie, who had bought a yearling, asked the " Mate," who was with him, what *he* had bought, and the answer was "an umbrella and a peacock."

Astute father certainly was, and he did not believe in giving high prices for his mares, Feronia, for instance, the dame of Atalanta, costing only twenty-five pounds. John Kent, trainer to Lord George Bentinck, declared Atalanta to be the finest animal of its age that he had ever seen. The Duke of Portland eventually bought her, and I believe he bought St. Simon on my father's recommendation. Father also had the distinction of breeding Tristan, who won the Queen's Vase at Ascot and the Ascot Cup in 1893, Ayrshire, St. Serf, as well as many other well known horses.

He had a few horses in training with Mathew Dawson,

2*

and later with Tom Jennings, but I think he found that it was far more profitable to breed horses than to race them. He betted very little, and fifty pounds on a horse he considered a prodigious dash. In one of his letters to mother from Newmarket he tells her that he has done this, adding, " Racing is an absorbing subject, to be treated with care and calmness."

Of course any amount of people used to come down to see the horses, and as I look back I can remember the doyens of the racing world, such as the " Mate," Captain Machell, the Duke of Portland, with his inimitable laugh, Sir Daniel Cooper, Lord Coventry and Baron Lucien de Hirsch. The last-named had come over to this country to race, and my father managed his horses. The Baron used to bring us large boxes of Marquis chocolates from Paris, so that we looked forward with great anticipation to *his* visits.

Moreton Frewen is another who was often with us. Father was devoted to him in spite of the fact that he persuaded him to put his money into a ranch and that it turned out a complete failure, but father always said it was money well spent—as he had made a friend he might otherwise never have met. Moreton Frewen was equally attached to father—he really loved him. Only the other day I went to see the Frewens at their lovely place at Brede, and Moreton at once began to talk of him —reviving old memories and recalling anecdotes and incidents of those far away happy days.

What an enthusiast Moreton Frewen is. He is as keen about his garden as he was about bimetallism, and though he had only just recovered from an operation he was still boyishly exuberant. He is immensely proud of his daughter, Mrs. Sheridan, and her work—justifiably so, and he showed me a little "statuette" they had of Diana Cooper by her, which was quite excellent.

It was Sir Daniel Cooper who gave me my first pony ! I only had a donkey to ride in those days, and on one memorable occasion he ran away with me ! I had no saddle, but I didn't fall off, so Sir Daniel, who was there at the time, said that I deserved a pony for sticking on so well. Zulu was his name, and his arrival meant that I could ride over with the others to luncheon at Normanton. This was where the Avelands* lived, a most typical jolly English family ; there were sons and daughters of all ages, all unmarried at that time.

Apethorpe, the most beautiful old Elizabethan house, belonging to Lord and Lady Westmorland, was also not far from us. Lord Westmorland was one of the best known and most attractive figures of his day. Lady Westmorland possessed an equal degree of charm, and I think it was Whyte Melville who said of her, " It's like opening the window to see her." They only lived in a corner of the house, but the lack of grandeur was far more impressive than a more ostentatious display in a less genial atmosphere would have been. The eldest daughter, Gracie,† was grown up and as popular as her mother ; the other, Daisy,‡ was in the schoolroom, and the same age as Sybil, who eventually married the only son, Lord Burghersh.

⊤   *   ⊤   ⊤   ✱

In the autumn we generally went to Dysart, but I never cared for living there nearly as much as at

---

* Afterwards Earl and Countess of Ancaster.
† The Countess of Londesborough.
‡ Lady Margaret Spicer.

Stamford. No paddocks, no riding, and, though we were by the sea, we were surrounded on every other side by coal mines and coal dust.

The Dysart coal mines were about the earliest ever worked in Scotland. A long time ago they had caught fire, and were supposed to have eruptions once in every forty years. The effects can still be traced by the calcined rocks, which go for more than a mile inland, and the old road from the harbour was called from this " Hot Pot Wynd."

My father was probably one of the first to attempt the alleviation of the miners' desperately dreary existence. The squalor of the old-fashioned houses was exchanged for more modern dwellings, and the Boreland, as the village was known, was built under my father's direction. As a child I used to wonder how the men could bear to turn night into day, but they seemed perfectly content to do it, and there was none of that carping unrest which has been engendered by modern Trade Union methods.

Dysart was a hideous, harled house, and its feature was a big square saloon, at the further end of which hung a portrait of my grandfather in " boots and breeches " Opposite him was the Lord Chancellor Loughborough in his wig and gown. He first practised at the Bar in Scotland ; but, after an acrimonious discussion in the courts there, he laid down his gown and said he would never grace those courts again !

From Scotland he came to England, where he made his name. In 1801 he was created Lord Chancellor, to which post he clung with such tenacity that, on the fall of Pitt's Government, he still insisted on attending the Cabinet Meetings when Lord Sidmouth had taken office, even though another Chancellor had been appointed! Finally, he had to be requested to desist from this practice. I wonder if Lord Birkenhead will follow his example!

There were no pictures of my grandmother, who, from all accounts, must have been rather eccentric. She had been very spoilt all her life, and when my grandfather retired from public life and said he was going to live quietly at Dysart and economize, she went to her bed and stayed there, I think, for five years. When the neighbours came to call she would sometimes see them, keeping them waiting whilst she dressed to receive them! She was a very clever woman and spent her time reading and writing. Volumes and volumes of leatherbound books were in the library at Dysart, all filled with MSS. in very fine but almost illegible writing; it is, therefore, impossible to discover, as one would like to do, what occupied her thoughts during her self-enforced inactivity.

The people of Fife are very boastful of their origin, and hundreds of years ago Fife was always regarded as a separate kingdom.

Many are the old sayings and proverbs about a Fife man, as, for instance, " To be a Fifer is not far from being a Highlander," and " They that sup with Fife folk maun hae a lang spune," which is scarcely complimentary to us.

Amongst the well-known Fife figures one stands out in my mind in very clear relief. This was Colonel Anstruther Thomson. He was one of the great sporting personalities, and in that world his name is as familiar as Jorrocks. Originally Master of the Fife Hounds, he went on to the Pytchley, and to the very last day of his life, though well over eighty, he was a familiar figure in the hunting field. I can remember him coming over to Dysart, very often bringing George Whyte Melville with him.

The Wemyss', our nearest neighbours, were cousins of ours. They lived at Wemyss Castle, which, standing on the cliff, forty feet above the sea, between Kinghorn and Elie, is one of the most beautiful places in Scotland. Below the cliffs the sea has made the most fantastic caves inscribed with the rude figures of mysterious pagan symbols and gods, and also with the Christian cross, carved by the unknown hands of some early missionary before ever history was written, and it was really from these caves that the name of Wemyss originated.

In the castle itself they still show you a room called the " Presence Chamber," where the ill-fated Mary first met, and lost her heart to Darnley, thus starting those years of misery which culminated in that final tragedy at Fotheringay.

Mrs. Wemyss had made some most fearfully ugly additions to the castle, adding a large hall panelled with light oak, and an entirely modern frontage. When she died she lay in state in this hall, and Randolph, until he married his second wife, would allow no one to pass through.

Sir Michael Wemyss was the first Scottish Admiral, and when he became too old to go to sea, he had a canal cut from his house at Largo to the parish kirk, and every Sunday was rowed to church in the most solemn state in an eight-oared barge.

They were a marvellously gifted and versatile family, some of their versatility coming, no doubt, from their

Lady Warwick's Bridesmaids.

V. l. Shaftesbury, Lad Beatrice   le arew and Lady Constance Butler.

ancestress, Mrs. Jordan. The eldest son, Randolph, had one of the most interesting personalities I have ever met, and became in later years one of my kindest friends.

Rosie, now Lord Wester Wemyss, has hardly changed at all. I can remember in my youth the same cheery smile, the same eye-glass and general air of jollity that distinguishes him now.

There were two sisters, Mary, who became Mrs. Cecil Paget, and Mimini, afterwards Lady Henry Grosvenor, both most beautiful to look at. Mimini, I suppose, was quite one of the most brilliant women of her day. She was a great gardener, and wherever she went she turned a wilderness into a paradise. She it was who started the " Wemyss Work School " and also the " Wemyss Potteries." Beautiful, and gifted with a marvellous voice, she was, nevertheless, an awe-inspiring element, and entirely ruled her family. Being so much younger I saw very little of them, but I can remember some of the parties at Wemyss. Lady Mary Mills stands out still freshly in my mind with her vivid colouring and attractive manners, and even more particularly, Lady Claud Hamilton with her amazing walk. She used to be held up to us as a model—she sailed rather than walked—but, to do it as she did, you would have needed all the gifts the gods had so kindly bestowed on her.

*   *   *   *

London, from May to Goodwood, broke the circle of the year. Every spring my father and mother took a house for the season, but to me London appeared a.very dull place indeed. The round of gaiety, which now fills the modern child's life, was unheard of in those days. Parties and matinées, which play a most important part in even babies' existence to-day, we knew little about, and the big children's party at Marlborough House and one or two others were landmarks in the summer of our schoolroom days. At one of the Marlborough House garden parties, when I was quite small, I broke the elastic which kept on my shoe—the shoe was, of course, two sizes too big, so as to allow for my foot growing—and any effort to retain it without was futile. This threatened to spoil my afternoon's amusement, and reduced me to tears till the Princess of Wales came to console me and sent it to be mended.

A variation to the routine of daily walks and daily lessons was playing in Hamilton Gardens, which was, in those days—it may be still for all I know—the chic place for children to congregate. Amongst the girls we used to meet there were the daughters of Lord Arran (the present Lady Salisbury, and Mabel, Lady Airlie), the Forbes, the Cadogans, and Edith Ward, now Lady Wolverton, who, we thought in those days, used to give herself great airs and suffered from a very moody temper! The games we indulged in were tinged with monotony, and consisted generally of Flags and Tom Tiddler's Ground.

An alternative to this orgy in Hamilton Gardens was going for a drive in the Park with Mamma. There were no hurrying, hooting motors then, and how much nicer those well-turned-out horses and carriages looked!

It is a refreshing relief now to see Lady Granard's stepping chestnuts, which remind one faintly of the evening pageants in the Park of bygone days. How well I remember the Londonderry barouche with its bewigged coachman and footman and Lady Londonderry's scornful beauty—the Cadogan steppers with their Eton blue browbands—Lord Calthorpe in the smartest of buggies and the most diminutive tiger in London and Lord Shrewsbury handling his perfect team, whilst a sprinkling of " pretty ladies " gave variety to the scene. The Bayswater-cum-Balham ingredients, of which the crowd in the Park is now composed, would have had something worth looking at in the eighties !

The Princess of Wales used generally to drive through in the evening, and whether from loyalty or snobbishness there was always a waiting crowd to see her pass.

The piebalds which we always drove used to attract a considerable amount of attention. They were a most perfect match and appeared to possess the gift of eternal youth—for they actually took me to church on the day of my wedding !

During the season father and mother always gave a number of dinners. My father was an admirable host, and epicures, I believe, considered his dinners the best in London ;˙ he and Lord Bath, I think it was, competed amicably for the honour of having the best chef. Certainly my father knew all about food and was a gourmet rather than a gourmand.

Before he was engaged to mother he went to stay at Easton and told her rather condescendingly that she had very nearly got a first-class cook ! All the same I don't believe mother ever ordered dinner when father was at home, but he used to go daily to the kitchen to interview the chef. He was extremely critical, but his was not merely a destructive criticism, for he knew what was wrong, and could say how a dish had failed. I used often to go with him, and after listening regularly to long gastronomical conversations, can I be blamed for being thoroughly greedy now ?

Apart from the excellence of the food at father's dinner parties, they were socially attractive, for he had the knack of collecting the pleasantest people around him. Without taking any active part in politics, he gathered to his house not only men of letters and distinction, but the heads of both parties. His aloofness from party controversy left him with a clearer vision, and he was therefore able to discuss a question from both points of view.

Watching the people arrive for dinner was one of my greatest amusements. I was generally able to slip out of bed undetected, but one evening I was discovered by Lord Rowton, who, seeing me hanging over the banisters, ran upstairs and carried me into the drawing-room in my nightgown.

Lord Rowton was a frequent visitor. He is better known, I suppose, as Montagu Corry, the intimate friend and devoted private secretary of Disraeli, while to hundreds of people to-day his name has been made familiar by the " working man's hotel."

I wish I could say that I remember Lord Beaconsfield, but I only know from hearsay that I sat on his knee, and of that I have no recollection.

He was one of my father's greatest friends, and he and mother used always to dine with him in Downing Street, on their return each year from Holyrood, when father was Lord High Commissioner of the Church of Scotland. This post he held under the Administration of 1874 and again in 1878.

There is an amusing story about him being given this post. Beaconsfield is supposed to have said :

" What shall we do with Rosslyn ? "

" Make him Master of the Buck-hounds," was the reply, " like his father."

" No, he swears far too much for that," said Dizzy. " We will make him Commissioner of the Church of Scotland."

I do not know if this is a true story any more than the other reason given for his appointment—" that he wrote pretty verses." Anyway he made an excellent Commissioner, and I do not think he shocked the Ministers or their sometimes starchy wives too much, although there are innumerable stories of his trying to do so. On one occasion a message came that Mrs. —— would be unable to dine as she was in bed with a housemaid's knee, to which my father promptly and cheerily replied " What the devil has she done with the rest of the house maid ? "

All his stories were told with the most delightful twinkle in his eyes, and no one seemed to mind them. If they sometimes sailed rather near the wind, they were never vulgar. Everyone listened to him with the keenest delight, and even Queen Victoria used to enjoy his jokes, which is saying a great deal ! Only my mother used to cry quite vainly from her end of the table : " Francis, Francis, remember the children are in the room."

My father always claimed to have been the first person to discover Mrs. Langtry. I rather think he met her in a studio, where she was sitting to some celebrated painter, I fancy Millais, but am beautifully vague about the exact details. He came home enthusing over her beauty and invited some of the connoisseurs of the day to meet her. She did not go down at all well, as she was suffering from a bad cold, and the Jersey Lily's nose on this auspicious occasion resembled a healthy peony in hue— while her clothes—well, they were not quite so wonderful as they afterwards became, and everyone laughed at my father, thinking that this time, at any rate, he had made an error in his usually perfect judgment. He remained, however, serenely confident, anticipating the verdict of posterity. And he was justified, for before very long my father's enthusiasm was shared by all London, and Mrs. Langtry had triumphantly arrived. These were the days when real beauty was deservedly ac- claimed, and people stood on chairs in the Park to see the celebrities pass by. Looking back at old photographs it seems difficult to believe that any beauty could have emerged triumphant clad in the monstrous garments that were then in fashion. Hair scraped back, leg of mutton sleeves, and voluminous skirts would have deprived the majority of the pretty women of to-day of any chance of success.

In 1878 my father went over to Spain to attend the marriage of Alphonso the Twelfth to the Dona Mercedes de Bourbon—the marriage which only lasted such a few months—Mercedes dying on the 26th of June in the same year. It was the most tragic ending of a genuine love affair. The King wrote to father signing himself " votre affligé Alphonso," and an extract from a private letter from Madrid describes the King's grief :

" The poor King remains leaning on her bed, and calling on her name : ' Mercedes ! Mercedes mia ! ' To the last her eyes were turned on the King."

Apart from his racing and his wide circle of friends father was intensely domestic, with a very deep vein of sentiment, as may be seen from his sonnets. His verse, if slight, was full of that tenderness which ran through his whole character. His sonnets were spontaneous. He would get an inspiration from the merest every-day trifle, which would be instantly transcribed on any half sheet, sometimes even on the back of a menu.

Inspiration used to come to him whilst he was dressing, and I would often find him sitting by the open window writing when I went to bid him " Good-morning." He had written a sonnet to all his children, and one day I told him I was very hurt because I was forgotten, so he promptly sat down and wrote this one ·

BEDTIME.

" 'Tis bedtime; say your hymn, and bid ' Good-night;
God bless Mamma, Papa, and dear ones all ; ◦
Your half-shut eyes beneath your eyelids fall
Another minute you will shut them quite.
Yes, I will carry you, put out the light,
And tuck you up, although you are so tall !
What will you give me, Sleepy one, and call
My wages, if I settle you all right ? "
I laid her golden curls upon my arm,
I drew her little feet within my hand,
Her rosy palms were joined in trustful bliss,
Her heart next mine beat gently ; soft and warm
She nestled to me, and, by Love's command,
Paid me my precious wages—" Baby's Kiss."

If his verses do not rank with those of the great Poets, they rendered, as he says himself : " Many hours of my past life happier and better." Almost the last thing he wrote was the Jubilee Lyric, " Love that lasts for ever." The Queen was delighted with it and commanded him to publish it, and she was supposed to have preferred it to the Laureate's tribute to the occasion.

LOVE THAT LASTS FOR EVER

A JUBILEE LYRIC

1887.

(Published by Command of the Queen.)

I

THERE is a Word,
　　A Linnet lilting in the grove,
　Keen as a sword,
And pure as Angels are above ;
This little Word good men call Love.

II

　It bears a Name,
Unsullied by the taint of wealth ;
　Careless of Fame,
And bright with all the hues of health,
It shrinks from praise, to bless by stealth.

III

　I join it now
To thine, Victoria !　Thou hast seen
　With clear eyes, how
To win it : blessèd hast thou been
With Love, as Mother, Wife, and Queen.

IV

　Love bathed in Tears,
To Love cemented, ever brings
　And ever bears
A chastened spirit, that in Kings
Is noblest among earthly things.

V

　Come, lasting Love !
For Sweetness in a moment dies,
　And all things prove
That Beauty far too quickly flies
From blue, or black, or hazel eyes.

VI

Youth is a snare ;
Like an awakening dream it speeds
  Nor cries, *Beware !*
A dream of unaccomplished deeds,
A hope of undetermined creeds.

VII

Is it Friendship then ?
The Tyrant of a summer day,
  The boast of men
Who loiter idly on life's way,
A band who neither work nor play.

VIII

Nay ! Friends, though dear,
Pass on their way—change—turn aside ·
  A transient tear
Dims Friendship's light—or some pale bride—
For Love was born when Friendship died.

IX

Thou, Grey or Gold,
Alone, Great Love, survivest all,
  All else grows old ;
Their birth, their growth, their rise their fall
Immortal only at thy call.

X

Love conquers Death
And is Life's portal, and the Soul
  Whose Heavenly breath
Inspires all Life, and ages roll
To ages, and yet leave it whole.

XI

Come then, Great Love,
To whom none ever plead in vain
  Come from above—
Where are no sighs, no tears, no pain—
And make us pure from selfish stain.

XII

Come, fresh as morn,
When golden sunrise laves the land,
And gilds the corn ;
Come smiling—come with open hand—
That brooks no chain—owns no command.

XIII

Thy voice sounds best
When faint the weary toilers sigh,
And long for rest ;
The tone is clear, but not too high
With just one touch of mystery.

XIV

Come, calm as night,
When Dian, with her stars, looks on
A wondrous sight—
A sleeping world :—Endymion
Slept thus for thee, pale Amazon !

XV

Be with us now ;
Illume our pleasures, soothe our woes
And teach us how
Thy sweet encircling spirit knows
The heart's unrest—the heart's repose.

XVI

Be with us now ;
A Day of many-sided thought
That curves the brow
With lines of memory, interwrought
With hope, and gratitude unbought.

XVII

Oh Queen ! this Day
Thy people, generous and just,
As well they may,
Confirm anew their sacred Trust
Enshrined in half a century's dust.

XVIII

For fifty years
Thy people's love has been content
(In spite of tears,
And bitter sorrows sadly blent)
To raise to thee Love's monument.

XIX

A Trophy, based
On duty done, on faction quelled
No deed defaced
By broken word, or faith withheld
No foe by stratagem compelled.

XX

Not stone or brass—
These perish with the flight of Time
And quickly pass ;
But Love endures in every clime
Eternal as the Poet's rhyme.

XXI

Not brass or stone—
These will corrode, and some day die ;—
But Love alone
Laughs at decay, and soars on high—
In fragrant immortality.

XXII

Thy Royal Robe
Is starred by Love : its purple Hem
Surrounds the Globe :
But true Love is the fairest Gem
Of thy Imperial Diadem.

XXIII

Queen of the Sea !
What prouder title dignifies
A Monarchy ?
The Orient owns it, and it lies
Amidst thy countless Colonies ·

XXIV

A wayward realm,
Yet ruled in Love for the world's gain;
Thou guid'st the Helm
That brings our commerce o'er the main
And makes us rich without a stain.

XXV

The Sisters Nine
Were all thy friends; a willing guest
Each one was thine,
In turn to cheer, or give thee rest;
Thy choice, they knew, was always best.

XXVI

And Science came
To meet thee, and enrich thy store
With Heaven-sent flame,
To burn—like Vesta's lamp—before
A sacred altar as of yore.

XXVII

Thy welcome gave
New impulse to her, and each day,
Like a freed slave,
She worked in Love such deeds, her ray
Shed light and truth around thy way.

XXVIII

No tongue can tell
Thy peaceful triumphs; mighty War
Has his as well;
But Peace has greater, nobler far
Than the chained victims of his Car.

XXIX

Thy Jubilee
Is marked by Love; 'tis all thine own
And given to thee
By all—a sweet flower fully blown,
The grace and grandeur of thy Throne.

Shooting Party at Houghton.

Lord Warwick, Hon. Evan Charteris, Lady Bettune Taylor, Lord Rosslyn, "Buck" Barclay, Lady Warwick, Willie Low, Tom Kenn t, Lord Guy de Wilton.

[Facing p. 36

XXX

'Tis thy just meed
For fifty years of righteous reign ;
    No heart doth bleed
In all thy kingdom, but the pain
Throbs in thine own, and not in vain.

XXXI

I pray thee take,
In some exchange for all the good
    That thou dost make,
The troubles thy brave heart withstood
Thy temperate yet undaunted mood

XXXII

These grateful lines ;
As the sweet myrtle wreathes the bay
    And intertwines
The classic leaf, e'en so I may
Entwine my chaplet with this Day.

XXXIII

'Tis a poor song,
By one whose heart has ever been
    Loyal and strong,
And who, like Simeon, now has seen
His hope fulfilled :—GOD SAVE THE QUEEN !

*   *   *   *

The landmarks in my childhood were most certainly
marriages, and my sister Millie's engagement to Lord
Stafford is the next memorable event.   It began through
the Duchess of Sutherland asking mother to let Millie
go and stay at Dunrobin, as a companion for her own
girl.   I was in mother's room at Dysart when she and
father were discussing it.   They were against the idea,
as Millie was in the schoolroom and Alix was grown up ;

and they thought it would have been much more to the point if the invitation had been sent to my half-sister, Blanchie.   But all the same, after some confabulation, Millie went, on the distinct understanding that she was not to be treated as grown-up.

Evidently her visit was a success, as we were all invited to spend the following Christmas with the Sutherlands at Trentham.   I shall never forget that journey.   The whole family, except father, who was joining us from London, left Dysart at dawn ; and you must remember that there was no Forth Bridge in those days, only a wretched ferry boat to take us across the Forth.   The journey was a cross-country one—I forget where we changed, but it must have been at least half a dozen times—and I think it was midnight before we reached Trentham, with Mamma reiterating most of the time : " Never, never will I come to Trentham again."

Trentham was a huge place, Italian in style, with beautiful grounds, but although later on in my life I spent many happy days there, it was to my mind a most undesirable possession.   The only other people I can remember staying there that Christmas were Sir Frederick and Lady Marshall and their two daughters, now Mrs. de Winton and Lady Hamilton of Dalziel.   I had caught a bad cold on the journey, so my Christmas Day was spent in bed, but it was enlivened by a visit from the Duke, who was delightful to me, and afterwards he specially sent me up a glass of champagne.   I think this was the first time I had ever tasted champagne, and I can remember at once writing a letter to my old nurse and telling her all about it.   When I woke up in the morning I found grapes and crackers beside my bed, and an envelope " with the Duke's love " written upon it.

When at last I was allowed to come downstairs, I went into the drawing-room and the Duke took me on to his knee and told me to guess a great piece of news, to which I replied with perfect sang-froid, " I suppose Daisy's had another baby."

The real news was, of course, that Millie was engaged to Lord Stafford. I wasn't particularly interested, though at the moment I queried as to whether she was old enough to be engaged, and I remember secretly wondering if my half-sister Blanchie wouldn't be very much annoyed at Millie, still in the schoolroom, being married before she was. Anyhow, everyone else was hugely excited about it all, especially as Millie was only just sixteen, a fact that was not lost sight of, and I believe she was made to go on doing lessons after she was engaged. Even in those days, before the Northcliffe Press was in being, the papers were full of the wonderful romance of a Marquis and a schoolgirl !

There was a curious coincidence relating to the houses from which my two sisters had been married, 7, Carlton Gardens, where Daisy's wedding took place, belonged to the Warwicks, whilst our house in Hamilton Place, from which Millie was married, had belonged to the Staffords and was full of Sutherland furniture with the coat-of-arms.

Millie's wedding was at St. Paul's, Knightsbridge, and she had a huge retinue of bridesmaids, of whom Sybil and I were two. We wore white frocks with " Cherry Ripe " caps and long mittens, and carried baskets of Parma violets, and it makes one smile now to think that Millie went away clad in a green velvet skirt with a crimson velvet bodice and *bonnet*, and was, I assure you, in the height of fashion !

After Millie's wedding, life fell back into its normal round.   There were few excitements beyong migrating, according to the seasons, between Stamford, Dysart and London.

We were kept very much in the background, particularly so in London. At luncheon we had to sit at a separate table when people were there ; this, I suppose, was really to prevent our hearing things we were not meant to, but I sometimes think the old adage about " little pitchers " was proved in our case, and I rather fancy we managed to hear anything that specially interested us. I am sure it would have been very good for us to have listened to some of the conversations, as among the people who used to be there, were such interesting Victorian notabilities as Alfred Montgomery, the best-looking man of his day, Maria ˙Marchioness of Aylesbury, almost universally known as " Lady A," who went everywhere and knew everything. A quaint figure with her bunches of obviously dyed side curls, of whom it was said, in no unkind spirit, let it be owned, that it was rare indeed for her to lunch or dine in her own home ; but she was always a welcome guest by reason of her very worldly versatility.

Then there was Frederick Locker Lampson, the poet, a very regular habitué of the house, and versatile Lady Dorothy Nevill, that brilliant eighteenth-century aristocrat who had known the great Duke of Wellington, and could recall the famous Count d'Orsay, had met Prince Louis Napoleon in the days of his exile, and whose long and close friendship with Dizzy by no means prevented her enjoying an intimate acquaintance with Gladstone. As a matter of fact, she was the friend and confidante of most of the celebrated men and women of her day, and the versatility of her mind can be appreciated when one hears that her regular Sunday luncheon parties included as her guests, amongst others, King Edward, Samuel Wilberforce, Lord Justice Cockburn, Richard Cobden, John Bright and Matthew Arnold.

When we were in London we generally rode in the mornings, but the fashionable time for riding in those days was in the evenings, between tea and dinner. Then everyone wore top-hats and very tightly fitting habits with a little tail behind—a fashion, by the way, that Mrs. Henry Molyneux still followed quite twenty years later in Leicestershire. If father took us himself we were sometimes allowed to go out in the evenings, and on a few rare occasions Colonel Brocklehurst (the late Lord Ranksborough) and Lord Ribblesdale were allowed to chaperon us. Lord Ribblesdale always dressed in the same picturesque fashion as he does now, with his square hat and butterfly tie. How well he looked on a horse, too !

Blanchie, of course, always rode at the fashionable time ! She was so much older than Sybil and myself that we saw very little of her. I think we used to watch her rather jealously when she was dressed for a party, and she certainly had the knack of knowing how to put on her clothes, and "Society Papers" have called her the best dressed woman in London, whilst someone (I believe the late Sir Arthur Ellis) said of her, " If she was undressed she'd still look overdressed ! "

Blanchie's marriage to Lord Algernon Gordon-Lennox, second son of the Duke of Richmond, which took place two years later than Millie's, made no difference to the rather even tenor of our way. It was a very quiet affair compared to the wedding of my other two sisters, and took place at Easton at the end of August, and my sister Sybil and I, with Lord March's two girls, Evelyn and Violet Gordon-Lennox, were the only bridesmaids.

I had become rather blasé about being a bridesmaid, always excepting the present, and the frock, incidental to the occasion. I think I appreciated the latter most, as one of the distinct disadvantages of being the youngest of a family is having to wear one's sister's frocks cut down, instead of having one's clothes made for one !

The following summer was Oueen Victoria's Jubilee, and we had a house that year in St. James's Square. Father was Captain of the Gentlemen-at-Arms, and as he had to attend all the functions at the Palace, was really terribly hard worked.

We went, of course, to see the procession, and had seats on the stand just outside Buckingham Palace, It is dreadful to think that I have nearly forgotten all about the Jubilee rejoicings, and I can only see a dream picture of the little Queen, wonderfully dignified, driving through the flag-bedecked streets thronged with the thousands of people over whom she ruled. Her popularity was then at its height.

The cream-coloured ponies that drew Queen Victoria's carriage I felt were intimate friends of mine, as Sir George Maude, my uncle, was Master of the Horse ; and very often on Sundays when we were in London we used to go round the Royal Mews and give them their Sunday feed of carrots.

Going to see Uncle Maude at the Stud House, Hampton Court, was also one of our outings from London, and I was there when the Queen's stud of race-horses was finally disposed of.

In spite of all the gaiety going on around, father used to strike me vaguely as being not quite in his usual spirits. He used to be so tired after some of the functions were over, and I often used to find him resting when I went to say "Good-night" to him; but no real premonition of the coming tragedy dawned upon me.

We were all up at Dysart when the first sorrow of my life came with overwhelming suddenness. Father had been to Harrogate, and had gone south for a few days to see his horses. Evelyn Fairfax was staying with him, when a wire came from her to say that father had been taken seriously ill, and for mother to come at once. I remember the hustle and bustle for her to catch the train, and then the suspense of waiting for news. In a day or two we also were sent for.

I shall never forget arriving at Stamford. There was a thunderstorm brewing; the air was hot and thick, with occasional growls of thunder and flashes of lightning. An indescribably desolate feeling came over me. It was as if the end of the world had come, for to me my father was my world.

We were not allowed to see him. Over the house hung a kind of hushed silence, and that dreadful atmosphere of serious illness. Specialists from London came to and fro, leaving us still in the throes of uncertainty and mental suspense. Then one day father asked to see me.

I was taken to his bedroom, and was standing by

his bedside, when he suddenly startled me by saying, in a perfectly normal voice: " You can ride White-lock to-morrow." I had not been allowed to ride my own pony, Zulu, as he had reared over on the stud groom. My father had evidently remembered this. From that moment he seemed to rally ; but it was only rallying. For two years he suffered with that fortitude and patience so characteristic of him.

Evelyn Fairfax stayed on with us for a time, and she was a godsend to us children in those days, as she took us out riding, and distracted our thoughts in a hundred different ways. She was quite a character, and known to everyone in Yorkshire. When she wasn't hunting she rode all day—even out to dinner, with her evening frock in a little bag !

As father gradually gained strength the question of a change arose, and from then on until he died, life became a pilgrimage in search of health, never to be granted to him.

Our first move was to Gunnersbury, lent us by the Rothschilds, and we were there for a few weeks. Being so near London it was within easy reach of doctors, and all father's friends used to come and see him. It was while we were at Gunnersbury that father sold his entire racing stud. He had what in those days was a record sale, and the Prince of Wales drove down to Gunnersbury to congratulate him personally. The sale meant a complete break with the old life, and must have caused father the most infinite sorrow—it meant, too, that he must have realized that he was doomed to remain a permanent invalid.

I think it was at the instigation of Moreton Frewen, Lord Houghton (now Lord Crewe) and Frederick Locker

Lampson that he began to rearrange and compile his second book of sonnets, and this gave him some occupation.

From Gunnersbury we drifted to the Solent and took a house on the Hamble river, and the Prince of Wales lent father his yacht *Aline*, on which we used to sail most days, sometimes cruising round the island. The sea, however rough, suited my father, so that later he chartered the *Miranda*, a large steam yacht which belonged to Sir George Lampson, and we started off to spend the winter in the Mediterranean.

I think father was the only one of us who enjoyed the passage through the Bay; unless one has been through it in a yacht one has no conception of the immense size of the waves. Our crossing was far from smooth, and at every moment I expected the yacht to be smashed up as the sea came crashing against the bulwarks, so it was with great relief that we put into Lisbon, an evil-smelling port !

The next point we touched was Gibraltar, where we were entertained to a picnic by some of the garrison staff, and explored the rock and its fortifications, which were very interesting.

I shall never forget my sensations when I first saw the " Rock ; " it looms up so solitary and grand, guarding that narrow passage of the seas, and it gives one a fearful thrill to realize that it belongs to England. I should hate to be there long, though, you do seem so dreadfully out of everything. The world " go down to the sea in ships " and you are left there—just watching.

From Gibraltar we toured the coast of Spain, crossing later to Algiers and Tunis. I suppose I was really too young to appreciate all I saw, and I often wish now, that I had inwardly stored a better recollection of everything we did, instead of which I resented sight-seeing when it savoured of knowledge to be acquired.

Looking back the whole of our time in Spain seems to have been passed under a haze redolent of goat's milk and red mullet, which greeted us at every port.

The trip was entirely spoilt for me by my governess being generally too ill to do lessons when we were under weigh, and being made to make up for *her* lost time when we were in harbour. All the same the story that I made a heap of all my lesson books and threw them overboard is quite untrue!

Sir Gerald Strickland was Governor of Malta at the time, and we had rather fun there, and went to tea on one of the battleships, where we made the acquaintance of Mark Kerr.

Father's health showed no permanent improvement. He was better one day and worse the next. It must have been dreadful for anyone whose body and mind were as active as his, to be obliged to lie still all day. His nature must have been stronger and finer than we any of us knew, for him to have borne it as he did.

Always the naughty one of the family, my punishments usually consisted of being shut up in my room without anything to do. This led to disastrous results once, for I found a pair of scissors and cut off all my eyebrows and eyelashes. I hoped that this would conduce to some more lively form of retribution in the future. But it didn't.

Once, when this special form of punishment had been meted out to me, and all the others had gone ashore, father rescued me from exile. When I came on deck to see him, anticipating a scolding, he just begged me to be good, because he said if I was shut up in my cabin, he was equally punished by not seeing me. After that I made a huge effort to avoid rows with my much hated governess.

Dr. Charcot had seen father, and wanted him to be under his care in order to try a new treatment ; so from Marseilles we went to Paris and settled down there for a few weeks. I much preferred being there, compared to London ; the bustle of people coming and going to and from the hotel was a change I thoroughly appreciated. The Paris shops were far more attractive than the London ones, and even at that age I discovered how very much better dressed the French women were than the English.

We saw a good deal of the Hirsch's, the father and mother of Lucien Hirsch, who used to race with my father. Baron de Forest was then quite a little boy, and he and his brother lived with them. No one ever quite solved the relationship, but when Lucien died, Touti, as he was called, became the Baron's heir. The Hirsch's were very hospitable and kept open house in their lovely " hôtel," and all the English and Americans used to go there when they came to Paris. Among them I can remember the famous Yznaga sisters, who included the Duchess of Manchester and Lady Lister Kaye, whilst of the English contingent, the most frequently to be met there were Gwen Lowther, Lady Georgina Curzon and her sister Lady Sarah Wilson.

But it was not only in Paris that the Baron was well-known. He entertained considerably at Bath House, and invitations to shoot with him in Austria were angled for with more brazenness than was always

compatible with dignity ! It was amusing to hear
the remarks made by some people who had not been
invited anent the more fortunate ones, and equally
amusing to hear the same people's excuses for accepting
an invitation if it eventually came !

My uncle by marriage, Count Münster, was at the
Embassy at that time. He was really a dear old man
and was always very kind to us. We had stayed with
him many times in the old days at the German Embassy
in London, when as children we came up for dentists
and doctors. I believe he was moved from London
as being too pro-English.

He had married my father's sister, Lady Harriet St.
Clair, and never, I believe, really got over her death,
and her room at Dernebourg was left untouched with
her books and things about exactly as she had always
used it. She died long before I was born ; in fact, I
think before my father was married. She must have
been a most remarkable woman, having lived at least a
generation before her time. She shot—a thing unheard of in those days for a woman to do—she was a
good horsewoman, a really clever artist, and she certainly possessed the courage of a lion. When there
was an outbreak of smallpox among the colliers at
Dysart she went down and nursed them herself ; and
when she had her fatal accident she held her own leg,
and refused to have an anæsthetic while it was "fired."
She was a most excellent cook too, and her book " Dainty
Dishes " is still one of the best cookery books going.

There is a story about my aunt that when she was
going to be married, the wedding was to take place in
the drawing-room at Dysart, and when they told her
everyone was waiting, she refused to move until she had

finished turning the heel of a sock that she was knitting !

There is a window in Rosslyn Chapel to her memory, but during the war the brass plate with the Münster name was left unpolished—so bitter were people's feelings at that time, there was a fear that a tourist seeing the German name might damage the window.

Count Münster's son by his first wife, Zander, like his father, was going to marry an Englishwoman, and was engaged to Lady Muriel Hay, and as they were both in Paris at that time we saw a good deal of them.

Prince Henry of Pless, who was one of the secretaries at the German Embassy, was very good about lending us his horses, which Sybil and I rode every morning in the Bois. He generally used to come with us, and I think there was some idea that he might marry Sybil, who was just grown up ; but this did not happen, and the following year his marriage to Miss Cornwallis West was one of the season's sensations. I confess I had not looked forward to him as a brother-in-law.

I was very sorry when we eventually left Paris, but father was getting restless, and though fairly well, he did not seem to be making the headway that was expected under the Charcot treatment. So we once more made tracks for England. Sybil was to " come out," and I was to be banished to Dysart to settle down to regular lessons.

My brother Harry's wedding to Miss Vyner made an excuse for me to emerge from exile, in order that I might take my part as a bridesmaid. I think that Harry's marriage was in some ways a disappointment to my family. He was only twenty-one, and had just gone into the Blues, and as the Colonel refused to have married subalterns in the regiment, it meant an abrupt termination of his military career.   His future mother-in-law, Mrs. Vyner, was one of the most fascinating women I have ever met ; and I've always been told that she and Mrs. Sloane-Stanley had more successes than any other women, but neither of them ever made an enemy—a record to envy.   Their charm did not lie in good looks, but in their personality, and they both had one point in common—a charming voice.

I heard a lot about Mrs. Sloane-Stanley later when I went to Leicestershire.   She was immensely attractive, and all the men, young and old, at Melton were in love with her ; but so well did she manage her love affairs that each thought himself the only favoured one.

       *   *   *   *   *   *

Almost immediately after Harry's wedding, father expressed a wish to go back to Dysart.   He had bought a yacht and was by way of going up by sea ; but he was taken much worse suddenly, so this was not practicable, and he was hurried North by train.   I think he must have had some sort of premonition of his death and wanted to be at home, for during his two years of illness he had expressed no desire to go to Dysart.

I had gone with Millie to their shooting lodge at Stack, in Sutherland, and I was still there when we were wired for to come back at once.   I can remember so well that forty-mile drive to Lairg Station, miserable with anxiety about my father, wondering if we should be in time, dreading and hardly daring to imagine the future without him, and haunted by the fear that I might never see him alive again.

We had the most marvellous weather during that first week of September, and I can see myself sitting crouched on the sill by the open window in mother's boudoir, which had been turned into a bedroom for father, looking out towards the sea, and listening to those last gasps for breath. Then came the end, the last drawn out sigh, and the horrible silence that followed, when the truth dawned on me that we should never again see the twinkling smile, or hear his cheery voice.

The funeral was at Rosslyn Chapel. No more beautiful spot can be imagined as a last resting-place. It stands, a gem, the most perfect piece of Gothic architecture in Scotland, overlooking Hawthorn Den, and under the shadow of the ruins of the Castle. The " Pocket Cathedral," as the chapel has been called, was built in 1446, and was restored by my father—an abiding memorial to his memory.

My father's ancestors were for many generations buried in the chapel in their armour without any coffin :

> Each baron for a sable shroud
> Sheathed in his iron panoply.

The soil is so dry that bodies have been found in perfect condition more than eighty years after they were interred. In some old family memoirs we read that " the late Baron Rosslyn was the first who was buried in a coffin, contrary to the sentiments of James the Seventh, who was then in Scotland, and of several other persons well versed in antiquity, and to whom my mother would not hearken, thinking it beggarly to be buried in that manner."

The grave of the founder of the family, William St. Clair, is marked by a sculptured stone representing the knight trampling two dogs. The story connected with the stone is that in a hasty moment St. Clair staked his

head in a wager with the King that the dogs would pull
down a certain stag before it reached the March burn ;
but the dogs only barely succeeded in accomplishing
the feat, so they were sacrificed in this way that their
master might not be led to risk his life a second time on
such a venture.

The legend of the " prentice pillar " is too well known
to need relating, but, as a child, I was never tired of
slipping in amongst the tourists and hearing the old
verger repeating it, to each successive party, in the most
parrot-like fashion. I used to hope he would alter his
phraseology, but it was always the same story, told in
the same words, and in the same monotonous voice.

Attached to the chapel is a queer legend immortalized
by Sir Walter Scott in " Rosabelle," telling of the red
light that is supposed to glow through the windows of
the chapel when a St. Clair dies. This is said to have
been verified the night father died, and again years later
when my brother and sister died. Whether this is
imagination or coincidence I cannot say.

*   *   *   *   *

I remember those days after father's death so well,
and it seemed to me that the world had come to an
abrupt end. Nothing seemed very much to matter,
and I heard without any enthusiasm that mother contemplated taking Sybil and me to winter abroad. It was
thought that a complete change would be good for
mother, and as my brother Fitzroy was going to South
Africa we went with him as far as Madeira.   ·

I had travelled so much already for my age that
there was no novelty about it ; and I should have preferred staying at Stamford.

We had an abominably rough passage through the Bay ; though it is a very different thing in a liner than in a medium-sized yacht, I was all the same very glad to arrive at Funchal. The bullock-carts I found amusing ; being carried about in a hammock was much nicer than going for a constitutional, and it used to be great fun going up the hills in this lazy fashion and then tobogganing home down the cobbled streets.

The climate was wonderful and the vegetation superb, with wisteria and bougainvillia growing like a weed all over the houses. In those days, I suppose, Madeira was very different from what it is now, and at that time there were only a few houses and not more than one hotel. The hotel was crowded with invalids, which was very depressing, and every week an empty chair would be seen ; this meant that its occupant was too ill to come out, and the next you heard of was a death.

As a race the Portuguese are not attractive, and their language, which I picked up out there, seemed a mixture of bad Italian and Spanish. Languages was one of the few subjects I did not jib at during lessons. I suppose I inherited this gift from my father. Many of the poems in his book were translations, and there seemed no language that he had not been able to transcribe with ease into English.

Life at Madeira was already beginning to pall when we started home. It was returning to Stamford that made one feel anew the immense gap that father's death had made, and the sense of loss which has always clung to me throughout the vicissitudes of my life. There was no one to rush to meet, as I used to do, when he came home ; no one to hang over as I watched him finish a sonnet.

I think that mother, too, felt life unbearable at Stamford without father. She decided that in future our life would be spent more in London, and she also hoped to get a little house at Rosslyn with the object of being near the chapel.

Harry was to live at Stamford and his horses were already in the paddocks. He had started his racing on very different lines from those followed by my father. The gambling instinct was strong in him and wise people shook their heads ; whilst others wondered if he would stop in time. Alas ! the good things in life had come to him too young and in unexpected quantity ; and if you have the gambling fever in your blood it is a disease that is almost incurable.

He started with phenomenal luck, but it seems that this was the worst thing that could have happened to him, as he was afterwards buoyed up with the conviction that his bad luck was only temporary. The inevitable crash came only two years after he had succeeded, and I think the " last straw " was when Buccaneer failed to win the Manchester Cup.

The love of gambling, imbued by some dead ancestor, lurked around me too ; and my first bet at the age of fourteen was on Father O'Flynn when he won the Grand National. Roddy Owen, who rode him, used to go with his mother regularly to church and sat in the pew behind us at St. Michael's, Chester Square. I had met him first staying with Millie, and we renewed our friendship over a hymn book which he gave me, and into which many a surreptitious note was slipped ! (What a horribly precocious child I must have been.)

Poor Roddy ! He had got into deep water and he came to see me one day to say good-bye. He was, he

said, determined to win the National and then to leave
the country, and he told me to be sure and back Father
O'Flynn. As he started at 40 to 1 I commenced my
betting career fairly successfully.

Sybil's engagement to Tony Westmorland was at
last announced. They had, of course, known each other
for years—since the days we had all played together
at Apethorpe; but the question of marriage had met with
stern opposition on both sides, for financial reasons.
The opposition had, through circumstances, broken down.
Sybil was nearly twenty-one, and the death of Tony's
father had made him his own master. It seemed, therefore, better to accept the inevitable with good grace and
they were married from Millie's house in Berkeley Square.
Our own house was let and we were spending the summer
at Combe.

Sybil's love for Apethorpe was one of her strongest
affections, and when the place had to be sold it really
broke up her life. Few people had a brighter personality
than Sybil, and no one had more loyal friends. She was
one of those rare individuals who are forgiven everything for the sake of a charm that is peculiarly their own.

Combe saw the arrival of a French governess for me.
As she had been with Mouche Duncombe, who was dreadfully clever and going to Girton, it appeared rather a
doubtful proposition from my point of view; but the
change of nationality was welcome !

I started her off well and put her thoroughly through
her paces. I took her out in my pony cart and drove
her straight across country, shaving gate-posts and
generally giving her a *mauvais quart d'heure*. Mlle.
Schott never turned a hair, and we became fast friends
and are to this day, whilst my opinion of the French

race rose to a height from which it has never dropped. Yet Mlle. Schott never inspired me with the desire to follow in the footsteps of Mouche Duncombe and go to Girton, and in spite of her good influence I was still rather an *enfant terrible*, and my betting transactions continued, mostly in shillings and half-crowns, and were carried on surreptitiously with the butler. I used to find the evening paper with the starting prices tucked under my pillow when I went to bed. I think I knew more about form than fractions !

Lord Bradford won the Derby that year with Sir Hugo. He had come down to Combe as he often did to luncheon, and the conversation turned a good deal on racing and on the Derby in particular. Both my brothers were there, and they laughed when Lord Bradford said that Sir Hugo had a good chance of winning. La Flèche that year seemed such a certainty—but I was tempted by the long odds and it was then my turn to laugh !

I remember, too, how once when the Prince of Wales came to dinner, I knew Mamma had taken a great deal of trouble about the dinner and the wine and had got out some very good Perrier Jouet. When I saw the Prince refusing the champagne I called out to him ·

" Do drink it, Sir, it's Mamma's best P.J. '74, specially got out for you."

King Edward rose to the occasion and followed my advice.

⌐   *   ⌐   ⌐   ⌐   ⌐

After Sybil's marriage, mother and I went to live at Rose Bank, the little house she had taken near Roslin Chapel, and I hated this period of my life more than any I can remember.

King Edward, 1895.

[*Facing p.* 56

Certainly Dysart was not far off, and I went over there a good deal, but I seemed to miss father more every day.

On one occasion when I went over to spend a day or two at Dysart, Harry, Fitzroy, and I went out hunting. It was an amusing episode and worthy of a Punch artist being present.

H. had a pack of harriers—which he took round Fife, but whether he ever caught a hare is extremely doubtful. The stud consisted of three old crocks who had seen better days. One of them, Oakstick by name, had been well known in Leicestershire and he was to be my mount; as he was 16-3, I took some hoisting into the saddle, and as neither Harry nor Fitzroy were experts, I remained poised half way for some time before finally reaching my destination!

The meet was just outside Dunfermline and we went by special train. On the journey Fitzroy, immaculately dressed in pink, white apron complete, but his spurs in his hand, was asked by Harry why these were not already adjusted, to which Fitzroy blandly replied that no gentleman put his spurs on until he arrived at the meet. Of course it ended in my having to put them on for him !

The procession started through the town, and I wondered why Harry persisted in wandering through so many side streets, until I discovered he was looking for a plate glass window in which he could see himself and his hounds reflected ! By the time the window was reached the hounds had vanished, and were only found after some difficulty, regaling themselves in the various butchers' shops in the town. Sport was nil and a hunt after the only hare in the vicinity came to an abrupt termination with the arrival of the luncheon cart.

II

I SUPPOSE my coming out really dates from a cotillon given by Lady Kilmorey at the " Savoy," although in those days coming out meant curtseying to the Queen, and before that event one was definitely and irrevocably in the schoolroom. My début might have been hastened had I agreed to finishing my education in Germany ; but having escaped from German governesses I had no desire to see their country or eat their food. At the last moment, though the cab to take me to the station was actually at the door, I jibbed, finally and firmly ; so my boxes were unloaded and as an alternative I was kept for another six months in the schoolroom in Scotland.

But to return to the cotillon. Blanchie took me. It was quite small and a " married woman's " ball, which meant that very few girls were asked. Gerald Paget led it—I can't remember who with, but I can distinctly recollect one figure, a Noah's Ark with pairs of all the animals that Noah had ever seen—and more besides ! The man had to find the woman with the corresponding animal ; an enormous number of animals came my way and I was introduced to so many people that evening that my brain positively reeled.

The Drawing-room was a week later. I had a lovely white frock made by Mrs. Mason. She was "it" in the

58

dressmaker line; all her models came direct from Jean Worth, and everyone who had any pretension to dressing well in those days bought their frocks from her. She was a most perfect old lady and might have been a duchess instead of a dressmaker. She lived in Old Burlington Street and always wore a black cashmere or taffeta frock herself, with a folded white fichu. She it was who revived the "picture gown," and she took her models for these from Romney and Gainsborough. Her prices were supposed to be exorbitant, but compared to those of to-day they were almost insignificant!

I was terrified of tumbling over my train, and I didn't like the feathers in my hair at all. We had the entrée, so there was none of that waiting about incidental to most Drawing-rooms. I had been carefully instructed to kiss the Queen's hand, and that she would kiss my cheek, but when it came to the point I quite forgot all my instructions and I kissed *her* on both cheeks. I realized too late what I had done, and felt distinctly foolish, but the Queen didn't seem to mind a bit. The Prince of Wales, who saw my dilemma, of course chaffed me about it, which added to my discomfiture; but I went on bobbing to the other Royalties until I suddenly found my train flung over my arm by a gentleman-in-waiting, and I was out of the room.

It was all over so quickly that it seemed a fearful waste of time to have dressed up for those few minutes.

After that I was properly launched into the vortex of the London season, and the days were filled up with the usual entertainments and other events which were crowded in between Easter and Goodwood. I went, of course, to Ascot, and enjoyed this almost more than any other part of the summer. Having been brought up in an atmosphere of racehorses, it was only natural that I should enjoy racing.

Lord Coventry was Master of the Buckhounds that year, and the Royal procession driving up the course on Cup Day was a lovely sight, but the procession was even more picturesque when Lord Ribblesdale was in office—his own appearance in the green coat giving an additional " old-world " touch.

After the races I rode in Windsor Park, on a big black charger belonging to Lord Tullibardine. Queen Anne's ride was the most fashionable rendezvous, and it was certainly a pleasanter place for seeing your friends than the crowded enclosure.

I had enjoyed myself so much at the Kilmoreys' dance that I had expected to do the same wherever I went, and at first I wanted to go to every lighted candle ; but I soon found out that there were balls and balls, and that what were known as the " married women's balls " were the only amusing ones, and in a very few weeks I became amazingly discriminating before accepting invitations ! Balls began much later in those days, and I found staying up trying to keep awake a most tedious performance, which took the gilt off the ginger-bread of the evening. Mamma had a great idea that an hour or two's sleep beforehand made one fresher, but I found that when I indulged in a siesta I had no inclination to get up, so that I very often used to turn over and go to sleep again and not go to the ball at all. I suppose I did not care enough about dancing, but the ordinary London ball-room is so small that the crowd would have spoilt it for even the enthusiasts. There were, of course, exceptions—Devonshire House, Stafford

House and Grosvenor House were the houses *par excellence,* and where one could not complain of a crush, however many people were there.

As I look back on that first season, there seems to me so very little of any importance to remember. I had looked forward to coming out so much that when it actually happened it fell rather flat. There was no such thing as liberty for a girl in those days, and I could not even walk across the street without my maid, though I never discovered what could have happened to me if I had done so in broad daylight. On the whole, I do not think I was really sorry when the season came to an end, and I went down to Easton to stay with Daisy for a fortnight, which included two week-end parties and a cricket week. Out of the big party there, I can remember Lord Houghton* who, of course, I had known as a child, and Prince Pless—he had grown fat and podgy since the days when I rode his horses in Paris, and the Asquiths—Margot impressive and generally hatless, but full of life and importance.

I was sorry for Daisy P., she was so young and so pretty that I was sure she could not have much in common with her German husband, and some years afterwards she told me how much she had suffered in her early married life. Before her first baby was born, " Hans Heinrich " used to drive her on his coach at breakneck speed down the very steep hill outside Baggrave, on purpose to frighten her. Isn't that typical of the German mentality ?

From Easton I went on to Cowes to stay with Blanchie, who had taken Egypt House for the summer.

* Marquis of Crewe.

The Kaiser had come over to Cowes that year, and his presence was responsible for an unusually gay week.

The races between the Kaiser's *Meteor* and the Prince of Wales's *Britannia* aroused, of course, much interest. Herky Langrishe and Philip Perceval were respectively in charge of them. Herky Langrishe was the wildest Irishman, up to all sorts of mad pranks, and he talked with a brogue so marked that I suspected it to be assumed. He was very good-looking in those days, and I should think, like the proverbial sailor, he had " a wife in every port." I was very lucky and got a good deal of racing one way and another, and I went out on both the *Britannia* and the *Meteor*. The Kaiser was on board his boat the day I sailed on her, and the party included Lady Ormonde and Lady Londonderry.

There is no gainsaying the glamour which was attached to the Kaiser in those days, and I confess that I was certainly one of those who fell under the charm of his personality. He was so wide-awake and interested in everything ; he was delightful to me, put me at my ease at once, and gave me the comforting feeling that he enjoyed talking to me. That gift of concentrating on the person he was talking to was shared with the Prince of Wales, and it was perhaps part of the secret why both were so popular. As I look back now, it seems to me as if there may have been a little jealousy between them, and I believe more fuss was made of the Kaiser at this time than of our own Prince. There was a certain picturesqueness about him, and though he did not strike one as catering for popularity, he had a well-managed press. Oddly enough, after this time at Cowes, I did not see the Kaiser again until I met him at a party the Londesboroughs gave at St. Dunstans, on his last visit to this country, and then I wondered if this could be the same man. He wore an ill-fitting grey suit, and seemed to have shrunk into an uninteresting old man with no sign of the War Lord about him. The withered arm, which I had never noticed before, seemed glaringly apparent. That he still remained a dominant figure in the minds of his own people may mean that he has *some* virtue ; or is it a proof of German sentimentality, for Mark Twain avers that no matter how cracked a voice may become with age, a once-famous singer still remains a hero in the eyes of the faithful German public.

I saw a great deal of Lord Dunraven at Cowes, and of his two daughters, who were both charming, Rachel, now dead, and Eileen, who is now Lady Ardee and as delightful as ever. We used to sail together in the smaller boats, besides amusing ourselves in many other ways. For Cowes week was a small edition of the London season and the Squadron Gardens were the scene of many revels.

From Cowes I went up to Scotland to Dunrobin and stayed with Millie. Dunrobin during the autumn was more like an hotel to which everybody came and went, with the result that the most incongruous parties would often be assembled there. Millie's interests were wide. She took life and things probably more seriously than other people, and while thoroughly appreciative of all the good things of life, she had an almost overwhelming sense of responsibility. She took a very real interest in the crofters in Sutherland and in the potteries in Staffordshire, whilst the silk industry at Leek was most successfully revived by her. She allowed everyone to propose themselves to Dunrobin, and was most indiscriminate in her invitations, so it would be no uncommon thing to find a Cabinet Minister, a poet, a parson and a social reformer sitting down to dinner together in perfect harmony.

I remember Lord Rosebery up .there that year, particularly because I wanted him to write his name in my Visitors' Book before he left. But instead of doing this he made Mr. Reggie Brett do it for him, as for some reason or other he strongly objected to giving his autograph. I was very angry when I discovered this forgery, too late to get it remedied, as he had left by the morning mail, but I made him sign it at a later date, even then under protest !

I have never seen anyone so spoilt as Lord Rosebery at Dunrobin. Everyone was kept waiting about until he had made up his mind if he wanted to go stalking or not, and by that time it was generally too late for anybody else to go out. I believe when he *did* go out he shot a stag under the recognized weight, but this mistake of his was officially concealed.

In the evenings we used to play the race game, and there was one horse we called Cicero, and if this horse did not win, Lord Rosebery was almost peevish, as he thought it was a bad omen for his chances for the St. Leger !

Roddy Owen, home for a few weeks from East Africa, was one of those who had found their way North that year. I had not seen him since he had said good-bye to me just before winning the National. The childish romance attached to Roddy had vanished, but he still

WAITING FOR THE MAIL AT DUNROBIN.
Lord Rosebery and Lord Chaplin on the platform.

[*Facing p.* 64

retained the hard, clean-looking appearance that had seemed to me at that romantic age so attractive.

Of all the people I had met I liked Lord Hardwicke—then Lord Royston—better than anyone. "Tommy Dodd," as he was nicknamed, was one in many thousands. He possessed good looks, which even a smashed nose, the result of a fall steeplechasing, did not spoil, and a nature as near perfection as could be found in a mortal.

When he gave up steeplechasing, he settled down to politics and became rather inaccessible. He lived with his mother in York Terrace, and though inundated with invitations he much preferred dining with her at home. Lady Hardwicke was very sweet to me, and I was always sure of a welcome from both of them.

October 1st, 1894.
Shooting party at Houghton.

How one hates to see these bald figures and dates in black and white, and one realizes suddenly that half the people one is writing about are dead, not killed in the war—just dead. Lord Grey de Wilton, my host, is one of these. He rented Houghton from Lord Cholmondeley, and as one of the gay bachelors of the day, his parties were very amusing, and he generally had his sister, Lady Bettine Taylor, to do hostess. She, Daisy and I were, I think, the only women there that week. The Houghton shooting is proverbially good, and all Lord Grey's guests were really first-class shots. Tom Kennard, the big-game shooter, Evan Charteris and Buck Barclay were amongst them that week.

As the Prince of Wales was going to Easton on his

way to Newmarket, Daisy had to hurry back there
before the end of the week, and I went with her.

With the Prince came Sir Donald Mackenzie Wallace,
M. de Soveral, the Portuguese Minister—I suppose no
foreigner has ever been so popular in this country—
Henry Chaplin and the late Lord and Lady Cork; the
latter, a most interesting old lady of the old school, was
always very nice to me, and used to ask me to tea with
her in London.

Daisy and I drove down to the station on her coach
to meet the party. D. was a very good whip, and I
believe it was Lord Charlie Beresford who originally
taught her to drive. She always had a beautiful team,
and her love of animals was one of her marked characteristics. The best of horses filled the stables at Easton
and Warwick, but she did not confine her attention nor
her affections to horses, for almost every breed of dog
was represented in her house. Now I believe she has a
collection of monkeys almost as varied as those at the
Zoo, and the question of their diet plays a most important
part amongst the household arrangements !

The Prince of Wales was a most easy guest to enter-
tain, one of his many charms being his interest in everything and everybody. Whether the strictness of his
upbringing had anything to do with it I don't know,
but I should think few people had more *joie de vivre*.
He enjoyed himself with the infectious gaiety of a school-
boy. That indefinable, but undeniable, gift of youth
remained with him all his life, yet no man took up his
responsibilities more definitely when they came to him.

I persuaded Brookie and Willie Lowe to take me to
see the Cambridgeshire run. It was quite an easy
journey from Easton, as the train used always to stop at

Elsenham Station to pick up a very large contingent of the Gilbey family. Old Sir Walter Gilbey looked just as if he had stepped out of an old sporting picture, in his funny, snuff-coloured clothes, most quaintly cut. This was my first visit to Newmarket. The attendance in those days consisted of a more or less family party of the racing set, everyone in the plainest of tailor-mades— very different from now, when the stand is full of a rather overdressed medley of females.

The late Duchess of Devonshire, Lady Cadogan and Lady Londonderry, with a few of their particular friends, occupied a corner of the stand nearest the paddock (Cadogan Place, I think it was called), and gave cold looks to intruders who dared to trespass.

Newmarket is the Mecca of the racing world, and is the most pleasant spot : that is, if you care about racing. The visitor from London does not know its joys, for besides the day's racing there is the morning work of the horses to watch, and riding over the almost boundless heath in the evening is yet another of its charms for habitués. Later, I used to go regularly to Newmarket, staying either with Lord Durham at Exning, or with Sir Charles Rose, and I remember being nearly knocked down one morning by Cyllene when he was doing a gallop on the heath !

As I look back now I realize what a tremendous difference it made having so many sisters, not only to take me out in London, but to stay with in the country ; what with Easton, Warwick, Trentham and Dunrobin, the year was nearly filled up. I have the happiest recollections of all of them, but particularly of Trentham and Warwick, as here I hunted, which was the thing of all others that I loved.

5*

My brother-in-law, Strath, was Master of the North Staffordshire Hounds. Before they succeeded he and Millie used to hunt from a little house at Market Drayton, and their return to Trentham had been joyfully welcomed after the régime of the " Mrs. Blair Duchess." The late Duke had married Mrs. Blair immediately on the death of the Duchess, Strath's mother, and this had caused a complete breach with his family. I never saw Mrs. Blair, but it is a matter of history that she spent some weeks in prison, for throwing a document in the fire in the very face of the lawyer.

The North Stafford was a rather rough country, but with a very jolly bit round Market Drayton, and on the other side it adjoined the Meynell. We used to hunt on Tuesdays with the Cheshire, where there was a more amusing field but also a very rough crowd from Manchester.

Mr. Corbet, the Master, was a dear old man, and he hunted the hounds himself. We used sometimes to go over to Adderley, where they lived, for a meet on the far side. Mrs. Corbet, an austere old lady (she is still alive), was very different from her husband, but they had a mutual adoration for their son Bertie—who became one of my best friends and one of my most constant partners.

It was in Cheshire that the wonderful Empress of Austria, piloted by Bay Middleton, did most of her hunting.

Besides the hunt horses which I had to ride, I had one horse of my own. He came from Ralph Sneyd with a big reputation as a timber jumper. He had, however, a very hard mouth, and was not altogether the horse you would have chosen for a beginner, and I had to ride him in a segunder bridle ; but he was a marvellous hunter and never gave me a fall. The first day I rode him in an ordinary double bridle, and from start to finish he took me just where he liked. Luckily hounds ran without a check, and I think we were first into the field just as they had bowled their fox over in the open. Here Royalist stopped dead, which was lucky, as I should have been soundly abused by Mr. Corbet if I had galloped into the middle of the hounds. He was a dear old horse, and years after, when he had broken down and was turned out, he used to jump over the gate of his paddock every Sunday morning and come into the stable-yard for his carrots.

As bad luck would have it, my first winter's hunting was hopelessly curtailed by frost, which lasted for endless weeks, and skating and tobogganing were a very poor substitute.

At Trentham there was always a big schoolroom and nursery party, for besides Millie's own children, the Chaplins practically lived there ; their mother, Lady Florence, Strath's sister, had died when her youngest child was born. Not only did the children make their home with Millie and Strath, but their father, Harry Chaplin, also had his own rooms at Stafford House, and used to hunt from Trentham. In spite of his great weight, he still went well, and from all accounts he must have been a wonderful man across country in his younger days. He had that rare gift of galloping a horse. Someone had said any fool can jump fences, but that getting over the ground between them is the test of horsemanship. How true—particularly on the Leicestershire ridge and furrow. The sensation of floundering over the fields is so often attributed to a faulty action on the horse's part, but it is more often the rider's. Even then the Squire of Blankney used to go as well as anyone, and I have never seen anyone enjoy it more—I am never quite sure if he enjoyed his food or his hunting most ! Besides giving me my first lessons in hunting, he encouraged my already prematurely developed taste for the good things of the table. As Milly and Strath were both rather indifferent as to what they ate, the kitchen arrangements generally devolved on Harry Chaplin ; he was consequently a most useful lodger !

Restaurants were very little frequented, and, in fact, hardly existed in those days. The " Amphytrion " in Albemarle Street was one of the first to be fashionable. It was not a long-lived venture, but it was patronized by the gourmets of London, and here at two o'clock you might be sure to find the Blankney Squire, discussing the latest dish with Emile, the presiding genius. Amongst the other habitués of this select and expensive rendezvous may be mentioned Monsieur de Soveral, Lord de Grey, and Major Wynne-Finch. Later Willis's rooms were reopened under the auspices of Algy Bourke and Edouard became an almost historical personage. Willie Lowe used to have a table reserved for him every day, with covers laid for twelve people. One day he, and I think Austin Mackenzie, were lunching together, when Willie thought he would ask for his bill. I believe it came to £1,200, but Edouard was quite pleased to accept half !

* * * * *

The New Year still saw me at Trentham. The Willie Grenfells*, Cardrosses† and Major Wynne-Finch (supposed to be one of the best looking men of his day)

* Lord and Lady Desborough.   † Lord and Lady Buchan.

THE BICYCLING CRAZE.

were all staying there. I remember being enormously
impressed by the vast amount of letters which Ettie
Grenfell wrote every day. I suppose this is one of the
secrets of her having more friends than anyone else;
though, after all, it is only a very small factor, for her
other qualities alone would make her what she is—the
most popular woman!

Who does not like getting letters!—but how very
few people are ready to gratify their friends' likes in
this direction! I think to write a daily letter is far
easier than an occasional budget. King Edward was,
I believe, a wonderful correspondent; but how few
people have been taught, or have the gift of writing
interesting letters! Those that had it certainly belonged
to the Victorian era, or earlier, and in these days it is
as rare as the blue bird.

Later Ettie was immensely good to me. Her
apparently boundless capacity for showing sympathy
is never tinged with pity!

A local ball and the bicycle craze added to our dis-
tractions while the frost still continued. The bicycle
craze was just beginning and I have got some old photographs of some of the party practising round the
Italian Gardens; one of Millie in a voluminous skirt,
being held up by a footman. How funny to look back
on that bicycling craze, and how universal it became!
Everyone had their bicycle painted a different colour;
bicycle stables were built and bicycles became a part
of everyone's luggage. There were bicycle parties for
breakfast in Battersea Park—bicycle parties by moonlight, to say nothing of trick bicycling. I wonder if
bicycling was a prelude to rather more reasonable clothes
being worn in the country?

The event of the winter of 1895 was the big fancy dress ball at Warwick which Daisy was giving as a sort of house-warming. She was having the most enormous party—enormous even for Warwick—which was saying a good deal. Daisy herself looked too lovely as a Marie Antoinette, Féo Sturt was gorgeous beyond words as Madame de Maintenon ; Daisy Pless with at least three tiaras on her head and her sister, Sheila Cornwallis West, a complete contrast to the other's fairness, were some of the people there. The men's clothes were, if possible, even more gorgeous than the women's. Humphrey Sturt made a marvellous Abbé ; the Neville brothers, Dick and Lord Bill, were splendid in brocades ; Count Deym, the Austrian Ambassador, was picturesque and stately ; Lord Lonsdale, thorough in everything he undertakes, had completely disguised himself by plastering down his side whiskers, and it must have taken some tons of grease paint to remove them, judging by the remains which I found left in the bathroom next morning.

Of course everybody for miles round brought parties, and no more perfect spot for such an entertainment could have been found. The snow was on the ground, and as one stood in the old hall, with its coats of arms and the men in armour, looking out across the river, the countryside decked in its glistening white mantle, the rich colours and fantastic costumes of the guests seemed enhanced by the romantic setting. It was a picture that no one who saw it was ever likely to forget.

In spite of the frost Millie and I went on to Leicestershire to stay with Doods Naylor for the Melton Ball.

My palpitating excitement over my first visit to Melton can be surely understood. I had been nurtured

on tales of Melton—had not Whyte Melville been a childish hero, " Big Brock "* an ideal, by which one gauged other men—had I not heard of the wonders of the Skeffington Vale and listened to the stories of the great " Chicken Hartopp " and of the " wicked Earl."†
Hadn't my imagination been stirred by the picture of Lord Waterford jumping his horse over a five-barred gate in the dining-room at Loseby, and of the gallant deeds of Lord Dupplin, in spite of the fact that he never went to bed ! Hadn't Lindsay Gordon's poems been the very easiest to learn and wasn't there a ring about Bromley Davenport's verse that had made one long for the " sublimest of ecstasies " under the sun ? Melton seemed teeming with romantic legends, and though most of the heroes of these reminiscences had passed the " unjumpable Styx " there were still a few of those amazing individuals left, for me to admire, whose deeds of daring were historical facts. Doggie Smith was still a past master ; Arthur Coventry, with his funny wrinkled face, went as well as ever ; Custance, not such a thruster as he used to be, for his mount was generally for sale, and must be nursed ; Sam Hames always in that little crowd that showed the way to the still younger generation. But alas ! the frost was so far in the ground that, even had an immediate thaw set in, the most sanguine could not have hoped to have a hunt.

The Plesses were hunting from Baggrave that winter, and had a large party for the ball, which, by the way. was excellent.

Daisy Pless was most proverbially casual over all arrangements, and some of her party were left stranded at the station, no sort of conveyance being available,

* Late Lord Ranksborough. † Earl of Wilton.

and I believe one woman had eventually to drive the
eight miles in a baker's cart. To make up for my
disappointment about the hunting, Doods insisted that
we should go to her for as long as we liked the following
year.

But all the same I did have one day with the Quorn
that season, for as soon as the frost broke up, Millie and I
actually went all the way by train from Trentham to
Leicester. Naturally I was immensely impressed with
the pageant. Lord Lonsdale was Master, and it would
be difficult to have seen a meet in Leicestershire for
the first time under better auspices. The chestnut
horses, the yellow carriages with their postilions made
it a most spectacular affair. The Yellow-man, as he
was familiarly nicknamed, was a picturesque figure.
His eye for a country was only equalled by his sense
of the dramatic, and his love of a picturesque setting,
and his facile imagination, that resulted in super Hans
Andersen tales, had always been a source of childish
delight to me. The ladies all, or nearly all, wore top
hats, but I do not think I liked the blue facings which
Lady Lonsdale had revived, as much as the Pytchley
white.

We only had a moderate day's sport—I think we
spent more hours in the train than actually hunting—
but I felt that none of them were wasted hours, and
I can well understand anyone who has hunted in
Leicestershire being spoilt for most other counties.

My diary is a Visitors' Book, full only of autographs
and old photographs, but it suffices to tell me where I
went and who I saw during the next twelve months.
However good a memory one possesses, dates are apt to

get confused, and though events may remain quite vivid, there is a difficulty in sequelizing and sorting them out ; but this picture diary not only brings them into chronological order, but reminds one of quarrels made and mended, of friendships formed and broken, and the wells of memory are stirred anew with ripples—not so faint and foggy as might be expected when one remembers the years that have elapsed.

I have deplored before that so many of the people one wrote about are dead, and as I look at my book now the fact strikes me with renewed force. I came just now upon Charty Ribblesdale's name and I remember the fun that we had together at Dunrobin. She and I and Lord Ribblesdale had the most delightful days on the Brora golf links. What a perfect companion she was ! so full of exuberant spirits that she made the world seem a jollier and better place. She had a more subtle, though not a less pungent, sense of humour than her sister Margot. She once called Margot the " Governess of the world," and used to laugh, though always with the greatest kindness and affection, at her busy " interest " in other people's lives. Through all her illness she still retained the same cheerful hopefulness, and no one is surer of a place in Heaven. She was not at Gisburne the only time I went up there. Her two youngest children—the Dolls, as they were called—Laura and Diana, were the most delightful couple : Laura,* with her brilliant looks, and Diana,† a perfect picture, either coursing with the greyhounds or riding over the country in her brown habit, with her flaxen hair tied back with a large black bow. They have remained indelibly printed on my memory.

* Lady Lovat.   † Hon. Mrs. Capel.

Laura, at the time I was at Gisburne, was the wor-
shipper of Augustus John. I ought to have known his
name, but it was from Laura that I first heard of it and
of his marvellous technique. She looked very lovely
in her blue sweater, and could not be torn from palette
and easel to join Diana, her father and myself on our
hunting expeditions. Lord Ribblesdale's buck-hounds
were an innovation and the country they hunted over
was big and wild, with a beautiful grass vale. The
rivers were rather disconcerting, and I did not at all
relish fording them. We had a day with—I think—
the Bramham Moor—" *some* expedition," and we ended
up by having tea at Leeds. One does not, somehow,
associate Leeds with hunting !

Bertie Tempest, so tragically killed in the Welsh
train disaster, is a personality who will be sadly missed.
He was certainly the life and soul of every party. Then
Lord Chesham, the most perfect type of English sportsman and gentleman, is another who has passed into the
ranks of the remembered. Roddy and Hughie Owen
have left us too—Hughie was killed out hunting, the
death he would have chosen—and Roddy had died of
fever in East Africa. Curiously enough, I had a letter
from him written in the best of spirits, congratulating
me on my marriage the very morning I opened the paper
and saw the news of his death. These names appear
again and again on the pages of my book, and they are
only a few, taken at random !

At that time, such books were the fashion, and it was
no uncommon thing at a country house to sign your
name at least a dozen times before catching your train
in the morning, but that old life is already so far away—

that life that seemed to consist of a visitor's book full of autographs ! Though it tells me where I went and whom I saw, it is such a continuous repetition of people and places that I am struck with the narrowness of the circle in which we moved.

Looking back, the social life of the late Victorian and Edwardian era seems to have consisted of a round of amusements which went to make up the rather futile existence of the bulk of society. What a wrong impression of our latent capabilities the public would have if they were to judge them by looking at this Visitors' Book ! But the war proved most conclusively that these butterflies were really made of sterner stuff, and with hardly one exception, they rose to the most unexpected heights of capability. When I went to France I could hardly make a cup of tea, and in three months I felt I could run Lyons' !

* * * *

The Yeomanry week at Warwick was an annual affair, and the park was converted into a miniature Aldershot for the time being : tents, horses, orderlies and all the rest of the military panoply, with Lord Roberts and Sir Evelyn Wood staying there. No two men could be more of a contrast. Lord Roberts was so gentle, yet he gave the impression of the wonderful strength of mind and purpose that we know was his. Sir Evelyn, full of good dinner, and good stories which he whispered into his neighbour's ear over the coffee—generally audible to all. Daisy's cats had all to be safely shut up during Lord Roberts's visits ; for it was no myth that he hated them.

Lord R. and Sir Evelyn were still there when the Prince of Wales arrived and the castle accommodation was taxed to the uttermost with over thirty people in the house.

Mr. Balfour is in tennis kit in my picture diary, and so is Lord Curzon (now Lord Howe), so we must infer that tennis formed part of our week-end diversions; but many of the other guests in the group are armed with croquet mallets, for it was about then that the game of crinolines and coquetry once more became fashionable, only a scientific element had been attached to its revival, and people took to going about with their own croquet mallets. Lord Cairns made one for me. He was most ingenious and clever with a lathe, and the mallet he made for me was elaborately turned out of ivory. It was not a very satisfactory implement to play with, and I discarded it when Evie Miller Mundy and I played our famous croquet match at Ranelagh. We were both supposed to be rather good and we were heavily backed by our respective admirers. I think she won one match and I the other.

A band was a *sine qua non* at all Daisy's parties, and no device which contributed to her guests' comfort or amusement was neglected. She had not developed her socialistic tendencies in those days, but entertained as thoroughly as, later on, she imbibed the doctrines of " the Comrades."

＊　　＊　　＊　　＊

It was at Easton that Elinor Glyn made her first appearance on the social horizon. She and her husband lived at Harlow and had driven over to watch the cricket. I can see her now, coming across to the tent where we were sitting, with her very red hair glistening in the

Party at Easton to meet King Edward hen Prince o Wales.

sun ; her frock (I must say it was only made of the very cheapest material) made her look as if she had stepped out of *La Vie Parisienne ;* we were all so thrilled over her appearance that we got Daisy to ask her to come and stay. The " creation " in which she appeared for dinner was another marvel, and after dinner she did the most wonderful imitations, for a select few, of Sarah Bernhardt !

Mrs. Glyn had not yet blossomed into an authoress, but the " Visits of Elizabeth " were, I fancy, in the making. I am not sure whether I should have been inordinately proud, or a little bit ashamed, of my photograph being used as the prototype of Elizabeth. *Enfant terrible* I may have been ; but I do not think I ever found myself in exactly the same exciting situations as Mrs. Glyn's heroine, though I believe I once made a terrible *gaffe*, rather on the lines of Elizabeth and the Ghost. On the other hand, it was head-turning to have had such an attractive heroine built upon what Mrs. Glyn imagined to be my characteristics.

I personally was very grateful to her because she gave me the address of her sister, Mrs. Wallace—" Lucille " of to-day's fame. I cannot remember where she lived, but it certainly was not in the present fashionable locality, and she made the most lovely frocks for £8 ! ! I really think she did a great deal to revolutionize dress in London : all her frocks, in those days even, were recognizable by her finishing touches, which generally consisted of minute buttons and little frills of lace and ribbon. She had a wonderful collection of old embroidered collars which she used to adapt, and she gave me a lovely one which she put on my going-away coat !

Another authoress I met at Easton, of a very different

type, was Marie Corelli. With her flaxen tousled hair, the sage green garments and the beads she wore, she put me instantly in mind of a very cheap doll. My father always said if you liked a book, you should never try to discover the author. He made this remark, having read " Coming through the Rye," then being bitterly disappointed when he encountered Helen Mathers, having taken endless trouble to make her acquaintance. I am inclined to agree with him. The few real authors I have met (I am not talking of the amateur memoir writers) have not inspired me with enthusiasm. Hitchens made me feel positively uncomfortable—in spite of his brilliance—or perhaps because of it. There are, of course, exceptions.

Well's personality grows on one tremendously. I met him first at Stanway, and again not long ago at dinner ; he was not sure whether he ought to be sorry or sad when I told him that his books were published in too small type for me to enjoy them ! We had great fun after that ; he has promised to convert me, and I am expecting a van load of his works to arrive any day— but of course I was only pulling his leg ! We discussed the " movies," and here we failed to agree, as Wells thinks Charlie Chaplin the greatest artiste and he bores me to extinction. We found, however, one great point in common, Wells refuses to eat haddock for breakfast without mustard, and I so agree with him !

ı   *   *   *   ᴛ

My second season was spent on the river. I persuaded mother to let the house in London and to take one at Windsor, but I came up for any good balls and entertainments that I wanted to go to.

Against the rather blurred background of the summer, my second winter's hunting stands out in pleasantly bold relief, and I was really delighted to be back at Trentham for the New Year. Jim Forbes, whom I afterwards married, was there. Millie had wired me to get a man who would dance at the local ball, and he was the first person I met as I went out for a walk. By such small things are the big events in one's life decided.

From Trentham, some of our party, including Jim Forbes and myself, went on to Warwick. I stayed on there, and Cecil Grenfell and Lord Kenyon, who were both hunting from Warwick, used to be very good to me. " Good hunting, little sister," was their morning greeting, and away we would go on some delicious expedition.

The Warwickshire Field included a good many interesting and amusing people, among them the Southamptons—both fine riders, Lord S. very silent but very good looking and never far from hounds, and his wife, Lord Zetland's daughter, though too short-sighted to ride her own line, was beautifully mounted on horses well over her weight, and she followed closely on her husband's heels. The Greville Verneys were at Kineton—he eventually succeeded his father, Lord Willoughby de Broke, as Master of the Warwickshire. I always liked him, and his rather theatrical manners were more amusing than annoying. Then there was the much-run-after Mrs. Tree, née Field, who so sensationally became what she now is, Lady Beatty. Her father-in-law lived at Rugby, and what he did not know about horses was not worth knowing ! He was a great character in Warwickshire, and not to know David Beatty was to admit your ignorance of who is famous in the equine world.

Lord Beatty was, of course, often out hunting, and

6

when he is held up to us as one of the few sailors who look as much at home on a horse as on a ship, people forget his parentage. He was almost born in the saddle. After he married Mrs. Tree, they came to Leicestershire, and I always thought she looked her best on a horse ; they were both light weights, and they rode a very perfect stamp of blood horse. Apart from being a fine horseman, Lord Beatty had those qualities of quickness and decision essential to the good man to hounds.

Millie and I were at last to spend that long looked forward to fortnight with Doods Naylor at Melton, and this time we had no fear of a frost as the weather was ideal for hunting. I had now got two horses of my own which I was taking with me. Besides Royalist, I had a little bay mare which Will Boxall, the North Stafford-shire huntsman, had bought for me from a farmer. She was only 15.2, and I thought I should feel rather lost on her in the big Leicestershire fields. We had tried her over some rails at Trentham, and had found her a perfect timber jumper, and she proved her extra-ordinary stamina the day Lord Lonsdale had a bye day at Thorpe Satchville. This bye day had been kept very quiet—we only heard of it at the last moment and nearly everyone had gone to London. Amongst the people that I can remember out were Buck Barclay, Mr. Biddulph, Arthur Coventry, Joe Laycock, Lancelot Lowther and the Hatfield Harters—surely no woman looked smarter than she in her " swallow tail " coat, and how well she used to go—but no woman ever had a better pilot than she had in her husband. We found a fox almost immediately at Ashby Folville ; he made straight for Adam's Gorse, and from there we ran over the cream of the Cottesmore Country with a satisfactory conclusion in Lady Lonsdale's garden at Cottesmore, as good a hunt as anyone could wish for. Most people's horses were dead beat, but when I started to ride home, after a most excellent luncheon with Lady Lonsdale, La Gloria, as the little mare was called, was as fresh as when she went out.

Melton was very full that winter. The Barclays were at Sysonby, or, to be accurate, he was there *en garçon* and Aggie was wintering abroad; the Lawsons were at the Manor House, the de Wintons at the Old Club, and the Manners' were as usual at Cold Overton, whilst the Henry Bentincks were somewhere in the neighbourhood. Tony Markham, Jim Forbes and Dick Fenwick had a small house in the town, and so had Joe Laycock and Max de Tuyll.

It seemed as if everyone was trying to give us a good time, and to make our visit especially amusing, and though I had only two horses I managed to get out hunting every day that I was there! The event of our visit was the ball Sir Ernest Cassel gave at Dalby. I have never seen so many lilies of the valley. They completely covered the walls and staircases. Sir Ernest had started hunting a year or two before in Warwickshire from Lord Willoughby de Broke's place, and he had only just migrated to Leicestershire. He was amazingly brave and seemed quite oblivious to the number of falls he took—and he was no light weight either. He kept open house at Dalby and it was amusing to watch the methods of his would-be exploiters!

Our farewell party was given by Buck Barclay and consisted of a huge dinner followed by fireworks. It was only marred by the fact that we were leaving the

6*

next day. How sorry I was to go ! A lot of us, however, were going on to Warwick for more hunting, which
was some recompense.

The Warwickshire meet at Shuckborough is famous,
and the country round, I think, is the biggest—some of
it, indeed, is practically unjumpable. They had a most
wonderful hunt, but I did not enjoy myself, as not only
was I hopelessly left, but I did not like the horse I was
riding. It wasn't fit, so I gave up all attempt at pursuit
and returned to the village inn and gloomily awaited the
arrival of the rest of our party. ˙ They came in one by
one all full of this marvellous day and found me morose
and unsympathetic ! The next day things were better
and I had a perfect ride on Jim Forbes' horse—Pilot.

I suppose that sealed my fate, for when ⏉. asked
me that evening to marry him, I said : " Yes ! if I may
have your chestnut horse." (I shudder to think of my
own callousness !) Lord Willoughby de Broke, when
he heard of my engagement, said he " hoped I would
surmount life's obstacles as easily as I had sailed over
those in the Ladbroke Vale that day."

' There is not much to write about the next few weeks ;
they were taken up almost entirely with trousseau-
buying in Paris. I went over with Mamma and we
stayed at the Hôtel Bristol. I don't think I had been
to Paris since father's illness and I found suddenly how
badly I needed him at this juncture of my life—buying
frocks and a pearl necklace from Boucheron was amusing
enough, but I can't describe my state of mind as happy.
The Marlboroughs were in Paris on their way back to
England, and I dined with them one night. Consuelo
very pale, and rather shy, and with only the promise of
the good looks which she afterwards developed. I

Col Anstruther Thomson

[Facing p. 84

came back in time for Melton Races to see Pilot, after refusing the water jump twice, win the Ladies' Purse. Jim also rode another winner that day, which pleased him considerably.

I was married on the 28th April, from Stafford House, at St. Paul's, Knightsbridge, and was driven to church with the old piebald horses which father had always been so proud of. My wedding dress, made by Mrs. Mason, was lovely. I wrestled successfully against the conventional satin frock, and she had designed me a dress of white chiffon with a very long satin train embroidered with sprays of lilies of the valley.

Geordie and Alistair, Millie's two boys, were my pages, and I had only two grown-up bridesmaids, Muriel Wilson and Helen Keith-Fraser; the others were all children and included my two nieces, Marjorie Greville and Ivy Gordon-Lennox, Edie Chaplin, Muriel Erskine and Diana Sturt.

I had rebelled against the conventional bridesmaids' dresses and had hit on the idea of their wearing red velvet capes slung over their white satin frocks. Every one was sceptical about the result at first, but when it came to the point, they all said that the note of colour in the church, if it was an innovation, was a success.

The big glass doors of Stafford House had been thrown open for the occasion and the whole of London seemed to have turned up. I had forbidden rice and slippers, but the Prince of Wales was determined that I should not be allowed to forego this orthodox custom, and I can still see him chuckling delightedly at having outwitted me, as he hurled a slipper full after the departing carriage.

III

ALMOST directly after I was married I went to Warwick for the Yeomanry week. Jim, in a fit of temper, because he couldn't get leave when he wanted it, had sent in his papers and left the 9th Lancers and gone into the Warwickshire Yeomanry. I remember being blamed for this step of his, but I knew nothing about it till it was a *fait accompli*. Naturally I should have opposed it, for, on principle, I believe that any man without an occupation is, to say the least of it, bound to be very difficult to live with.

Warwick was, of course, crowded as usual. Major Douglas Haig was staying there. I believe Daisy had met him out hunting, and we were told then that he was supposed to be a rising soldier, but certainly no one guessed what his ultimate future would be, and I am afraid we were not as impressed by him as we ought to have been. It was some years after this that he met and married Miss Vivian, Queen Alexandra's Maid of Honour, and from that time his advancement began. Though not so pretty as her sister Violet, she has proved an admirable wife for him—in fact, one might say that in the matter of his marriage Lord Haig first showed his generalship.

We were eventually going to have a house in Leicestershire, but in the meanwhile we spent the summer at

Stafford House. Were there ever two people so kind and hospitable as Millie and Strath, and I wonder how many houseless members of their family, to say nothing of their friends, found a welcome with them—surely Stafford House was well named " The Stafford Arms ! "

We went to stay with the Marlboroughs for Ascot and the party included the Churchills* and Lady Randolph. I never remember her as the brilliant beauty she is described by those who saw her when she first came to this country. Her eyes were the most arresting feature of her face.

The Churchills seemed so absurdly happy in those days and for years after, and I certainly had plenty of opportunity of judging, for later, when they went to live at Rolleston, I used to see a lot of them, and their dependence on each other must have struck the most casual observer.

This was Consuelo Marlborough's first Ascot, really almost her first appearance in England. She had a great success, and looked quite un-American with that very small refined head on that very long neck. She had, of course, the most wonderful frocks—an array to choose from every day, suitable for all possible weathers and emergencies. She was quite the thinnest person I have ever seen, and she used to wear her pearls sewn up in a horsehair bag as a bustle tied round her waist—this was partly to insure their safety and partly to make her look fatter.

*　　　*　　　*　　　*　　　*　　　*

Finding a house in Leicestershire was not as easy as we thought, and we made several fruitless pilgrimages

* Viscount and Viscountess Churchill.

before we eventually took Kirby Hall. It was a horrible looking barrack of a house, standing on the road close to Kirby Gate and three miles from Melton, so we had, at any rate, the compensation of being excellently situated for hunting with the Quorn. There was also good stabling for sixteen horses, and, in spite of being quite unable to afford it, we very seldom had an empty stall.

Our nearest neighbours at Asfordby, only a mile away, were the Lancelot Lowthers and the Max de Tuylls. As Mrs. Bunbury, Baroness de Tuyll was well known in Cheshire, Ireland and Leicestershire, as one of the finest women to hounds that had ever been seen. She had not long been married to Max, and at first sight they seemed a rather ill-assorted couple, but, as a matter of fact, no two people could have got on better. Max really liked the social side of hunting, and seldom left the hard high road ; but how well *she* used to go, and not always on the best of horses.

Years later, when her health had suffered so much from her many falls that she was obliged to give up hunting entirely, I asked her if she missed it ; her eyes filled with tears, and her reply was : " If I could only have one more winter's hunting I would gladly die " Sometimes I feel like that myself !

It was at the De Tuyll's that I first saw Eva Wellesley, who became one of my best friends. She came down to Asfordby to hunt several times not very long before she was engaged to Randolph Wemyss. Though not really good looking, she had wonderful red hair, and a delightful voice and smile, and I think looked most attractive in the Beaufort blue and buff.

Gettin into one's own house for the first time must

art at **Warwick** in **1895** to meet King Edward , then Prince o Wa es.

[*Facing p.* 88

be an interest and amusement to everyone, and I used to go for long shopping expeditions with Caryl Craven, who had just taken up decorating and furnishing people's houses for them. I think he was the first gentleman to make this a profession, but amusing as was the choosing of carpets and curtains and the searching of old curiosity shops for bargains, the getting together of a stud of horses was an even more enthralling occupation, and a great part of our time that summer was spent at Tattersall's, at the Repository at Leicester, as well as in visiting the dealers' yards.

Almost the best horse I ever had was one that Jim bought at Daisy's sale and gave me as a birthday present. I had never ridden him, but I had seen Lord Timmy Paulet* on him often in Warwickshire the year before, and knew what a wonderful jumper he was. He was rather inclined to be impetuous, but it was the impetuosity of youth, and though there was some doubt as to whether I should be able to ride him, I found him perfectly easy, and he only gave me one fall in ten years.

In order to get rid of some of his old horses, Jim had a sale at Leicester. I hated to see his new owner sailing over the country on Pilot, instead of being on him myself, but there were compensations, as another very good horse was returned after the sale as having navicular, which I appropriated. He certainly used to come out a bit stiff in the mornings, but after a short time he would be quite sound, and there was no better hunter. One hunt I remember particularly on him was in the Quorn Monday country; the meet was at Lodge-on-the-Wold, a rather unfashionable rendezvous, and no one was

* Marquis of Winchester.

anticipating much sport—indeed, when the fox went
away, most of the field were having lunch.   I was on the
left of the wood with two or three others, among them
Lord Lonsdale and Lady Gerard, and I can see the fox
now, stealing away from the covert, with only a few
couple of hounds—the body of the pack were, I think,
hunting another fox in the wood—then a few more hounds,
a blast of the horn from Lord Lonsdale and away we
sailed !   The field, including Tom Firr, had not heard
the horn, and were hopelessly left.   In all the years I
hunted I think I enjoyed that day as much as any I have
had—all over Monday Quorn country to Asfordby Osier
beds—not a bad point, and the most perfect country to
ride over, but I think it was such fun because there was
no crushing, crowding field to compete with l   •

I confess the crowds in Leicestershire *were* distracting,
to say the least of it, and generally proved a difficulty
to the new-comers, for to slip through a crowd is an art
in itself.   In the Pytchley and North Warwickshire
country they were infinitely rougher, and one really had
to struggle, and not mind being knocked about.   I can
remember one day when a lot of us went from Melton
to have a day in the Pytchley Wednesday country, I
was riding a horse of Joe Laycock's.   Oh ! the banging
and scrambling that took place at the small bridle gates.
I had given up all hope of seeing any sport, and I think
I was the last to get away from Crick.   Hounds checked
a field or so ahead, and the crowd were scattered in every
direction.   By this time I discovered I couldn't hold
my horse, and that I should have to be either in front
or else probably kill someone.   My horse settled the
question for me, and conveyed me, a mere passenger,
in *front ;* but I can remember nearly jumping on Georgie

Curzon,* who was floundering on one side of a brook
with her horse on the other. I wasn't altogether sorry
to change on to my second horse, and there is a sequel
to my story. Not long after I saw a lady having a most
unpleasant ride, and I recognized a friend, who was
trying the same horse with a view to purchase, because
it had carried me so well! I may say she did not buy
the horse!

The Quorn field had been wheeled into line by Lord
Lonsdale. He ruled them with an iron hand in a velvet
glove—not that he didn't have some *contretemps*, and one
day I believe he took hounds home at one o'clock
because of someone's misdemeanour—rather hard on
the rest of the field! But I think all good M.F.H.'s
must lose their temper occasionally, and considering the
ignorance of some people who go out hunting, it is
really wonderful that they do not do so oftener. I
remember Lord Willoughby de Broke once being furious
with Lord Timmy Paulet for going on down a ride
whilst he was drawing the covert "Come back, you
moon-faced man on a white-faced horse!" yelled Lord
Willoughby, but still Lord Timmy went on, and when
asked if he hadn't heard, he said he was riding a hireling
and hadn't looked at its face. Both Lord Willoughby and
Lord Lonsdale were such past-masters of the art of
hunting, that no one should have felt any resentment
at being reprimanded by them. They both taught me
a lot about hunting, for which I cannot be sufficiently
grateful, as I soon found out that the man or woman
who only thinks of the ride misses half the joy of hunting.

There is nothing so boring or so alarming as following a straggling crowd a couple of miles behind hounds.

* Late Countess Howe.

Gaps on these occasions seem to me more frightening obstacles than a post and rails when hounds are only a field or so ahead of you, but one cannot hope always to get a start, and a little attention to hounds and a little intelligence will often enable one, when one has been left behind, to make a fortunate turn, and nick into a good place again.

It is curious, though, how the same people could almost always be seen in the first flight ; Jock Trotter, utterly oblivious of the number of falls he took ; the veteran Doggie Smith, Sam Hames, Buck Barclay—as quick as anyone for a fast twenty minutes, Johnnie McKie, who was always there, no matter the horse, and Walter de Winton are a few that leap instantly to my mind. Year after year they were in the front rank, and the younger generation never seemed to take their place.

The sportsmen of to-day will probably think it is heresy of me to say so, but I always feel that about that time there was a small coterie of men who stood out as a wonderful type of the best that England could produce. They stood as an almost unique group. There are others who have followed them, wholly as brave, whose morals and whose brains may have been superior, but whose personality seemed to lack something which that little gang most undoubtedly possessed. They were not a very small group either, and their names have lived, like Bay Middleton's and Peter Flower's, not actually by their deeds of valour, but by their personal magnetism which radiated.

When we hear of the days of hunting being over, I cannot imagine a greater calamity for the country than for " the sport of kings, the image of war with half its guilt and only ten per cent. of its danger " (one per cent. would be nearer the mark now) to cease. Hunting is, apart from anything else, a great character former ; it teaches you decision, presence of mind and unselfishness. Just think of hounds streaming in front of you, a man falls—he's either hurt or not, but his horse passes you—it *does* require unselfishness to stop and lose your place, and take it back ; yet I affirm that there is no man worthy of the name who would not perform this act for friend or foe in the hunting-field.

*   ⊤   ⊤   *   *   *

We spent Easter that year at Monte Carlo. I had been to the Riviera as a child during our yachting trip, but Monte was quite different to anything I had ever seen. I took to Roulette and Trente-et-Quarante like a duck to water, and was almost compensated by this new recreation for missing the last weeks of the season's hunting. It seemed difficult to associate that lovely garden looking across the bluest of blue bays with the stories of suicides, but I suppose everyone feels like that on their first visit to the gambler's paradise. I was told a rather charming story the other day of how Monte Carlo was supposed to have started its present notoriety. In the old days it was a quiet little place, and chiefly famous for the monastery that stood on the hill, overlooking the sleepy little town. This monastery got rather heavily into debt, and one of the monks, clever at astrological calculations, invented a combination of " chances " which seemed to ensure success, but which was not applicable to any card game then known. He therefore set his wits to work and planned a new game, which he called " Roulette," and with this he set about

to repair the fortunes of his monastery. He went down
to the little inn and explained his game to the innkeeper,
M. Blanc. They arranged that the game of roulette
should be played at the inn, and there at that game
the monk won large sums from the soldiers and inhabitants of the neighbourhood every week. When he died,
he handed over the secret of the combination to another
monk, who went down the hill, as his predecessor
had done, to exploit the system. This man, however,
was younger than his instructor, and, as ill-luck would
have it, he sat down to the tables next to a charming
lady, with whom he entered into conversation, and with
whom he at once fell in love !

He struggled with his conscience, but found the
temptation too great for him. The relaxation from
monastic rule implied by his visits to the tables had
weakened his asceticism, and he succumbed to the
snares of the world and the flesh. He returned once
more to the monastery to lay before the Abbot the
proceeds of his gaming, and then he escaped from the
monastery to journey across the mountains, with the
object of rejoining his love.

That night a terrific snowstorm came on, and the
monk sank under the snow. He was never seen again.
Not only was his life lost on the mountains, but also
his knowledge. Though he had taken the money
to the Abbot before setting out on his fateful journey,
he had not confided to anyone the secret of the system,
for he had not divulged his intention of escape. Therefore, on his death, the secret perished, and never again
were the monks able to take advantage of the discovery of the founder of roulette.

Yet the game continued to be played, and the fame

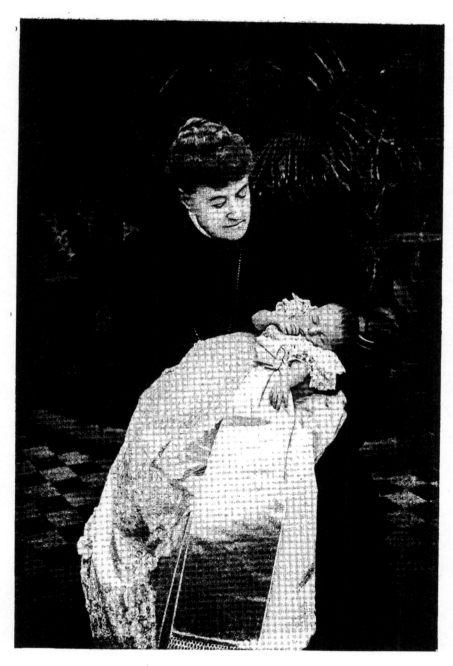

Marigold with Madame de Falbe.

[Facing p. 94

of the roulette tables at Monte Carlo is now known
from end to end of the world.

*   *   *   *   *

We spent the summer with Madame de Falbe, in
Grosvenor Square. She was by far the most human
of all my near in-law relations, and I think she saw
already that my marriage was not going to be a very
successful one. I was realizing this myself, but as I
had embarked so lightly on the sea of matrimony I felt
it was my own fault, and that there was nothing for
it but to try and make the best of it.

Madame de Falbe's own life had not always run
on smooth lines, a fact which she herself confided to
me. She had been separated from my husband's
grandfather, Dudley Ward, owing to his very violent
temper, and I remember her giving me a bit of advice,
which was, that separated women were always at a
disadvantage. I almost think that she must have
anticipated something of the sort happening to me, or
why should she have dwelt on this, for eventually her
own life had altered to one of complete prosperity.
When Dudley Ward died she had married Gerard Leigh,
who had left her all his money, as well as Luton for
her life, and she had settled herself happily for the third
time, with M. de Falbe, the Danish Minister. As her
tact was proverbial she made an ideal wife for a diplomat.

Madame de Falbe died in 1899. I wish I had seen
more of her in later years, but family troubles intervened. I had some charming letters from her to the
end, and I look back with deep gratitude on her kindness to me.

Gerard Leigh, who inherited Luton, died just a

fortnight after he succeeded.   His wife, Smikie, was one
of the nicest of women.   I had known her well before
I married. , I think one never forgets the people who
were nice to one as a girl.   When I came out the young
married women were not always too amiable to girls.
I can look back, though, on several notable exceptions,
amongst them Lady Alington and Mrs. Hwfa Williams.
Mrs. Hwfa is one of the Social Landmarks of the Victorian and Edwardian reigns.   Even now few people
many years younger possess her charm, her vitality and
her energy.   She has god-mothered many of the new
social celebrities, and has been the very centre of the
jolliest parties, whilst the youngest can still feel they
are talking to a contemporary.   I found her one day
only last year playing tennis with Gerald Paget's grandchild.   Her house at Combe bears testimony to her
artistic skill, for she has herself painted most of the rooms.

Hwfa is another most perfect friend.   The years
may pass by but he seems just the same—frailer, perhaps, but with that dry humour which always made
him such a delightful companion.

His sister, the Duchess of Wellington, possessed
much of his charm—I spent many happy days at Strathfieldsaye, the home of practical jokes and nicknames.
Strathfieldsaye is an ugly house and interesting only
from its associations with the Iron Duke.   The Duchess
had always been lame and could only walk on crutches,
but she rode everywhere, quite alone, surrounded by
her pack of deerhounds. The Duke was the fattest
man I have ever seen, and went by the nickname of
" Spurgeon."

Lady Angela Forbes, the year she came out.

[*Facing p.* 96

The Jubilee season was, of course, wonderful, and characterized by Queen's weather, but mingled with all the rejoicings was the thought that it must be the last national thanksgiving of a woman who had meant so much and for so long. Queen Victoria was probably idealized by me. The very close friendship, and the many letters from her to my father, had surrounded her with an atmosphere and a rather particular glamour.

There were balls and parties every night, but the biggest social event of a most crowded season was the Devonshire House Fancy Dress Ball. To be invited to Devonshire House in those days, or not to be invited, was a question of burning importance. The old Duchess of Devonshire was a personality neither preceded nor succeeded. Her approbation counted for success, and her approval secured perquisites, in the way of invitations, for many who might otherwise have remained in comparative obscurity. She had the strength of an eagle, the wisdom of the serpent and an intimate knowledge of the frailties of human nature.

The Devonshire House Ball was almost a repetition of the Warwick one, but as an actual spectacle it missed the historic setting. Most people were bedecked with jewels, many of them hired and borrowed for the occasion, but my two sisters, Millie and Sybil, were a striking contrast in their simplicity, relying for their success entirely on their own beauty. Millie, as Charlotte Corday, in a perfectly plain scarlet *crêpe-de-chine* frock, and a mob cap, looked delicious, and I never saw Sybil look more beautiful than she did that evening as Hebe, in white draperies, with a huge eagle poised on her shoulder, its outstretched wings forming a background to her head. There were, of course, period quadrilles, and the most fantastic display of dresses. Muriel Wilson and Helena Keith Fraser both looked quite dazzling among the crowd of Orientals. After this pageant the rest of the season's entertainments seemed comparatively flat.

＊　　＊　　＊　　＊　　＊　　＊

My eldest child, Marigold, was born that August, while I was still in Grosvenor Square, and we went on to Luton to stay with Madame de Falbe for her christening. There we found a family party, including the Dudleys, Lord Dudley being one of Marigold's godfathers.

I always thought Luton a rather dreary place, and better fitted for a hydropathic establishment than a private house. It was in the winter garden there, by the way, that Prince Eddie proposed to Princess May.

From Luton we went to Scotland for a round of visits—to Dunrobin, where the usual autumn crowd were assembled, and on to Invermark, the shooting lodge which the Dudleys and Hindlips took together, a deliciously wild place.

I didn't go out stalking personally, as it is a sport which does not appeal to me immensely. I am not fond of walking, and I think crawling on one's tummy through bog and heather, to be almost murdered if you breathe, is not the happiest way of spending a day. I never can understand why people are so keen about it—unless, of course, you do your own stalking—but that is an exception, and the day is spent following a gillie, who first chooses your stag, and then, without further explanation, expects you to trail after him blindly till you are within shooting distance. It is curious how many stags are missed in the season : they seem such a big target. I suppose it is a form of stage fright, or else the uncomfortable position you find yourself in at the last moment. I was lucky, and killed the only stag I have ever shot at. I was so surprised to find the rifle did not kick at all, whereas practising at the target I had bruised my shoulder horribly. I believe this is quite an ordinary experience, but the reason for it has never been explained to me.

We came back to Leicestershire in time for Kirby Gate, the opening meet of the Quorn. The horses had summered well, and I looked forward to the season's hunting more than I can say. The daily irritabilities of life are so enormously accentuated in the rather stifling atmosphere of London ; with hounds streaming in front of you and with a good horse on which to sail over the country one recovers one's sense of proportion, and incidents, which might be tragedies, become almost farcical instead, and the worst row is forgotten in the joys of a good hunt. The Dudleys and Jock Trotter stayed with us a good deal that winter, and Sandy Fraser, just back from India, was the very kindest of cousins-in-law. I had got a new chestnut horse called Merrymaker, that we bought from Lord Cowley. He was one of the very best, with only one crab—that of kicking badly in gateways. It kept one always on the alert, but he was such a perfect fencer that I jumped fences on him to escape the crowd that I should never have dreamt of doing on any other horse.

I stayed on at Kirby as long as possible, as we were to spend the summer in my mother-in-law's house, which quite frankly I was not looking forward to. Domestic troubles are trying enough in any circumstances, but particularly so in other people's houses. Jim had inherited his grandfather's temper, and lost it over such unexpected trifles. I remember once his being absolutely furious with me because I forgot to order any visiting cards, and then when I had retrieved that error I forgot to leave them!

Though Mrs. Forbes was a charming woman she was without much sense of humour, and with an intensely narrow point of view, and my sister-in-law, Ida Edmonstone, told me that until she married—and she was well over twenty when she did—she had never been allowed to write a letter or read a book without first showing it to her mother. If Mrs. Forbes did not actually disapprove of me, I think she disapproved of all my friends. When I was first engaged to Jim, and she heard we were dining somewhere, she came to me quite seriously, and begged me not to let Jim get into a fast racing set. At the age of eighteen I did not quite know what the fast racing set consisted of!

Just as things were reaching an impasse in our joint establishment Madame de Falbe came to our rescue, and took me off to stay with her in Grosvenor Square, and she eventually gave us a flat of our own in Mount Street.

Another year of Kirby and then Jim went to India. I remember suggesting going too, but to my secret relief my offer was not accepted. We let Kirby for the season, and I was left with a small house at Melton, and three horses of my own.

I got any number of mounts and on off-days I amused myself driving a pair of mules tandem, in a coster cart. I hadn't driven a tandem since the long ago days at Dysart, when I had surreptitiously borrowed two ponies, one from the butcher and one from the blacksmith, and harnessed them together with the assistance of ropes. All had gone well until the leader fell down and broke its knees. After that further concealment was impossible, as my exchequer could not meet the amount required by the blacksmith for damages !

Max Angus, a farmer-dealer, was particularly kind about mounting me. He said I brought him luck and that he always sold the horse afterwards. I know that I very seldom rode the same animal twice, which I regretted when it was a good one. The variety in my mounts gave me lots of experience.

I was revelling in my newly-found freedom, and it would have been a very jolly winter but for the South African war. French's victory at Elandslaagte filled us all with our British optimism, but it was followed so soon by a reverse, and the fact of our troops being concentrated in Ladysmith was depressing. Our reverses at Magersfontein and Colenso had quickly wiped out Lord Methuen's victory at Belmont.

In December came a cry for more men; practically everyone one knew at once volunteered, particularly amongst the hunting men. The Yeomanry were all going out under Lord Chesham, and Jim had to join the Warwickshire direct from India; but apart from the regular Yeomanry Alwyne Compton had raised " Compton's Horse," and amongst the people who went out with him from Leicestershire I can remember Lord Cowley, Lord Hamilton of Dalziel and one of Lord Derby's brothers.

Leicestershire was becoming deserted, the field consisting very largely of women. The Brocklehursts were at the Spinney; Alfred B. was a host in himself, and much run after by the ladies, and he always rode home surrounded by a party of "fairies." Lady Wilton, the Queen of Melton, and Mr. Prior, were, of course, at Egerton Lodge, and gave their usual dinner parties; it would have taken more than an earthquake to disturb the Egerton Lodge routine.

Hilda de Winton was another grass widow with a house in Melton—her sense of humour contributed towards keeping us in as cheerful a frame of mind as possible—Walter was in South Africa, but we still had Lord Cholmondeley and dear "Pickles" Lambton to keep us cheery. Alas! he is one of those who have gone for ever. What fun he was that winter! He always used to chaff me for never getting tired! Once he and I rode fifteen miles home together and I had been keeping up a rather one-sided conversation, but failing to get much response had dropped into silence. As we jogged along the road I was startled by "Pickles" suddenly calling out to me: "Angela, I don't believe you could be killed with a hatchet!"

A new arrival at Melton about this time was a foreigner, Rodakowski by name; he had married Lady Dora Carnegie, who did not hunt. He, however, made up for it by never missing a day and jumping all the most impossible places, so much so that when someone complained of being unable to pronounce his name Hughie Owen declared it wouldn't matter, as he would break his neck in a week.

Another Melton personality was Lady Cardigan. She used to come to the meet in a brougham, her saddle

From Lady Angela Forbes's   isiting Book.

on the top, a leopard skin coat over her habit and a tiny billycock perched on her yellow curls. She used to ask everyone if they had seen her horse, but the horse, of course, was a myth—she had not been on one for years !

I had known her in the old days at Deane, as we used to go over to luncheon there from Apethorpe, and the first thing you saw there on going into the hall was " My Lord's charger " that he rode at Balaclava—she had had it stuffed ! Then she used to take everyone to see her bridal chamber, which contained a bed surrounded with looking-glasses and draped with white net, roses and satin ! Her feet were supposed to be the smallest in the world and she made a point of exhibiting these, calling for the butler to change her boots for her in the drawing-room. Most people thought her an oddity, not in the least appreciating her humour and reminiscences. At Melton she led a most lonely life, but occasionally she would be asked out to dinner, and nothing pleased her more than being asked to dance afterwards.

Lady Cunard, by the way, made her first appearance in this country under Lady Cardigan's chaperonage, and it was Lady Cardigan who arranged her marriage with Sir Bache.

The season that year in London somehow dragged itself through. Nobody was feeling very cheerful—the long list of casualties included Lord Airlie, whilst Lord Roberts and Lord Chesham had both lost their sons.

Lady Chesham and Lady Georgina Curzon's Hospital was the only recognized Unit of the kind, but a few venturesome spirits had found their way over to the Cape, and Randolph Wemyss and Sir Samuel Scott were amongst those who had their yachts out there.

Scandals galore drifted home, and there were plenty of stories of the "goings on" at the Mount Nelson Hotel, mostly centred round a few important personages.

No real balls were being given in London, but there were a few dances for the boys and girls. The girls were gradually coming into their own and having the time of their lives. Whether this emancipation tends to the ultimate good of the individual is a question open to doubt ; the very tight Victorian rein under which I suffered obviously needed relaxing, but the flinging away of all restraint has become almost too emphatic.

Chaperons were beginning to see the end of their career in sight, but there were a few mothers who still clung tenaciously to their office. In many cases, though, they were glad to escape, and I have always felt a profound pity for those unfortunate middle—or past middle—aged ladies leaning uncomfortably against the wall of a ball room in a drowsy condition in the small hours of the morning. Many of them were probably hungry too, no one having even asked them to go to supper.

The Westminster wedding was causing a good deal of stir—to be or not to be was the question ; but when it did come off as a "show" it was quite ordinary.

"Bend Or" was very young and very charming—he was obviously marked out as one of the victims or favourites of fortune. His happy-go-lucky character made him able to appreciate his luck and come up smiling through all vicissitudes.

I was very little in London myself during the South African war, but spent a delightful six weeks with the Londesboroughs on the river. Glancing back over the past years I can think of few people who have shown

me greater kindness and hospitality, than the Londesboroughs. Their home seemed my home and those
who only knew Francis casually, missed discovering the
depths of gentleness and sympathy which were his
dominant characteristics.

I was back in Leicestershire when the news of the
Queen's death came. Her passing meant the end of a
very great era. She had watched her Empire grow,
probably to the highest pinnacle which it will ever reach,
and the Victorian tradition and all that it meant went
with her.

IV

I SHIFTED my headquarters during the South African war from the Melton side of Leicestershire to the Cottesmore country. They were only ten miles apart, but one felt immediately the difference in the atmosphere of Melton and Oakham. The Oakhamites looked rather sourly on the Meltonites, whilst the Quornites rather rudely called their sisters on the other side "Cottesmore Cats" When asked why, they said it was because they were such "stay-at-home tabbies," and the "Cats" retaliated by dubbing the Quornites "Quorn Kittens."

Certainly the "Cats" seldom invaded the Quorn territory and were mostly content to hunt with their own pack, and if they had any scandals, they kept them in their family circle. The majority of them had been established in the district for many years, but the Melton crowd, on the other hand, were an ever-changing population who took their hunting-boxes for the season, and departed as soon as Melton Races were over. Most of the scandals emanated from Melton, or were supposed to do so—I wonder whether a psychologist could explain why Leicestershire was responsible for so many. A visitor to Melton once said: "I hear there are only two things to do in Leicestershire—and I don't hunt!" It is certainly difficult to think of many couples who really survived more than two or three seasons. A good many ended in the divorce court, though I can remember one notable case when a reconciliation after much negotiation was effected. But all the same, if the tales one hears are true, our grandfathers and grandmothers had no right to look askance at us! They had pretty good times themselves, but perhaps their methods were more circumspect. They must have had a lot of harmless fun too in the old days at Melton, and I always think that the moonlight steeple-chase, when all the hard riders at Melton set out attired in their nightgowns, must have been a great joke. I have got a copy of the original pictures that Angus McNeill did of this event.

As for situation, from Melton you could hunt with the Quorn, Cottesmore, Belvoir and Mr. Fernie in their best country without having more than a few miles to go to the meet. This probably accounted for the extra popularity enjoyed by Melton as a centre.

Personally I liked my new surroundings. It was rather a respite from the constant crowd to have a comparatively small field on two days in the week, and this we got on Mondays and Thursdays, but even on these days the fields began to grow in dimensions when the new huntsman, Thatcher, arrived. His reputation of being almost a second Tom Firr, spread like lightning, and the Cottesmore soon became the most fashionable pack.

Barley Thorpe, the Lonsdales place, was only a mile from Oakham. Lord Lonsdale's individuality is entirely apart from his intellectual abilities. A picturesque sense of imagination is strongly developed. If somebody once said to him that he suffered from constitutional inaccuracy, his inventions were generally arresting and without the smallest tinge of ill-nature. His organizing powers and attention to detail are almost superhumanly developed.

The tour of the stables on Sunday afternoon was performed with much pomp and ritual. No stables were better kept or contained a more perfect collection of weight-carrying hunters. A basket of carrots awaited Lord Lonsdale's arrival and was handed him at each stable door.

Sometimes we would see a horse put into the school and it would obey Lord Lonsdale's voice, almost like his dogs did, which is saying a good deal, as they in their turn are as well disciplined as a Guards' Battalion. On one occasion a young horse from Ireland was put in the school for the edification of Lord Ribblesdale and myself. We watched Lord L.'s methods of making hypnotic passes, and saw the rebellious animal become gradually docile, though I confess I shared Lord R.'s scepticism as to this being the horse's initiation into the ring !

All animals love him, and he has undoubtedly a mysterious power over them. I think it has something to do with his voice, which is one of the most charming I have ever heard.

A description of Barley Thorpe would not be complete without mentioning the custom of sitting round the horseshoe table in the dining-room in front of the fire after dinner, when the toasts of " The King," " The Ladies " and " Fox-hunting " are always drunk.

The Bairds, Blairs and Calandars were a much inter-married clan. Mr. Baird, who hailed from Fife, had been master of the Cottesmores for years, and his sisters and their husbands had been established round Oakham for an equally long period. They were supposed to look on all new comers with suspicion, and I was rather frightened of them when I first migrated, but they were all very nice to me.

The Noels seemed to be interned behind the walls of Catmose. I used to hear of their ultra-Victorian régime from their pretty daughter-in-law, who divided her year between Catmose and foreign travels ; I think she was surprised herself that her intelligence survived her *milieu.*

Two members of the Brocklehurst family, Lord Ranksborough and Annie Fitzwilliam,* had built houses in the neighbourhood. Lord R. had built his under the shadow of the famous covert. He will be one of the most missed figures in that part of the world. Immensely tall, one's ideal of a cavalry officer, he had the gentlest and sweetest disposition, and he seems to have been almost the last link between the present and my childhood. The Fitzwilliams were at Barnsdale—a house where I have spent many happy days. It is not often that the charm characterizing one member should run through an entire family, but in the case of the Brocklehursts each one of them seemed to possess it.

The Guy Fenwicks had established themselves on the further side of the country. Elsie Fenwick was distinctly social and filled her house with all the youth of the countryside. She was the soul of cheerfulness, while he was quite unexpectedly intelligent on a variety of subjects. A very large contingent of Fenwicks were dotted round Leicestershire, some of them having been rather unflatteringly nicknamed—one of them rejoicing under the appellation of Foul Fenwick !

Two of the very few gentlemen riders who have won

* Hon. Lady Fitzwilliam.

the Grand National both hunted with the Cottesmore —Lord Manners and Mr. Maunsel Richardson. The Manners' came regularly every year to Cold Overton, and Mr. Richardson and Victoria Lady Yarborough had given up the Brocklesby hounds and taken Edmond-thorpe—a few miles from Oakham.

Two more different types of riders to have won the National it would be difficult to conceive. The "Cat," as Mr. Richardson was called, was one of the finest horsemen, and he really lived for horses and hunting. Though by no means a young man when I knew him, he always preferred making a four-year-old himself to buying the finished article. He took an enormous amount of trouble about his horses, and spent his spare time schooling them—he was a great believer in driving them on the long reins over fences. I rode several of his horses, and though they were not of outstanding merit, they had been so perfectly made by him, that one was sure that they would take off on the right spot. Mr. Richardson was a very great friend of Lord Minto's, and the story goes that they both loved Lady Yarborough—and in order to decide which of the two should propose to her, they took off their coats and settled the question then and there.

* * * * * *

The house I had taken was at Manton, and I was living there when Jim returned from South Africa.

The return of husbands from South Africa and the consequent re-adjustment of life was, of course, not only felt by me, but one's own circumstances, in one's own eyes, are generally assumed to be more difficult than other people's.

But life jogged on as it has a way of doing in the same accustomed groove, and I found myself once more doing the same monotonous round.

The summer of 1902 I spent in London. Jim was very little there, as he was doing galloper to Lord Chesham, who had been given a Staff appointment connected with the Yeomanry. With the exception of a week at Ascot, I hardly went away at all, as my mother was dangerously ill.

Mrs. Forbes had a house at Englefield Green, and I went to stay with her. I did not go to the races, but amused myself riding in Windsor Park and playing golf with those of the party who were staying with Lord Grimthorpe, next door, and who were also not inclined for the crowd of the Enclosure. He had, I remember, a large party there that year, including Lord Lonsdale and Lord Elcho, the Islingtons and Lady Gerard.

The arrangements for the Coronation fixed for June were all cancelled at the eleventh hour owing to King Edward's illness. No end of foreigners had come over, and there was a boom in London houses ; we had let our flat for £250 for the fortnight of festivities that were to take place, but our tenants only stayed two days. I offered it to them for nothing (the least I could do) when the Coronation eventually took place, but they could not come back, so I stayed on and went to it myself !

Even a Coronation suffers from postponement, and it was shorn of much glory, but all the same it was a most impressive sight. I had got a seat in the Abbey and Lady Maud Ramsden and I sallied forth at about 8 a.m., as we had to be in our places at a very early hour. Imagine some of the jaded faces in full evening dress

and tiaras at that hour of the morning! The Queen
of Roumania stood out on that occasion—not only for
her good looks, but because she was so much better dressed
than any one else.   It was a long, weary wait, and we
were very thankful that we had brought a provision of
sandwiches and biscuits.   We were rather ashamed of
taking them, but found that we were in the fashion;
all the same, a picnic in Westminster Abbey does sound
a little incongruous, if not exactly profane!

*   *

My daughter Flavia was born that winter.   Jim was
very much disturbed at her not being a son, as in his
heart I think he imagined that he would one day be Sir
James Forbes of Newe, but that idea has since been
knocked on the head by the certainly belated arrival
of several sons into his cousin Charlie Forbes' family.

I had lent my house at Manton to Margot Asquith
for the winter.   Jim was going abroad, and I was to join
Margot as soon as I could.   She usually hunted from
Cold Overton, but this year the Manners' had given it
up and gone into a small house at Oakham.   I think,
too, Margot wanted to have the children with her; Elizabeth was then about six, and Anthony only a month or
two old.

Our joint *ménage* was the greatest fun.   Barbara
Lister* and Lord Ribblesdale were down there a great
deal, and who could want better company!   Rib was
delightful anywhere, and in that hunting *milieu* he
excelled.   His superb sense of the ridiculous made the
most trivial episode into a fantastic adventure.   Barbara

---

* Hon. Lady Wilson.

Tom Firr and the Quorn Hounds.

[*Facing p.* 11

had a combination of her mother and father's wit. She was waspish one moment and mellow the next. I think her criticisms of people and things were tinged by her personal feelings towards them, but they never failed to be entertaining.

Margot has been blamed for hunting so much. Her friends were inclined to be critical of her, and said she was not doing her duty to her husband, which meant she was not entertaining his party! "Peter has been my love; Asquith is to be my life," was her method of announcing her engagement to a mutual friend.

I don't think Margot was ever so happy as when she was hunting, and she would probably have made a much better M.F.H.'s wife than a Prime Minister's—it possible. She still went well, and if there was any sign of her nerve going it was imperceptible, except possibly that she rode a little too fast at her fences; that is as a rule such a tell-tale signal.

• Margot is always kindness itself to her servants, and Barbara and I used to be quite annoyed because she would insist on our letting our maids go out for the day before we were dressed ourselves. She thought her servants liked hunting as much as she did, and used to pack them all off to the meet in a wagonette. How we all fitted into my tiny house I don't know, but Margot has the art of making a small house expand to her requirements. She was good nature personified, and when (as we generally did) Barbara and I used to take all the hot water, she went bathless without a murmur !

Marigold and Elizabeth did lessons together and were most amusing. They used to have many arguments, and Elizabeth was overheard in the train telling Marigold that Mr. Asquith was very superior to *her* father

8

as he " spoke in the House " ; to which Marigold replied :
" You should hear *mine* speak in the house ! "

There is not much more that one can say about
Margot. She has said almost too much about herself ;
but then, Margot is superbly tactless, and in her memoirs
she has been even more tactless about herself than
about her friends, and with an almost unpardonable
lack of reticence she has written about things which
most people would hesitate to discuss with their nearest
and dearest. I am sure she was never immoral in the
accepted sense of the word ; she is one of those people who
might smile at indecency, but who would scowl on im-
morality. I have seen nothing of her in the last few
years, but remembering her genuine wit, her book disappointed me terribly. Like a good cook giving you a
badly ordered dinner, she has chosen the dullest stories
and selected the most unattractive episodes of her life ;
she has concealed the most interesting details and has
given place and prominence to domestic anecdotes which
would have been most happily ignored.

Mr. Asquith came down for week-ends and I used to
wonder if he was bored by the luncheons and dinners
that Margot hurried him off to on Sundays, or if he
enjoyed them as a relaxation. He never talked his shop,
but listened to our description of a day's sport, and asked
endless questions on the subject, and he was apparently
as interested in the doings of the " tally-hos ! " as in
the annals of the Kit-Cat club. He didn't know one
end of a horse from the other, so it must have been pure
kindness on his part.

      *   *   *   *   *   *

Instead of going to Scotland for the autumn, I went
to America to stay with Bridget Guinness in August,

1903. I was really to have gone earlier, but Flavia was ill and I could not possibly leave her. The Shaftesburys and Lilah Paget were the only people I knew on board. Lilah was on her way out to see some of her American relations, but seemed quite vague as to where they lived or what they looked like. The Shaftesburys were going to stay with Sir Thomas Lipton on the *Erin* for the Cup Races. Cuckoo S. took a sentimental interest in the fortunes of the *Shamrock*, as she had apparently christened her in Belfast.

Robin Grey met me in New York, and took me on to Long Island, where Bridget's house was. Her mother, Lady Bulkeley, Lady Charlie Beresford and Prince Troubetskoy (Amelie Rives' husband and a very fine looking man) were staying there, as well as Hugo Baring.

Bridget had already made herself very popular on the other side, though at first I think they did not quite understand her Bohemian ideas, which were the antithesis of the rather conventional New Yorkers. Her house was of course delightfully comfortable ; you could trust Bridget to see to that, and also to have most excellent food.

The heat and the mosquitoes were our great trial, and the minimum of clothes was the order of the day. Our first expedition was to Sheepshead Bay to see the Futurity Stakes (the big American two-year-old race).

Here I met the great Mr. W. C. Whitney—the most hospitable man in America, which is saying a good deal. I could quite understand his popularity, for he had great charm, and he certainly seemed to be adored by his entire entourage. He amused me with his rather caustic criticism of Englishwomen who had gone to

8*

America. He thought they were more interested in finance than in anything else.

Mr. Whitney's entourage included, amongst many amusing people, Peter Dunn, of "Mr. Dooley" fame. Some of his stories are inimitable, and I loved the comparison he drew between the American and English accent, "though we speak in the same language it is through different organs of the face."

Mr. Whitney talked with pride of his son Harry, who was already a polo enthusiast, and eventually came to Leicestershire and took the Burns-Hartopps' place, Dalby, joining the ranks of the other Americans who were already established at Melton, and who were making hunting very difficult for the individual of moderate means.

The power of money was making itself forcibly felt. No sum was too high to be paid for a good horse by these new comers, and the prices of horses, good or bad, went up automatically. Owners were tempted to part with the best out of their studs, dealers began to overrate the quality of their horses, and I expect that the visitors from over the water were occasionally badly stuck. In the same way rents went up, and the local tradesmen reaped a golden harvest, whilst the poor man was left lamenting.

The racing in America was quite different from that in this country. One missed the grass, and the dust from the dirt track often completely hid the horses from view. I had never seen the starting-gate before ; no one could understand why we hadn't got it in this country. All the jockeys rode *à la* Tod Sloan and looked just like monkeys. Their methods seemed different from ours ; there was no question of riding a waiting race or of any particular horse making the running, but just what looked like a wild scramble to be first to get the inside berth on the rails. They discussed the form of the horses by the stop-watch as much as anything else. The Futurity that year was won by Sidney Paget's Hamburg Belle and we were all on !

Mr. Whitney asked us all over to stay at his " Cottage." Anything less like a cottage it would be difficult to imagine. Everything was done in the most wonderful way and diversions planned for every hour of the day

The Hitchcocks lived not far off and were mad about horses and riding. Mrs. H. rode astride. They asked me if I rode, so, of course, I said yes. Had I ever hunted ? Yes. Had I a habit ? Yes. Would I ride to-morrow ? Yes. So out I started on a horse of Mr. Whitney's that had won the 'high jump' at the New York Show. I had a rather uncomfortable saddle, but as I presumed we were only going for an ordinary ride, I didn't think it mattered much.

I was soon disillusioned and found that nothing so dull was contemplated. There are no hedges bounding the dusty roads, but slat timber fences that we should have thought a fair size in Leicestershire and should *not* have selected to " lark " over, but before we had gone many yards someone quite calmly turned and jumped one of these palings out of the road. We were a biggish party, and I watched them all jump, realizing that whatever my feelings there was no evading, and I must follow suit. But the worst was yet to come. One after another came these gruesome obstacles, all of which had to be jumped, and if there had been a gate no one would have condescended to open it ! As the only Englishwoman I could not disgrace myself by even showing surprise, but I thought myself rather lucky to get home safely.

My horse had been schooled for high jumping and got right " under " the timber, bucking over without touching it, but all the horses did not jump in this way. The Hitchcocks' horses went rather fast and stood away like Leicestershire hunters. Most of their hunters were thoroughbreds, too slow for racing, which they schooled themselves. This they do most thoroughly, taking them loose into an enclosed ring with a movable bar, that they have to go over at different heights. As they do this regularly one would have thought the horses would have got stale, but apparently they don't. When I asked if they didn't get a lot of falls when they went out with the drag, Mr. H. told me not many, but he also told me of several people that had been killed !

When I got back to England I felt a curious affection for a post and rails, and I am not sure that on a good horse it isn't safer than a fence you can see through.

I went on to stay with the Hitchcocks, and their house was more like a home than the so-called cottages of New York Society. The ways and customs of the Hitchcock household were those of the South, and the food was characteristically Southern, and, to my mind, delicious. Sweet potatoes and corn on the cob are fare for the gods, to my thinking, and I remember, too, a wonderful little bird, something like a quail, the name of which I have forgotten, but whose flavour is an abiding memory.

I met Lady Astor for the first time in America. She was then Mrs. Bobbie Shaw, very pretty and full of fun. When she came over here later with her sister she had a great reputation for wit, and sometimes I thought it was almost a nuisance to her, as she had to live up to it !

I remember her on one occasion asking a man who wore the red, black and orange Zingaree ribbon why he wore such bright colours. He told her what it was. " What's that ? " she said. " Some kind of marmalade ? " Within half an hour she repeated the same remark, having led up to it with the same question to someone else ! But even the gods are caught napping sometimes, and there is no doubt she was a great success here. Both she and her sister looked awfully nice on a horse, and the number of men who wanted to marry " Mrs. Bobbie Shaw " were legion. She took a house at Market Harborough, and the eligible members of the Pytchley field were all supposed to have succumbed, but apparently she preferred to marry a fellow-countryman, even if he is a naturalized Englishman.

I have not seen her lately, but, judging from the reports of the House of Commons, I can't help thinking that she has changed a good deal since the days of my trip to America.

I certainly think she showed a dog-in-the-manger spirit over the Divorce Bill. She need not have grudged her English sisters their freedom, having herself benefited to no small extent by the American law !

Of course I saw the yacht racing, but it was not very amusing and it meant a long, tedious day. I spent the night before in New York, and Hugo Baring and I started at a very early hour in the morning. We lunched on the *Erin*. Sir Thomas Lipton had a huge party, with champagne and speeches. The water was thick with excursion launches, and the lack of any breeze made the race a fiasco. Personally I was content to read about the others, and one could be sure that the minutest description would be given in the papers.

The Sunday papers were the most amusing things I have ever seen. Eighteen years ago the English newspapers were very much more restrained than they are now, but the American papers gave such details and said such things that I cannot think how anybody dare breathe in New York !

Winter is the New York season, and when I was there American society was scattered and Newport was the social centre of the moment.

A little colony had been formed round Roslyn on Long Island. One of the show places (but equally enjoying the name of cottage) was the Clarence Mackay's ; Mrs. C. M. considered herself an intellectual and was very exclusive and admitted very few into her circle of friends. Her children's nurseries were decorated like a Mayfair drawing-room, there were very few toys about, and they were all *en suite*, whilst silk and lace abounded. What an atmosphere to grow up in l

The hen luncheon parties, whilst the men were working, were most depressing affairs. The average American husband struck one as the most tolerant money-making machine ever invented. It was a case of men working and women spending—not weeping !

Burke Cochrane was a curiously arresting personality, who seemed a primeval in that rarefied atmosphere. He was an idealist and a fine talker, and whatever his politics there was something about his rugged appearance that stamped him at once as an individualist, and he made the rest of the community look puny.

I returned to England in the autumn just in time for the Newmarket Meetings and found Flavia busy cutting her teeth and grown large enough to have got a prize at a baby show.

I should hate to live permanently in America, but I had enjoyed myself so much and everyone had been so kind that I was genuinely sorry to leave. I came back on a German boat ; Mr. Drextl was on board, and I thought him rather blatant over the insinuations of his successes in England !

An unfortunate *contretemps* occurred to me on my way home. I rang the bell for my maid and a fat German stewardess appeared, telling me that she was not available, as she had produced a " fine boy " during the night ! Tableau ! Naturally I was entirely oblivious that such an event was even anticipated.

*   *   *

We had still got our house at Manton and I was overjoyed to be out hunting once more. The fences looked comparatively small and I was full of courage after my recent experiences in America.

I don't think there were many new additions to the field. Lady Suffolk, then Miss Leiter, was almost the only one I can think of. She and Margot were hunting together from Oakham. Poor Eustace Crawley—killed in the war—was very much in love with her, and we all thought she was going to marry him, when her engagement to Lord Suffolk was announced.

It seemed as if this was to be our last winter's hunting. There had been a financial crisis in the affairs of Forbes, Forbes and Co., and as all Jim's money was in this business it meant having to sell all the horses. Jim proposed going to India ; but in the meanwhile our plans were absolutely uncertain.

We drifted through part of the summer in a rather

detached fashion and drifted finally to a complete separation. Incompatibility covers a wide road of wretched hours, and yet whilst secretly looking forward to freedom Madame de Falbe's words still remained as a warning to me. It was her advice which made me accept the arrangement which Jim insisted on, only under protest, and which later made it much easier for me to obtain my complete independence.

Meanwhile life had to be lived and the question of finance to be seriously reckoned with. Hunting cost money, and life without hunting seemed to me like bread without butter ; yet I have grown used to doing without horses and to eating margarine !

Had I graduated in the school of cheery philosophy in which I have now almost taken my honours degree, I should probably not have sold my jewels to buy horses, for that is what I actually did. Of course the horses went lame, and my pearl necklace was irretrievably gone !

I am not even now quite sure that I am entirely to blame for this utter absence of philosophy. Education in my childhood was such a dreary affair, that unless one was particularly serious-minded one was apt to look with scorn on the other side of life as presented to one in its unalluring garb. A child thinks its mother much more attractive in bright colours than when dressed in black, yet later the same child probably comes to realize that black suits its mother better than colours ever did.

But to return to my horses ! Like money earned by oneself, those horses, bought by myself, gave me far more pleasure than the ones given to me in my earlier days, and I had at least two jolly winters to which I look back with a happy recollection. I spent one of these at Oakham and another at Ashwell. Has anyone, I wonder, changed their abode in such a short space of time as I did! I enjoyed those two winters hilariously, with no regrets for the past and taking little thought for the future. But all good things come to an end. So did my money! So did the pearls!

*   *   *   *   *   .

Most of my autumns had been spent at Wemyss, and Randolph and Eva, who had been the best of friends to me, wanted me to go and live at Balfour. It was close to Wemyss, and Randolph had taken it for his mother to live at when he married; there were still a few years of the lease to run, and between them they persuaded me to move there. My last winter with only two horses, and otherwise dependent for my hunting on the kindness of friends, had made me realize the futility of trying to hunt without money, so I gladly accepted the offer and settled myself in my new home!

A delicious house of typically Scotch architecture, full of legends of the " Queen's Marys," for it had been Cardinal Beaton's home. The big drawing-room was panelled with oak from his chapel in Paris, and the old stone kitchen had been converted into the dining-room by Mrs. Wemyss.

Stories of the Cardinal's ghost, who walked with his head under his arm, were rife, but I never saw him, though I confess that I had some difficulty in persuading my lurcher Smoker to come into my bedroom. Every night he would get into a corner of my sitting-room, and refused to move until I had pulled him out, and he used to wake me up by groaning loudly at one o'clock.

My sitting-room led out of the drawing-room through a lobby beyond my bedroom. There was no one else sleeping anywhere near, and people used to ask me if I wasn't frightened ; but the only thing I was frightened of was that if the ghost did appear, it would vanish if I spoke, so that, after all, I should be none the wiser if I saw it !

The nearest approach to seeing a ghost was hearing one hammering on a glass bookcase in my doctor's consulting-room ; I knew that he was psychic, and we were discussing the subject of reincarnation, when suddenly the rat-tat, making exactly the same noise as human knuckles hitting glass, made me look quickly round. I was bound to accept the doctor's explanation that it was a frequent occurrence. It was a perfectly quiet room, removed from the sound of heavy traffic and with a curtain hung over the door. It was apparently an uninteresting ghost, confining its attentions entirely to the medical tomes.

The old walled-in garden at Balfour was a feature of the place, and here Mimini Grosvenor's hand could be easily detected in the broad herbaceous borders with their flaming mass of colour.

I think nothing was more tragic than Randolph's illness. He knew he was a doomed man, yet sheer pluck kept him alive for longer than the doctors ever thought possible. How well I remember his telling me of his illness. I had gone to Wemyss to open a bazaar for Eva, and he took me into his sitting-room and told me that he had got diabetes, that he could not live more than two years. I could hardly believe it ; he seemed perfectly well, and had come himself, in spite of pouring rain, to meet me at Thornton in his Mercedes car. His one idea seemed to be to keep the truth from Eva—she was always his first thought, and he knew what it would mean to her as she absolutely adored him.

Through all his illness he showed no sign of depression, and he very seldom talked of it. He had the most vital personality, brimming over with energy, and it was almost impossible to be with him and ever to realize that his days were numbered. He seemed, indeed, to be almost defying fate, trying to prove that a will such as his could conquer in the end. Eva was wonderful, too ; a sword hung over her head, but she never allowed it outwardly to make any difference, and her anxiety was so veiled as to deceive an onlooker.

The miners testified amply to their affection for him. Theirs was a saner attitude then, as they stood bareheaded at their cottage doors to watch his funeral cortège, or followed him to the grave, than in their flooding of the mines to-day.

V

I MISSED my hunting much less than I expected, and found that farming, gardening and golf filled up a very large portion of my time, and the fact that the Wemyss' were so close to me meant that when I wanted human companionship, it was always available.

The children were growing up and had passed from the tiresome age of babyhood into the more amusing stage of childhood. Marigold promised to be very pretty. Flavia was fat and without any pretensions to good looks, but she was jolly, and amusing enough to be forgiven for her lack of this important commodity. The amicable separation between my husband and myself still continued, and though we were on perfectly good terms with each other, I felt that both of us were still young enough to wish to be free, or else that we ought to make another effort to once more resume a joint *ménage*, but when I made this suggestion it was received without enthusiasm.

It seemed ridiculous for both of us to be permanently tied when the Scotch courts, with their very much more humane and sane divorce laws, were accessible. I had excellent instances within a few miles of me of two most happy marriages after two most unsuccessful attempts, and I pointed them out to Jim, suggesting that it was within the bounds of possibility for us to do likewise.

The great objection he had to a divorce was that in Scotland the " guilty party " was treated as dead. This meant that if I divorced him, I should be quite well off, but that he would probably become bankrupt ! In order to avoid this catastrophe, I offered to forgo my claim to the settlement during his lifetime, and to continue on the same allowance he was then giving me. After a considerable amount of discussion it was arranged, and I was, at last, free ; the divorce was for desertion only, and so we were saved all the sordid details which apparently are necessary in the English courts.

Eva Wemyss came into Edinburgh with me, and the whole thing was over in about five minutes—it seemed almost incredible that one's freedom could be obtained in so short a time. There is no decree nisi and no decree absolute, and you can walk out of the Scotch court into a church or registry office without any interference from the King's Proctor or anyone else !

The difference in my circumstances was only technical. Though I talked glibly of the possibilities of a second marriage, it was probably the last thing I contemplated.

I went south to spend Christmas with Millie at Lilleshall. She and Strath had lived there a good deal when they first married, and were doing so again, as Trentham was more or less shut up, or in the throes of being pulled down completely. The potteries had extended almost to the front door, and the chimneys and smoke had made it the most unattractive place to live in. I had to take a house in London after Christmas, as something was supposed to be wrong with

Flavia's heart. After taking her to various doctors and going through weeks of the most ceaseless anxiety, she was mercifully passed sound. I got a few days' hunting that winter, but I am not sure that it was worth it. Going down with the milk train and having a bad day's sport and hearing all about the good ones one had missed, not to speak of the stiffness, was a doubtful pleasure.

I was destined to spend only one more autumn at Balfour, as that summer Randolph Wemyss was taken suddenly much worse, and his death occurred only a few days after his return from doing a cure abroad. I lunched with them just before, and his courage and energy were the same. Dorothy Dalmeny,* a lovely creature, came in after luncheon. Randolph had always been devoted to his sister Mimini, and was equally fond of her children, and he seemed both pleased and touched at Dorothy coming to see him. Randolph's death meant an entire reconstruction of my future plans. The lease at Balfour had almost run out, and as the trustees were anxious to wind up the estate, we decided that I had better make arrangements for moving, and the next few months were spent with the children at Easton, as Daisy had asked us to stay with her until I settled down in the new house.

London seemed the best place to establish my head-quarters, but before I was in a position to settle anything I had various unpleasant lawsuits to tackle, a tiresome and expensive job ; and when one has divorced one's husband, one's budget does not as a rule allow for any further litigation on the subject.

* Now Mrs. R. Brassey.

A succession of tragic comedies took place. J. at
first threatened to stop my allowance altogether, because
I refused to give up my maternal claims on Marigold!
An attempt on his part to kidnap her was frustrated by
a prompt move on my part! It was important, if he
was going to be tiresome, for the children to be in Scotland, under Scotch jurisdiction. They were at that
moment at school in London, but by the time J. or his
agents arrived to abduct M., she was safely on her way
to St. Andrews! The threat about the allowance was
at once put into force, and we were left penniless! Then
followed an entirely new development in the shape of
a melodramatic announcement that our divorce was
null and void, as my husband was not Scotch, but
English. Coming from J. it was more than comic. He
was never quite happy out of a kilt, added to which he
was going to be married himself in a few weeks. It all
entailed endless complications, and it eventually devolved
on me to get him out of the mess that he had got himself
into, and to prove that he was still entitled to his kilt.
It was a lengthy process, and during the weeks that followed I can never be grateful enough to the Elchos (now
Lord and Lady Wemyss) for all they did for me. The
children and I spent a great deal of our time at Stanway,
and Marigold eventually went to Dresden with Mary
Charteris and her governess.

Stanway, which is one of the strongholds of the Souls,
is a most perfect type of Elizabethan architecture, with
its beautiful gatehouse built by Inigo Jones. It is not
only lovely to look at, but delightful to stay in, and
its literary and domestic atmosphere, as represented
by its inmates, was in no way enervating, and though
the Précieuse might be there, it was far removed from

9

one's conception of the Precious. I had rather scoffed at the intellectual games, probably through fear of being unable to shine in them, but I fell under their charm directly I played them. The guessing game is particularly amusing. Having selected your victim, you describe him or her by the scent, the flower, the architecture, even a good dish of which he or she may remind you. It is a game calculated to add to your list of enemies—to be described as resembling a cauliflower, a toad, macaroni and sage green, is not likely to make you feel friendly towards the author of such an uncompromising word-picture. The fact that the most libellous portraits were the most easily guessed is a proof that people's idiosyncrasies and faults are more easily noticed than their virtues. Another amusing game is presenting an historical scene by dumb acting, and leaving it to the audience to discover who and what you are—Beb Asquith and I were particularly successful in our representation of Madame Steinheil and Monsieur Faure !

Lady Wemyss shares with her sisters the very special gift of motherhood, coupled with a very clear understanding of the things that matter in life. Her children possess unique and varied gifts, and a solidity which is not always the accompaniment of charm.

Cynthia's* charm is so subtle that, in spite of her having sat as a model oftener than most people, no artist can reproduce it. John confesses that he found it only once, to lose it with the next stroke of the pencil. I think it lies in the quiver of the mouth, which seems to turn up and down simultaneously, and gives the idea of wandering virtue which made me once describe

* Lady Cynthia Asquith.

The Saloon, Dysart.

[*Facing p.* 159

her as the Madonna gone wrong. She is alarmingly observant, which makes her super-critical even in a critical family.

That lives so full of promise as those of both Ego and Yvo should have been cut off in the very heyday of their summer is one of those non-understandable workings of a Providence we are taught to believe in.

*   *   *   *

I was lucky, when my various lawsuits were eventually disposed of, to find a rather unique house in Devonshire Terrace, just off the Marylebone Road. It had been for many years the home of Charles Dickens and the centre of his social life. In it he wrote some of his most famous books, including " David Copperfield," and from there he waged his battles against the stupidity, harshness, and smugness of his age. Dickens took himself most seriously as a social reformer, and it seems to me his value in that connection has never been fully recognized, nor sufficient homage done to him along those lines. His age was certainly the age of *laisser faire*, and social service, except for the select few, merely a name. Later on, I know, it became almost a fashionable pastime among a certain set, but in Dickens' day it was in its infancy, and Lord Shaftesbury was considered a mad crank by most of his friends.

The house seemed at times full of ghosts, kindly, cheery ones, I am glad to say ; Maclise, Foster, McCready, and even Douglas Jerrold had a softened humour.

I had not, however, fully recognized the significance of the charming little blue medallion placed on the wall of No. 1a, by an almost too thoughtful London County

9*

Council. Various respectful little groups used to gather
round the house, while a lecture on Dickens, his times,
and his influence was evidently in progress—at least
I judged so by the looks of rapt attention cast from
time to time at the windows of my residence. I didn't
mind that at all, it was a tribute to the great writer
and that pleased me, but societies at rather inconvenient
times requested permission to go over a part of the house
and to see the London garden Dickens had loved ; it
was more than awkward occasionally, but had to be
done. The Americans were horribly persistent. They
appeared and flatly refused to budge until they had
saturated themselves with the real Dickens atmosphere,
as they phrased it. The fact that my own great works
were being perpetrated meant nothing to them, and
they poked about everywhere armed with notebooks,
floating veils and all the rest of it, ending with effusive
thanks and making straight, I suppose, for Westminster
Abbey.

Whether the ghost of the great writer or a diminutive
bank balance was responsible for my taking to literature
is a delicate point. Quite frankly, I am afraid it was
a commercial rather than a literary instinct which
prompted me to first take up my pen. Imagination,
hitherto, had not been my strong point, and I found
considerable difficulty in extricating heroes and heroines
in an artistic, and at the same time commonsense,
fashion from the difficult situations into which I had
somewhat thoughtlessly placed them.

My earliest literary effort was at the age of eight,
when I won a prize in a " Little Folks " competition,
and my next attempt was at Madeira, when I embarked
on a novel. The report that it was too improper to

be published was based on the fact that my heroine was married on a Monday and on the following Saturday a baby had duly appeared upon the scene—excessive innocence or absurd ignorance would have been better criticism.

In the interval I had edited a *Natural History Magazine.* It was, of course, a purely childish effort, but it contained some quite interesting contributions, and my father wrote this sonnet for it :

WRITTEN FOR

ANGELA'S NATURAL HISTORY MAGAZINE

WHAT a dull World 'twould be, if only Man
    Were in it ! Man the Tyrant ! Man the Slave !
The vocal woods all silent as the grave,
And Nature cursed by some Almighty ban ;
No swarm, ephemeral, that lives a span
Yet lasts for ever ; the dark Ocean's wave,
No more aglow, from crest to inmost cave,
With fiery atoms, lustreless and wan !
Oh ! what were life without a horse or hound
(The Race, that makes the dullest pulse beat quick
The Chase, that stirs the energies of Youth)—
Those dear companions of our daily round ?
Oh ! cherish them with love, tend them when sick
And learn from them the honest ways of truth !

I was also given a hitherto unpublished poem of Elizabeth Barrett Browning's, but alas, I cannot reproduce it, as I have no copy of the magazine. The idea of the magazine was a crib from Eva Baird, now Mrs. Graham-Murray, who started an anti-cruelty to animals paper and asked me to be a contributor. Its contents consisted principally of articles dealing with the woes or the intelligence of cattle and sheep.

My first real book, " The Broken Commandment,"

was banned by the libraries, a fact which my publisher told me ought to elate me, as it would undoubtedly have a good market in consequence. I really don't think it was a bit more improper than most of the books which were selling regularly on the bookstalls. The criticisms amused me immensely, but after reading them I was not sure whether it was a work of great literary merit, or the most immoral book that had ever been published. The *Times* was short and sharp in its notice and summed it up in a few words, " a compound fracture of the seventh commandment " !

My next two novels (I am really not writing of them in any spirit of pride) were published during the following three years. If they were of no literary merit they certainly kept me occupied and gave me a glimpse into another side of life. The spade work of writing was thoroughly distasteful, and I finished up by dictating them to the typewriter, but my amanuensis used to take up nearly as much time telling me stories of Fleet Street as I did of hers dictating rather mediocre fiction.

Her mother had been Lord Northcliffe's only " hand " in the days when he first ran *Answers*, and as a child, she used to go on Saturday afternoons to sort the postcards for his postcard competition—the competition which attracted so much attention, and helped him on to the first step of the ladder he has so successfully climbed. The day *Answers* was able to run to a cover, he was so overcome with joy that he took his " Sub-Editor " to have a " steak and porter " at the nearest Chop Shop.

The result of hearing this story was to surround Lord N. for ever with a romantic halo. I have read of people who have made fortunes out of nothing, but they always seem very intangible and as remote as Dick Whittington—there is nothing the least remote about Lord Northcliffe.

Scribbling did not occupy all my time, and I was beginning to take a rather more intelligent interest in politics and history. I realized regretfully that the development of my education had been seriously handicapped by my father's death, when I was at an age to have benefited most from his companionship, and I determined that Marigold, who was really rather fond of her lessons, should be encouraged to take an interest in present day events and happenings.

We engaged a history lecturer, and, as we were all sublimely ignorant about the rights and wrongs of Ireland and as the Home Rule Bill was on the tapis, this was selected as one of the subjects. My knowledge of Ireland was practically limited to a visit to the Head-forts, and I was horrified to learn the part my ancestor, the Lord Chancellor Loughborough, had played in the affairs of that unfortunate country.

The cult of the politician was becoming general, and an attempt to revive the salon was a fashionable occupation. Somewhere about now F. E. Smith was being talked about as the new discovery, and he availed himself of his discoverers to promptly climb the ladder !

I was at the next table to him and Lady Pembroke at the " Ritz " one night, and could not help hearing some of their conversation. She was busy talking politics, and he was trying hard to talk hunting !

I amused myself reading the Parliamentary reports, but was undecided in my mind over the Die-Hards and the House of Lords reformers ; I even dug up Lloyd George's Limehouse speeches in a wild endeavour to

preserve a perfect balance of view. Can Lord Derby
have forgotten them entirely, I wonder, when he cheer-
fully suggests that Mr. Lloyd Géorge may be the next
Conservative Leader ? On the other hand, of course,
the convert is always more zealous than one born in
the Faith.

Mr. Lloyd George, with his keen sense of humour,
must laugh heartily sometimes when he sees himself
surrounded by the pillars of the party who would once
gladly have seen him gibbeted and who now hang on his
words hoping for his favours.

The Prime Minister's success has obviously not
turned his head. He has, apparently, no leanings
towards intimacy with so-called smart society, and
so far no social star has succeeded in inveigling him
away from the domestic hearth.

I suppose if one lives in England, London is the
best headquarters for a lone woman, but I confess I
did not appreciate the atmosphere. Desolate as the
country may be, I don't think one is ever so lonely as
one can be by oneself in a big town. Somehow, when
the birds go to bed and Nature has settled down to await
the dawn of another day, one drops quite naturally
into a dreamless sleep at an absurdly early hour, whereas
the rattle of the horses and cabs and the town lights are
vaguely disturbing. In the same way, I know of no
more depressing entertainment than supper after a
play—a thing since DORA almost unheard of. One
is not hungry if one has dined a couple of hours previously, and there is a note of false gaiety about it ;

Easton Lodge. 'Where I lived as a child.

[Facing p. 136

one needs to be very young to prolong in such fashion either a boring or a merry evening.

One of the " philosophers of life " that I saw a good deal of in those days when I lived in Devonshire Terrace was Ralph Nevill, Lady Dorothy's son. I know no one with whom one could spend a more entertaining hour—whose mood fitted in with one's own more truly, or who coloured dinner-table conversation more brightly than he did. " A student of human nature " he called himself, and he had evidently studied to some purpose !

I spent two winters at Biarritz and enjoyed myself, though I don't rave about the place as some people do. The wind was to my mind a great drawback. An occasional gale, as I remembered in my childhood at Dysart, when we used to stand on the end of the harbour pier and watch the waves dashing themselves at our feet and soaking us with spray, is divinely exhilarating, but in everyday life a perpetual wind becomes singularly exasperating.

The Orloffs and Demidoffs were at Biarritz both winters, and I liked them immensely. I had known both the Demidoffs in Leicestershire and in Paris. Prince D. was quite charming to Flavia, who shamelessly announced one day at luncheon that she prayed for Princess Demidoff's death, in order to marry the Prince herself. I am afraid that he was the person who started her on the path of flirtations !

We had some very amusing foursomes at golf, both at St. Jean de Luz and at Biarritz, when Massey and I played Hugo* and Prince Demidoff. St. Sebastian was a rather nice place, and on one occasion George

* Earl of Wemyss.

Vernon*, Hugo and I motored over to gamble. We had all lost our money and were just going home, when I found a louis counter in my pocket. I threw this casually on number twenty. To my intense surprise, I heard the croupier announce it had won. I plastered the number with my winnings, and once more had the satisfaction of seeing it come up. For about ten minutes I couldn't go wrong, and when George came back to see what I was doing, very cross at being kept waiting, he found my pockets bulging with counters. I was torn away before I had time to lose them again!

One of my most scatterbrained adventures was a night trip in a balloon with the Dunvilles. The D.'s and Mrs. Assheton Harbord spent most of their time ballooning, and I was dining with them in Portland Place, when the suggestion was made that we should dash off to Chelsea Gas Works and embark.

When the balloon left her moorings we rose slowly and steadily without any sensation at all—the helplessness of the pilot to direct our course was entirely lost sight of by me, when I suggested that the tail rope was extraordinarily near the top of some trees in a wood we were skimming, but the only means apparently of averting any disaster was to throw sand out of the balloon! There was not enough wind to make it really exciting, and on one occasion we touched the ground in the middle of a corn field. I could not help thinking how uncomfortable it would have been if we had landed on the goods station at Paddington instead! The trials of not being able to smoke were compensated for by seeing the day dawn above the clouds. Though

* The late Lord Vernon.

one was in the middle of it, it seemed to happen without any consciousness of what was taking place. From complete darkness we seemed suddenly wrapped in a mantle of rose colour, and the next moment was day-light.

We came down in a most orderly fashion at Colonel Hall Walker's training ground near Swindon. I was not sorry to emerge from the basket; a sand-bag is a most uncomfortable seat on which to spend the night —even in the best of company!

A chain of minor accidents led my wandering foot-steps to Le Touquet. Flavia was a most inconsiderate child, and invariably developed some infantile com-plaint, generally at the most inconvenient moment. From her point of view her periodical illnesses were a considerable asset, and she became in consequence almost a connoisseur of seaside resorts! Sandwich, Margate, Brighton and the rest of them were all sampled, and most of them, with the exception of Sandwich, very much disliked by me! I think there is nothing so dreary or depressing as the ordinary English South Coast watering-places, and I felt entirely unable to cope with it when the usual change of air was ordered for Flavia after her tonsils had been removed!

A sudden inspiration came to me to try Le Touquet. I had been to Paris Plage in 1898, when the golf links were hardly laid out and Paris Plage was a diminutive village, consisting of little more than half a dozen wooden chalets, which you could not dignify by the name of houses. I remember going over from a yacht at Boulogne to see Lady de Trafford and Lady Norreys, who were there with their children. The journey then was a bit of an adventure, almost a pilgrimage, but there was something very captivating about the huge, almost boundless stretches of sand, and the utter absence of anything regulated or planned—its very inconsequence was its charm.

When I went there again, a few years later, time and speculators were hard at work doing their best to change its aspect. The golf course was completed, but you still only needed a niblick, a driver and a putter ; now things were different, and it is greatly to the credit of those who had the course under their charge that they were able to induce grass to grow in that sandy soil. The links had undergone drastic changes under Vardon's supervision, and a rather gimcrack and extremely unpicturesque hotel was crammed to overflowing. Vardon was looked on as a tin·god—at one moment it looked as if he might be going to spoil the course by adding too many artificial bunkers and spoiling what Nature had already effected. Later on the course was considered good enough for the championship to be played there. Of all the pros, I liked Braid the best, and I played several foursomes with him, and also with Robson, who came to Le Touquet for quite a long time with Lord De La Warr.

On my first visit to Le Touquet I had been stranded for hours at Etaples Station, unable to get the most humble of conveyances ; but when the children and I arrived we were met by an hotel motor bus, and the station was full of *voitures* and taxis, testimony to the popularity of the place. Certainly its popularity was well deserved when you think that in those pre-war days you could leave London and have a good round of golf in the most delightful surroundings, to say nothing of a gamble, before dinner without any inconvenience. The old château where we gambled would no longer accommodate the inquisitive and increasing crowd, and plans for a gigantic Casino were in the process of development, whilst in Paris Plage shops and chalets had grown up like mushrooms in the night. I always wonder why such astute people as Mr. Balfour, Lord D'Abernon and Lord Wemyss did not see the potentialities of Le Touquet, but the fact remains that years ago they all came, saw and condemned it ; but they have all since confessed that their judgment was very much at fault.

The Wemyss', the Elchos and Mr. Balfour came over for Whitsuntide, and Mr. Balfour divided his time between the golf links and the tennis courts ; these were another sign of the civilization that was fast conquering Le Touquet's seclusion.

The Stonehams practically owned the entire place, he having bought the property for a mere song, and it was to him that much of its rapid development was due. They had built their own house almost adjoining the golf course, and Mrs. Stoneham was justly proud of her rose garden. (Mr. Balfour was the recipient of a basketful on his arrival.) They had two demon children who have grown into nice boys. The youngest one, asked by a General during the war if soldiering was going to be his profession, replied firmly · "No." The General, by way of inducing him to change his mind, suggested he might eventually be his A.D.C. The boy saw no attractions in the prospect—if he was a soldier he said he wanted to fight. The General assured him he would get plenty of that. "No I shouldn't," said the lad. " Your A.D.C.'s stay at the base and get decorations."

Another " accident " led to my staying considerably longer at Le Touquet than I had anticipated. On the very eve of our return to England a telegram came to say that there had been a fire in my house in London ; the result, apparently, of a fused wire. This was followed by a letter from my landlord, asking me to let him make some alterations to the house, and as these alterations meant improvements, including a new bathroom, I asked for nothing better. The alterations, he told me, would take at least three months to complete, so after bargaining with the hotel management I decided to spend the summer where we were.

It was then that a wave of inspiration came to me. A small building syndicate, one of the many being then floated for the improvement of Le Touquet, had been formed, and two villas, just completed, stood as the outward and visible sign of the syndicate. Were they to let ? I made anxious inquiries, and found they were still available. I saw a chance now of living rent free. By taking one and letting it in the season I should probably make money, and I should equally have no difficulty in letting my house in Devonshire Terrace when I wanted to.

This seemed such an attractive scheme that I at once put it into operation, and my luck at the Casino made it easy. I really did have phenomenal luck that summer. With one louis I made a hundred one afternoon before dinner, having looked into the Casino on my way back from bathing—and from that day for several months I never used to go out of the rooms a loser. It was one of those extraordinary runs which come sometimes once in a lifetime. The gambling, except at Whitsuntide and Easter, was very limited, but I made several expeditions to Paris and went out to Enghien, always followed by the same amazing good fortune. I made enough to furnish my villa, and eventually my prognostications regarding the rent were correct, and I let it every season for six weeks for more than I paid for it by the year.

But apart from the financial success of the enterprise I loved the life out there. It was never dull, and without any of the tiresome conventionalities of London. Of course, the crowds at Easter and Whitsuntide were tiresome, for, as the place became better known, the riff-raff of London found its way across, and the crowd made the links rather impossible to play on with any degree of comfort—but this was only during the holidays, and the course was improving each year.

A few enterprizing people were beginning to build villas. Amongst these were the Kemps, who had already spent some weeks at the Golf Hotel and had fallen under the charm of Le Touquet. They had bought some ground quite close to my villa, so I was assured of pleasant neighbours. Mr. Kemp was a very nice American and Mrs. Kemp a beautiful woman with blue-black hair and marvellous eyes. Isabel Kemp was a delightful child, and she had had the advantages of a combined American and French education.

I had started golf in a rather desultory fashion when I was living at Balfour, where I had the advantage of being close to St. Andrews, but I now took it up with great seriousness. I cannot say that the results are as good as I might have wished for, though I actually had the impertinence to play in the French Ladies' Championship.

Quite a large number of the female lights came over for this event, amongst them the Leitch sisters and Miss Ravenscroft. I liked her the best. She was so very unconceited over her game and did not appear to make such a business of it as some of the others. Mdlle. De Bellet was much the best of the French competitors. She is very pretty and her style excellent, but has not got the *beef* which is behind most of the others—always excepting Elsie Grant Suttie. It was wonderful how the French were taking to golf. The hotel used to be full at week-ends of Lille merchants, their wives and families, who nearly all played with a varying degree of excellence. They were so tremendously keen that the pro.'s time was always fully booked ahead for lessons.

I was immensely struck by the superior education of the French *bourgeoisie* over the English of the same status; the difference is particularly noticeable in the Casino, where the second-rate Englishman appears sixth-rate with his blatant self-complacency and his faltering aspirates or country dialect in comparison with the polite Frenchman, who speaks good French, no matter what his vocation in life might be. The average Englishwoman you meet at the seaside in this country is generally impossible as a companion. Frenchwomen, on the other hand, and I met many, and got to know some well, are all well-read and well up, not only in their own politics, but in those of other countries, and their knowledge of English affairs very often put me to shame when I remembered how little I knew of theirs.

A most delightful woman, Madame le Blanc—her husband owned some big cotton mills in Lille—was a regular visitor to the Golf Hotel. We often played golf together, and one day I was talking to her of Germany

Lady Angela Forbes, 1897.

and the Germans, and I asked her if the proverbial cry of hatred and *revanche* was genuine or merely *blague*. The year 1870 seemed so remote and far back in history that I found it difficult to realize the terrible feeling of hatred which was supposed to exist in every man, woman and child in France. " Do you," I asked, " personally dislike every German you meet ? " Her reply was unmistakably genuine, and she pointed to her sons just then strolling down to the club house and said · " I would gladly see those boys die on the field of battle so that France might avenge herself for 1870." They were very fine looking boys, almost English in appearance, and I have since heard that the two eldest were killed. Madame le Blanc was in Lille through most of the German occupation.

She went on to tell me how the " day " must come, possibly sooner than any of us dreamt ; the politicians in both countries were blind—wilfully or stupidly blind, she did not know which, anyway as far as England was concerned. Of her own country's Government she had not much opinion. Our conversation took place at the moment when the period of the " Service Militaire " was the burning question. She looked on it as the height of folly and said that all patriotic Frenchmen were of the same opinion, and that it was purely a political move.

Since Napoleon I. the French had been used to the idea of conscription, though it was only in 1889 that the Military law of " Service obligatoire " was actually passed. The law then was that every Frenchman, if fit at twenty-one, had to serve in the army three years, but by passing certain examinations the period was reduced to a year, in order that the men who were to adopt other careers should not be needlessly hindered. In 1905, owing to the Socialistic influence at work, the Government passed another law, reducing the term to two years, but with no exemption. The idea of this was to reduce, little by little, the military charges ; the French Government then in power did not *want* to see the danger signals in German politics and preferred to pander to the Socialists and to the Radical electors. Germany, however, persisted in her efforts to irritate France, till at last public opinion, under the influence of the real French patriots, realized how suicidal this policy was, and in 1913, in spite of a strong Socialist opposition, M. Barthou managed to carry the day, and the three years' " Service obligatoire " came into force with no exemptions.

Caillaux and his clique were, alas for France, still far too influential, and were doing their best to rescind the Barthou Bill. Politics were corrupt and tinged with drama, which reached its height with the Caillaux-Calmette murder. French politics are carried occasionally far into the law courts, and no one anticipated any other verdict than one of acquittal for Madame Caillaux.

Time has convicted Caillaux himself, not only by the High Court of Justice but by every right-thinking citizen —at Vichy the other day a wounded *poilu* attacked him with his crutch and he was no more seen in the streets.

PART II

WAR! How one remembers those early days when a curious heart-sickness seemed to have fallen on everyone—one remembers them with almost more vividness than the years that followed. All one's senses seemed strung to a nervous tension and strain.

I had only just come from Le Touquet—having let my villa as usual for the season—when the Arch-Duke's murder and the German Note gave the first dim warning of future troubles. Even then one did not realize how soon the storm would burst.

I can remember my German kitchen-maid telling me there would be no war; that the Germans hated the Kaiser and that he would be assassinated before he could marshal his armies in the field—so much for her knowledge of the German mentality.

The news of the hurried flight from Le Touquet and Paris Plage reached me through Mr. Butler, the Secretary of the Golf Club, who came to see me in London.

Le Touquet and Paris Plage had just started their season, and the Polo week was in full swing. The new ground which the Millers had superintended was being opened, and the Duke of Westminster and Lord Rock-savage had got their ponies there, but when war was declared English, French and Americans fled in absolute confusion. The manager of the Golf Hotel, a German, had disappeared, but a waiter of the same nationality had been pushed overboard, in the Harbour, by the mob and left to his fate. Mr. Butler also told me that all the men in the district had reported themselves at their Depots—only to be sent back as there was not a pair of boots or a single rifle available. This, for a nation that had been crying *revanche* for a generation, seemed incredible, but there is no gainsaying the fact that the French were quite as unprepared for war as we were.

Official circles resolutely refused to realize the nearness of " the day." Although the Opposition spent their time warning the Government of the danger of this apathetic policy, they continued to shut their eyes to the probability of war, as resolutely as did the English to Lord Roberts' prognostications.

The French Government wanted to inspire the people with confidence and established a false security. Caillaux influence was at work, and his policy was to pander to Germany, always hoping to break down the natural antagonism of France towards that country, which would one day end in an alliance against England. One of the most reassuring incidents sometimes used for the justification of the unpreparedness of the French for the war, was the presence of the President, and other members of the Government, at a reception given in June, 1914, by the German ambassador, M. de Schoerr. It was the first time since 1871 that the President had ever crossed the threshold of the German Embassy. It was almost an unwritten law that he might not set foot on " German soil," and the German Embassy is, of course, legally such. To such an extent was this fetish carried, that whenever the President went to see his ally the Czar of Russia he had to make the journey by sea in order to avoid crossing German territory.

The fact that this habit of years had been broken appeared more indicative of peace than war.

* * * *

Then came those days fraught with tense anxiety and suspense as to England's rôle in this world-event. The doubt was felt rather than expressed. " When are we going in ? " rather than " Are we going in ? " was the haunting question in every breast.

There were Cabinet meetings, rumours and speculations as to what transpired at them—Lloyd George and Lord Morley were commonly reported to be the pacifists —and then on the 4th August the tocsin sounded! The face of London was changed, and at one stroke the habits of years slipped from the populace. London, usually a dusty wilderness in August, was crowded—no one wanted to go away. Overborne with a new sense of grave happenings, people ceased to concern themselves with changing their clothes. The hotel grill-rooms were crowded, but to dress for dinner became banal, almost an outrage. At nights the people poured into the streets—and no surer proof of the loyalty of British citizens could have been found than in those throngs, that gathered round Buckingham Palace, to cheer their King.

Meanwhile the military machine started moving and the great mobilization began. Not only the secrecy, but the swiftness with which it was carried out, constituted a *chef d'œuvre* of organization.

At the London depots men confined to barracks could be seen talking to their wives and sweethearts through the railings. They had cheery, jolly faces, and, poor devils, they all expected to be back again

in a short time. A few of them, doubtless, knew better
the true nature of the great adventure upon which
they were being resistlessly hurried ; but their women's
courage must be kept up at all costs, and all sections of
society feverishly strove to connive and to keep the
national moral to its topmost point.

Everyone was delighted that Sir John French was
to command the Expeditionary Force. Up to the last
moment it was not absolutely certain that he would
do so, as he had relinquished his position as Chief of the
General Staff the previous April, owing to the affair
at the Curragh ; and there were rumours afloat that Sir
James Grierson, whose knowledge of Germany and of
the German mentality was so profound, might be sent
in his stead.

Sir John French, however, was duly appointed to
the supreme command, and the nation felt that our
fate was in competent hands. The First Hundred
Thousand were flung at the invader. Few realized
more surely than Sir John French how the issue hung
in the balance, and no one could have done better than
he, with his inadequate material, and his handful of
men, against the terrific onrush of the German hordes.

Those early days, with all their bull-dog endurance
in the face of overwhelming odds, will not easily be
forgotten—at any rate, by those who were associated
with the epic retreat from Mons. French's superhuman
efforts in rallying his forces when things seemed to
have reached breaking point are now matters of history,
and when at last he left the Army, he left it admired
and beloved by his officers and men.

I dined with the P.'s the night before the Grenadiers
left ; one or two of G.'s brother officers were there.

It is interesting to recall the point of view at the moment : back in six weeks and the Germans beaten into cocked hats ! I was shouted down when I suggested the possibility of the Germans winning the war ; their argument was not that we could wear them down with determination, as we eventually did, but that it was unthinkable that they should even win one battle ! I suppose it was this wonderful spirit of confidence, or optimism, that helped that handful of men to stand up, as they did, against the overwhelming majority of the enemy. Another thing ·which was frequently propounded in those early days was the impossibility for human nerves to stand more than six weeks of the hideous and ferocious violence of modern warfare.

No sooner had the war-cloud burst than a general desire to take some part evinced itself. First Aid classes were inaugurated, and everyone who owned a house in any way suitable instantly offered it to the War Office or the Admiralty to be used as a hospital. There was a rush of women to the London hospitals to be taken as probationers, and every shop that sold a cap or apron was literally besieged by those who wanted, at least, to possess a uniform.

Millie lunched with me a day or two before we knew definitely that England had come into the war. She was very busy getting letters off in the Foreign Office mail-bag, but she did not divulge that she was off to France herself, and one night she vanished. What happened there after that she herself has written. I went with her after luncheon to the first-aid class at Londonderry House, where I found " Society " making gallant attempts to master the intricacies of the capelline bandage, and how *not* to tie a granny knot, and if the bandages *did* roll from one end of the ball-room to the other, as they escaped from amateur fingers, the efforts to succeed were so genuine that no one could have ridiculed them.

There was something singularly eerie about the big room in all its party panoply, with its summer-clad occupants grouped round an anatomical model or a blackboard inscribed with medical terms and diagrams, and one afternoon I remember seeing Lord Kitchener pass through the room to have tea with Lady Londonderry.

Constance Richardson was a striking figure in her " desert " garments—she had just taken to going about in draperies and sandals. Constance is certainly an extremist in dress. She was the pioneer of the no-back sleeveless frocks many years before they were formally adopted by the multitude. Will women, I wonder, ever adopt her new style ? She had brought her boy there—an overgrown child of seven, to act as a living model on whom the students were to practice bandaging. Constance has an idea that her son is a reincarnated early Celt, and, in consequence, his hair is not cut, but bound round with a broad band, and he walks through the world bareheaded and with a very short kilt ! Poor child, I was quite sorry for him !

A rather curious thing happened about a week after. I was at home trying to get a number on the telephone when I got on to a crossed line, and accidentally heard the most interesting conversation between a man and a woman. The man was a member of the Turf and the Athenæum Club, a curious combination. I knew this because he told the woman, obviously a great friend, that he was dining at one or the other. He had been staying with Lord Grey for the week-end, and when I tell you that he was describing Lord Grey's mental attitude during that fatal first week in August, will any of you who read this call me dishonourable when I tell you that I did not put the receiver down ?

It appears that during that week Lord Grey was torn in two directions. I gathered that he felt that by boldly declaring that England would come into the war he could have stopped Germany ; but, on the other hand, he was convinced that once France was absolutely confident of our support, she would not have allowed anything to deter her ; his hope lay in France averting the war herself by not knowing whether we should support her or not—that, at least, was what Lord Grey's visitor told his friend. He also said that we were making ourselves very unpopular in France by declaring that, but for Belgium's neutrality having been violated, we should have remained neutral.

When people talk of our unpopularity with the French, I think they forget the point of view that was adopted in those early days. In French eyes it must have seemed an ungracious way and an ungracious attitude to adopt, and whatever hypocrites may say about our reasons or our obligations for going into the war, it was entered upon, and it was necessary that it should be entered upon, for the ultimate safety of England herself. A little less cant and a little more honesty, and we should have heard nothing, because there would have been nothing to hear, of the unpopularity of the English in France.

Certainly some measure of English unpopularity in later days resulted from the unfortunate selection of officers for base jobs. With some naturally obvious exceptions, the " Jacks-in-Office " were bad examples of our race, and I have often had to blush and apologize for my compatriots. Apart from their insular prejudice outside their own island, they displayed a lamentable lack of tact in their dealings with the local French population. I can recall one glaring example of rudeness. I had been dining at a café in Etaples, started by a lady with the primary object of providing funds to run a canteen for the French *poilus* who were stranded at Etaples Station on their way home on leave. Two officers called for something to eat—it was just closing time, and the M.P.'s on duty battered loudly on the door, ordering them out, but telling them that they could get anything they wanted—including drinks—at the English Club round the corner. The patrone, who was very pro-English, and has since married an Englishman, for the moment saw red—and who can wonder ? Imagine the picture reversed ! A Frenchman in England telling a man in front of a publican that he might not drink at his bar, but could do so in a French estaminet a little further down the street. I tremble to think of the Frenchman's fate in such circumstances. Incidents of this description were perpetually occurring, and were accepted in a spirit of comparative resignation, as part payment of the debt they owed us, for their recognition of our services in the field was unstinted It has since been explained to me that the base was used as a dumping-ground for the undesirables out of most regiments—hence the " riff-raff " that literally fell over each other in some departments.

I have often told Frenchmen of the conversation I overheard, and their opinion is more or less unanimous, that if the German Government had been warned by our Ambassador in Berlin, that in the case of an attack on France we should be solidly behind her, Germany might have thought twice about forcing the situation and making war inevitable; and that if England *really* feared France being aggressive, *she* need not have been told of our friendly intentions.

I asked a French friend of mine at a later period what the feeling in France had been when England's ultimatum still hung in the balance. She described it rather quaintly: " We were sure of you really, but it was as if someone told you Flavia would not kiss you good-morning ! "

I became rather interested in the First Aid classes and went to some more, rather more serious ones, at Mrs. FitzGerald's house in Cadogan Place. I confess I had no intention of being a nurse, or of even going to France at the time, and my amazement was great when I got an urgent telephone message from Mrs. FitzGerald telling me that she and I had been asked to go over to Doctor Haden Guest's hospital in Paris. She implored me to go, and, more stirred with the spirit of adventure than with anything else, I agreed, and rushed to Garrould's to get some sort of an outfit. Imagine my feelings the night before we were due to start, getting a note from Mrs. FitzGerald, to say that her son had returned and that she was chucking the expedition altogether. My excitement and my spirits fell to zero. I frankly hated going alone, but I had not the moral courage to give it up. By the most marvellous luck, I managed to get a passport for the children's governess, and she and I went off from Victoria on, I think, the 1st of September.

The Folkestone boats were not running and we had an abominable crossing—very rough and a very crowded small boat—via Dieppe. Sarah Wilson was on board, and let me share her cabin. She had still nowhere to put her hospital, and I believe was meeting some of her staff in Paris. I had begged her to take either the Hermitage or the Golf Hotel at Le Touquet, as they were both on offer ; but Winston Churchill apparently had said that that district would be quite impossible for any hospital, owing to the difficulty of embarkation at Boulogne.

At Dieppe we were met by a friend of Sarah Wilson's, who gave us heartrending accounts of the conditions for the accommodation of the French wounded. The only doctor was run off his legs, the sanitary arrangements were abominable, amputated limbs were left in the dustbins, and anæsthetics were a negligible quantity.

It was pitch-dark when we arrived in Paris. I went with the Haden Guests to the Hôtel Majestic, where the hospital was installed and where I was to have accommodation. Supper was ready for us, and we went into the barely-lit passages through smells of chloroform and iodoform, into what was the staff's mess-room.

I was hungry, but I could not eat the very nasty looking food that was produced for me. How I wished that my moral courage had not failed me, and that I had never left England !

Mrs. Guest asked me if I would like to go straight into the ward and see some of the men. Longing to say " No," I said " Yes," hoping no one would discover what I was feeling.

The mess-room was only just outside the ward, which was the big ball-room in the Majestic, and groans could be distinctly heard. As we passed in, it seemed as if my heart almost stopped. The chandelier had only about two lights in it and they were thickly shaded, making the figures in the beds all round look more terrible than any ghost. Some of the men were sleeping and in their dreams their screams were terrible to hear. " They hear the taxis," said the nurse, " and they think it is the Germans." The men were nearly all French, with here and there an Englishman. All were badly wounded. They had been left behind, a great many of them, after the retreat of Mons, and there were several cases of tetanus, whilst two men died as I stood in the room. The lack of tetanus serum at that time was pathetic. I felt myself utterly helpless and only in the way, and the nurses looked at me, as all nurses did at amateurs in those days, with suspicion, and it was with a sigh of relief that I at last crept up, with the light of a tallow dip, the great gloomy staircase into a small apartment which was to be mine whilst I was at the Majestic.

The next morning I came down to breakfast, having spent the most miserable, sleepless night, haunted by the sounds that I had heard and the faces I had seen.

The meals with the staff were a rather trying experience, and I used to escape to a little restaurant as often as possible. We were a most heterogeneous collection of human beings. Haden Guest himself, a man of parts, struck me as being a bit of a crank, probably only due to his theosophical convictions, which, by the way, were shared by a considerable number of the people surrounding him. His wife appeared to have as many varied interests as himself, and his secretary, Miss Osborne, who was extremely capable, found time to deal with and disentangle the many muddles which arose from day to day. I must say I was immensely struck by the gentlemen orderlies, who performed their duties in the most professional and devoted manner imaginable.

＊   ＊   ＊   ＊   ＊   ＊

I was in the ward one morning, feeling singularly incompetent and horribly in the way, when the surgeon asked me whether I could stand seeing the dressings and take notes on the cases, as the man who was doing it had something else important to do.

Naturally I said I could ; my tummy by that time feeling absolutely empty !   He was extraordinarily kind to me and told the nurse to put a chair handy for me as he said anyone might faint without being ashamed when they saw their first amputation dressing.

This was cheering !   However, the courage of the man who had a leg and arm amputated, and who insisted on holding the stump of his leg himself, gave me the impetus which I needed.   There was no need for a chair ; I became suddenly businesslike and almost professional.   Apparently my notes were written satisfactorily, for after that I was asked to go down to the theatre and do the same work.   I hated the smell and I hated the groans of the men under chloroform, and I remember one terribly bad case of a man who was suddenly taken ill with a hæmorrhage and had to be operated on immediately.   His wound was in the face, and the doctor told me that I had come through the test well, as face wounds were far the worst to see.

It was utterly impossible to sleep at night, so I used to get off in the ambulance that went to pick up wounded at Aubervilliers Station.   There was a little woman working in the hospital ; she was gay and pretty, and had since married a Scotchman, but before I left the Majestic rumours were flying about that she was really a German and probably a spy. Anyhow she had a way with her, and used invariably to get the password for us to get through the gate of Paris. Once arrived at Aubervilliers, what they called body-snatching began. There were ambulances from all the hospitals and each one vied with the other in their efforts to get the worst cases. These body-snatchers were quite unscrupulous in their methods and would often send one of the " competitors " on a fruitless journey. " There is an interesting case over there," they would say—and unless you were an old hand you would probably hurry off to find the man already dead.

Directly I got to Aubervilliers Station, I was taken in charge by the Duchess of Camastra, Madame d'Hautpoul, Mrs. Marshall and others who had a canteen on the platform.

The platform itself looked gay and like a village fair with its tents and twinkling lights—but, oh, to see those trains come pouring in with men dying, packed like sardines into cattle-trucks. Such a thing as a hospital train did not exist.

These cattle-trucks were used for transporting men and horses to the front, and the wretched wounded were sent back in the same dirty wagons. This entire lack of hygiene accounts for the many cases of gangrene and tetanus, which were so terribly prevalent in all the hospitals at this time.

A nurse in charge of the corridor carriages groped her way about with the light of a candle doing what she could, but the trains made the most prolonged detours, which meant that the men were on their journey for endless hours before they eventually reached hospital. How she welcomed the refreshments we had got, but, alas! numbers of the men were far too ill even to look at a cup of coffee.

The trains only stopped a few minutes and they followed each other in quick succession from eight at night till eight in the morning. One hardly thought there were so many men in the world. On all sides one heard of nothing but disorganization in the transport and of the difficulties to find anywhere to put the men, and yet there were hospital units like the Duchess of Westminster's and Lady Sarah Wilson's wasting their time and their money because no location could be found for them.

There was the most terrible amount of red tape and jealousy between the hospitals, and there was one thing on which the French authorities were determined—and that was to have as few wounded as possible in Paris itself. Whether they thought the Germans would get there, or whether they thought that the French temperament might sink to dangerous depths of depression if they saw the wounded, I do not know.

The battle of the Marne was, of course, in full swing when I was in Paris. I had seen the men despatched in the taxi-cabs and motor-buses, but I wonder if any of them knew how nearly the war might have been over then and there. It was a long time afterwards that I met an old retired English naval officer at dinner, and during our conversation on the war he told me that he had just come across a Dutch officer on his way through Paris. At the outbreak of hostilities the Dutch officer had been sent to Germany by his Government and had been attached to Von Klück's army during the retreat of Mons and the battle of the Marne. The Germans, it appeared, had been most disagreeably surprised, after their encounter with the English. The enemy's losses had been colossal, far heavier than the most optimistic reports would have led one to believe. The Dutchman told my friend that when the Allies retired, they marched as far in two days as the Germans could in three, and that on every occasion in which the armies came in contact the enemy casualties must greatly have outnumbered ours. As a result of these losses Von Klück had all his reserves in line, and he was obliged to reduce his front by a half, and was consequently unable to maintain his original plan of advance. And this is the real explanation of Von Klück's apparent change of direction when nearing Paris. So badly had the German army been knocked about, that at a war council the generals were unanimous in their wish for peace, but the Kaiser and the Crown Prince carried the day in their desire for a continuance of war. The Dutchman was later attached either to the British army or navy, so there is probably nothing new about this story.

It was only much later that the full significance of the battle of the Marne was fully realized by the public generally, and that they grasped the fact that the war had been won then. But when the big guns were finally silenced the names of Joffre and French were acclaimed in the hearts of those who knew, though seemingly forgotten amidst the honours and titles which were bestowed in random profusion on their successors.

Year by year the part which Joffre played in the destinies of the world is becoming more and more impressed on the minds of the French people. The anniversary of the Marne celebrated at Meaux is a pretext, not only of honouring the dead, but of paying tribute to the man who at the critical moment was morally brave enough to take the entire responsibility of using all his troops and reserves against the enemy. He had counted the cost of failure for France, but he never for one moment hestitated to consider what that failure might mean to his own future, and his reputation.

" Quoi qu'il en soit, la lutte qui va s'engager peut avoir des résultats décisifs, *mais elle peut avoir aussi pour le pays en cas échec, les consequences les plus graves,*" was what he wrote on September 5th.

Colonel Fabry writes :

" La Marne est faite à l'image de Joffre, elle est *une victoire d'équilibre*, d'équilibre *réalisé* sur un front immense et *maintenu* au cours d'une crise redoubtable par la volonté la plus ferme, par la foi la plus convaincante dans la destinées de la France. Elle est bien la victoire de Joffre."

In 1921 M. Barthou, Ministre de la Guerre, has added another well-deserved tribute to the great man.

Whilst he points out that much honour is due to Gallieni and Foch and to the superb fighting forces of France and England, he ends up by the words, " *mais qui donc commandait.*"

The last time that I went to Aubervilliers we brought four of the worst cases back to the hospital. Two I remember distinctly, as they were put in a little ward, where I was working. One, a boy of fifteen, was dying of tetanus ; he was wearing an English uniform, and until his mother came the next day—just too late to see him alive—his case was a mystery. I was called in to act as interpreter, and she told me that one day he had gone as usual to play with his little brothers and sisters, but had not come home with them. They had eventually found a note from him asking their forgiveness, but saying that he felt that he, too, must go and do his duty. It appears that the French Army would not take him, but that an English Officer had taken him on as his servant.

The other man had both arms and legs amputated immediately on arrival ; he was a hopeless case from the start, but till the very end he did not realize it, and he asked me if I thought his sweetheart would still marry him. He had not even realized that he had lost his legs, but said he wished he had his hands, as he would like to have played a *jeu de carte* to amuse me. I should never end if I were to tell you the simple thoughts and amazing cheerfulness of these men, for all of whom, even if they lived, all the joy of life must have been taken from them.

Outside the hospital one saw astonishing changes. Paris was very empty. You could walk from the Majestic to the Place de la Concorde, meeting only here and there a pedestrian, while hardly a taxi or a *voiture* was to be seen. The Rue de la Paix was equally deserted, its shops boarded up and without a trace of their former glories—yet surely never had Paris looked more calm and beautiful. The emptiness made one appreciate the glory of her buildings and the wideness of her thoroughfares.

The Government had flown to Bordeaux, accompanied

by most of the big administrations. This was not a popular move amongst the people, but it was obviously inevitable. Amidst the tragedy of the departure there were humorous incidents. Two special trains were reserved for certain important personages and their wives, and the ones who were not legally married found themselves a little embarrassed! An important official of the Foreign Office, who is a frequent visitor to London owing to the number of conferences, had to be married by special licence an hour before the train started!

This sudden influx made it extremely difficult to find accommodation; important people were glad of a shake-down anywhere, and Bordeaux quickly became a small Paris. Some of the principal newspapers had transferred their offices to the South, and miniature editions were printed in Bordeaux.

The community was not limited to the " makers of history," but such notabilities as Cecile Sorel, of the Comédie Française, and M. Alexandre Duval, of the " Bouillon Duval," had followed, and found Bordeaux a pleasant place in 1914.

Most of the Conservative representatives for Paris accompanied the Government; this was a strategic move on their part. Rumours were afloat that sooner than see Paris destroyed, peace would be made; but these representatives trekked to Bordeaux, armed with mandates from their constituents that this was not to be; better see Paris in flames than surrendered to the hated Boche; and it was these *députés* that were mainly instrumental in bringing about the pact that no ally could sign peace without the other.

Very few of the Paris hotels were open. The Red Cross had established their headquarters at the Hôtel d'Iéna, and the Women's Hospital was installed at Claridge's; it was entirely staffed by women, with Dr. Garrett Anderson in charge—a daughter, I think, of the first well-known woman doctor of that name. Everyone spoke in terms of praise of the women's skill, not only in the administration of the hospital, but also in the operating theatre.

I saw Lord and Lady Esher once or twice, and Hubert Cox came to the hospital, and almost collapsed at the smell of the chloroform! Vera Arkwright and Mrs. Addison were both working in hospitals, the one at Neuilly with Mrs. Vanderbilt, and the latter at the English Red Cross Hospital, but otherwise there were very few English people about. Mrs. Addison, whose husband was in the 9th, has the most beautiful red hair and looked lovely in her nurse's clothes.

Before leaving Paris I lunched with the Duchess of Camastra at her house in Passy. Everything in it was beautiful, including the Duke, one of the best-looking men I have ever seen. The house is situated in a huge garden and might have been a hundred miles away from Paris. It was crammed with art treasures, and the Duchess's own suite was enchanting in every detail, down to all the little lace-edged sachets which lined her lingerie cupboards.

I was very interested to see where they had hidden their jewels and treasures when the Germans were practically in sight of Paris. They had been buried in the garden. The Duchesse told me of her sister, Princess Murat, who had actually been in her château when the Boche arrived. She had had an interview with the German general, who had given orders to his men to behave themselves, and on looking at the order,

Princess Murat found that it had been signed by Von Klück himself. Eventually she and her boys escaped in a small motor car.

Near Epernay, Chandon, of champagne fame, was in his château, towards which the Boche was advancing. One morning some enemy staff officers took possession of his house, leaving him two rooms on the top floor and announcing the imminent arrival of one of the Kaiser's sons. When he came, he asked who was the owner, and on hearing it was Chandon, and that he was upstairs, he expressed the wish to see him as they had met the winter before at St. Moritz. Chandon refused an invitation to dinner, or even to speak to the Kaiser's son, which caused an outbreak of furious temper, and the château was at once looted from the cellar upwards.

After four days of drinking and wrecking the result of the battle of the Marne came to them, and their departure was much more precipitate than their arrival.

I went over with Countess d'Hautpoul to Aubervilliers and had tea with the London Scottish. They had already been there for some time, and were expecting daily to be moved to the line. They were very bored with their job, which at the moment consisted of looking after prisoners and deserters. Some of the officers came over to the hospital to dinner the next night. McNab, who was afterwards killed, told me he had been up to the front, " having a look at things." It appeared that the distance between our line and that of the enemy was so slight, that the commencement of a German attack could be anticipated, as it was heralded by crackings of whips and German oaths as the soldiers were driven on by their officers.

There were more nurses than patients in the hospital, and, quite frankly, I was utterly miserable, and after the early rush had subsided almost equally useless. I was genuinely homesick, so to dally longer in Paris seemed mere waste of time.

II

ONCE back in London, I found myself in a general atmosphere of unrest. Everyone was in the throes of war-work of some sort or another. Only one woman of my acquaintance deplored this enthusiasm, and I must say she fully lived up to her lights, and at the end of the war, as far as I know, she still maintained her passive attitude of spectator.

It was astonishing to find the number of unexpected people who had taken up nursing, not merely because it was the right thing to do, but who actually enjoyed it. Of course, knitters were to be seen everywhere, in every possible or impossible place, until shapeless socks and other grotesquely fashioned garments became almost a nightmare. Lady Colebrooke belonged to the strenuous contingent, and she had pioneered society into the munition factories. She had always been clever with a lathe in the old days at Abingdon, so I expect she found the work easier than some of her followers did. I saw her one day at the " Berkeley," and she was immensely proud of her overtime and piece-work earnings.

My place among all these energetic ones seemed particularly vague. There was certainly no guiding torch beckoning me with a certain light towards either munitions or nursing, and I had most emphatically no tendency towards knitting, whilst rescuing Belgian refugees, of whose ingratitude I had heard so much, did not appeal to me as a permanent occupation. I did go to Charing Cross Station to act as guide, philosopher and friend to some of those stranded individuals, who certainly were a most pitiable sight ; but as I had no car of my own I was obviously less useful than all the lovely ladies who were there with their Rolls-Royces. What, after all, is any amount of sympathy in comparison to a motor car ! I did not even faintly resemble a woman, who wrote to me much later on when I was in France, plaintively asking for some employment that entailed danger (her letter was accompanied by a huge photograph, even the size of the photograph hardly took in the size of her hat) : " Do let me do something that others are frightened of doing," she wrote. I almost replied · " The only thing people are frightened of, apparently, is spoiling their hands ! "

My ultimate destiny was soon settled for me. I had not been at home very many weeks when I found myself starting once more for France. Rachel Dudley wanted me to go with her to see the Golf Hotel at Le Touquet, with the idea of using it for the Australian Hospital, with which she was closely connected. Having lived out there I knew the directors well, and had been able to arrange for one of them to meet us and talk matters over.

I was not sorry to get out of England and, incidentally, to see what had happened to my villa, as my tenants had been amongst the first to fly when war was declared. The sailings between Folkestone and Boulogne had just been resumed, so that I had a much pleasanter journey than before. Lady Wolverton was, I remember, on board, but I cannot recall anyone else. I have a clearer recollection of the piteous sight of the wounded that were crowded on to the quay. It had seemed at one moment so very probable that the Channel ports might be in German hands, that no preparations had been made for the possible use of Boulogne as a base. The battle of Ypres had made a virtue of necessity, and the most energetic measures were at work dealing with the situation.

On our arrival we found that the Australian Hospital was already installed at Wimereux, but Rachel still wanted to go and see the Golf Hotel for herself, in case there was any possibility of moving there. We arrived at Boulogne at about mid-day, and after lunching at the Station Buffet we at once motored out to Le Touquet. It was a most perfect day—a day when such a hideous thing as bloodshed seemed utterly unthinkable.

I had not been on the Etaples road since the war began, but it seemed to be singularly unchanged. On the hill, just outside Pont de Briques, some old wagons were shoved across the road to form a barrier, and two gendarmes in blue stopped the car and spent a long time examining our permits. It was the most horrible place to stop a car whichever way one came, as I discovered later when I was driving a big Daimler *down* the hill. The brakes were not working, and we shot past the astonished sentry, who got out of our way just in time to avoid being knocked over! But *la dame avec la cigarette*, which was me, had become so well-known by then, that I did not get into any trouble. I had found out by then that cigarettes were a *douceur* much appreciated by the French! The scarcity of cigarettes in the early days was acutely felt and at one time a Woodbine was worth its weight in gold.

My villa was unlocked, but exactly as I had left it, plus, of course, a considerable accumulation of dust ! After inspecting the Golf Hotel we went on to the Casino, where the Westminster Hospital was just being installed.

The Duchess of Westminster and Mrs. Whitburn had been lent the Hôtel des Anglais, and they were living there with the rest of the doctors and nurses. The Duchess had some rather elaborate brassards for her staff embroidered with the Westminster badge, a wheatsheaf and a coronet. Personally, I thought them rather vulgar, and though she looked very pretty in her nurses' clothes they were too theatrical, and I have never been able to reconcile jewels with a cap and apron.

After looking round everything we motored back to Boulogne, and, having nothing particular to do, I strolled down to the quay. Another train of wounded had come in and as many of the men as possible were being put on to the hospital ship to be brought back to England. The rest were lying on the quay or in the Douane, which had been converted into a temporary hospital, but there were no beds, and the men just lay on the ground. I cannot say how many there were, but the place looked absolutely packed. Two or three volunteers, including Miss Holman, were doing what they could, but they had an utterly impossible task. " If only someone would come and help us ! " was Miss Holman's cry.

Hospitals were being equipped as quickly as human hands could do the work. Lady Sarah Wilson and Mrs. Keppel brought their Unit from Paris, and were getting into the Hôtel Christol, and the wounded were moved in practically as the furniture was moved out. The Red

Cross were doing invaluable service, but the suddenness with which Boulogne had been turned into a Base was bound to upset the most perfect organization, and the arrangements for the wounded were for the moment naturally chaotic, and the exigencies of the moment were met only by prompt action on the part of the Red Cross Volunteers.

I think it was seeing the crowd of unattended wounded on the quay and in the Douane that gave me the idea for a " Canteen " on the lines of the one at Aubervilliers. I was informed it was necessary to secure permission from the Officer in Charge of the Station, and accordingly I put the suggestion before him. He welcomed it enthusiastically, and, burning to get to work, I decided to go back at once to England, and return as quickly as possible with some stores.

On the boat home I told Blanchie, who happened to be on board, that I was going to do this, and for some reason or other she appeared to take it as a personal grievance. She had come over herself with, I believe, the view of spending the money that Otto Kahn had given her on comforts for the hospital into which the Douane was being converted. " You cannot do it without leave from Sloggett," she told me. " Have you got it ? " I told her " no " and thought I had better drop the subject, as far as she was concerned. But I felt it was a case of acting instantly or not at all, and if I was to be of any use I had to start at once, so that there was no time to make any elaborate preparations.

Accordingly, buying stores and saying good-bye to the children occupied only twenty-four hours. Imagine, too, going to Fortnum and Mason's for canteen stores !

Yet that was where I spent the large sum of £8, which represented the original capital of the " British Soldiers' Buffets." When I look back now and remember the gigantic cargoes of tea, coffee, cocoa, sugar and other groceries which used to arrive weekly and almost drove the Military Transport Officer to distraction, I cannot but laugh at my absurd initial effort.

As I was on the point of starting I received a wire from Blanchie saying, " Miss Holman is in charge of all refreshments at the station under Captain Norrington," but, fortunately, the wire came too late, when all my plans for departure were already completed.

Directly I arrived, I went in search of Miss Holman, with the object of offering her my stores and my help if she needed it. Miss Holman, looking so pretty in her blue veil and working with almost superhuman energy in the Douane, absolutely denied the truth of the wire, so I at once established myself in the waiting-room. I was, however, advised to make my position perfectly secure by obtaining the D.D.M.S. permission. This I did, and I also took the precaution to get the much-needed permission in writing.

My £8 worth of stores did not take long to unpack, and I started feeding the men on the very next train that came in. M. Gerrard, the manager of the buffet on the station, was more than kind and helpful. He gave me the waiting-room which adjoined the restaurant for my canteen, and supplied me with jugs and various odds and ends, and to M. Gerrard I owe much of the success which eventually came to the British Soldiers' Buffets. No one can possibly imagine the discomforts under which we worked, so different from the elaborate arrangements which were eventually found in every canteen. At first I had to borrow all the hot water from the restaurant, and for a long time our *batterie de cuisine* consisted only of an iron boiler, two or three old tin jugs and a pail for washing-up in.

But if my stores did not take long to unpack, they certainly did not take much longer to be consumed, and I promptly went off to the Hôtel de Paris and threw myself on the mercy of the Red Cross, with the result that they kept me supplied until an appeal which I put in the papers was most generously and spontaneously responded to. People were simply wonderful, their help and their practical sympathy at times almost overwhelmed me, and I can never be sufficiently thankful to them for their kindness and generosity in those early days when I had not the slightest idea of what the canteen would be to so many hundreds and thousands of weary and wounded men. At the moment I was only thankful to be of use to them, of expansions or future development I had no thought ; the moment was all that mattered.

In spite of official permission, however, things were not going to run absolutely smoothly for me, and on the second day I got orders, presumably from Sir Arthur Sloggett, that I was not to feed any more wounded men ! I shall never forget seeing a crowded train of men clamouring for a drink, and having to refuse it, but I did not dare to disobey orders as it would have given my enemies a handle to use against me. Luckily, Lord Wemyss, who had just come out, was there to see it, and he was as much distressed as I was. He went off to find Blanchie at the hotel. I don't know exactly what they said to each other, but I know it was war to the knife ! Meanwhile, I dashed back to England,

and went to see Lord Esher.   He and Colonel Barron had
already seen me at Boulogne.   He was very sympathetic,
at once grasped the situation and wrote a line to Sir
Alfred Keogh.   In it he said · " I have told Lady Angela
that unless things are amicably arranged, I shall ask
Lord Kitchener to have them both sent away " (Blanchie
and me).

This was the most diplomatic thing he could have
possibly done, as in spite of Blanchie being reported
to have said she would not rest till she had forced me
off the platform, she would rather have seen me there
than have run the risk of being sent away herself.   Why
she had taken me *en grippe* goodness only knows,
as I had had a perfectly friendly luncheon with her
only a few days before.

I saw Sir Alfred Keogh ; I knew something of him
and of the influence used to get him to the War Office
as " the ablest man for the job," so I felt in safe hands.
He promised to do what he could ; though the officials
in France were really under the officials in England, it
was not considered etiquette to issue definite orders
from this side, but " a request " generally achieved
the desired result.

It was in September, 1914, that I first met Colonel
Barron of the Army Medical Service Temporary—very
much temporary—as I cannot imagine anyone more
typically unlike the cut and dried R.A.M.C. officer.   As
I see that Lord Esher has referred to the fact in his book
on Lord Kitchener, it may not be indiscreet to remark
that Colonel Barron had a very great deal to do
with the rapid improvement which followed on Lord
Kitchener's permission to let private enterprise supplement the efforts of the R.A.M.C. as regards the care of

the wounded.   It was his report backed by Lord Esher
which, if rumour speaks true, very nearly caused a
cabinet crisis.   At any rate it drew Lord Kitchener's
abrupt attention to a phase of the war which owing to
his overwhelming duties had rather been overlooked.

The immediate result of the report was the recall
of Sir Alfred Keogh from civil life to his old post of Director General.   Civil hospitals were allowed to open
for the reception of wounded.   Red Cross and other
ambulances were hurried out and a great flood of unofficial
assistance was quickly made available.

These happenings did not exactly endear Colonel
Barron to the official mind, but, fortunately, he is one
of those irritatingly benevolent gentlemen whom it is
so impossible to annoy and so hopeless to suppress.

During the very early days I frequently met Colonel
Barron and frequently sought his advice, which, summed
up, was to do as I was told, if possible, but, anyway,
to do it.   Colonel Barron believed heartily in speed.
Later I went several times to his office in Rue Edouard
VII., where every sort of record and chart connected
with the wounded was kept.   This office was, I am
told, financed by Messrs. Cox and Co., Bankers, which
is a fact as greatly to their credit as it is a tribute to
Colonel Barron's determination to get a thing done
unofficially, if he failed to do it officially.   I remember
him saying to me : " Lady Angela, when things right
themselves, as they will, you will get kicked out, and
so will I.   We are not part of a system, but there has
been no time for a system and no money.   Meanwhile,
get on with it and get in the way as little as you can."

Colonel Barron had himself an odd system of persuading the high and mighty ones to attention.   They

won't listen and they have no time to read, if they can see a picture. He therefore drew pictures. I saw some of them in preparation, showing the loss of men due to disease, as opposed to the loss due to wounds; pictures showing the way the different battalions reacted to exposure, and even pictures showing the resisting power of English, Scotch, Welsh and Irish. " They will look at these," he said, and they did. But whether they liked the ones showing two dogs labelled respectively D. G. and A. G. pulling in opposite directions I hardly dare think.

Colonel Barron and I have remained firm friends, and he wrote me the other day :

" So you are writing your memoirs. Well, judging by any information I have relating to you, which came my way, they should be exciting. .Let us off as lightly as you can ; the A. G. is in all probability a charming man in private life. Looking back, I cannot help feeling a strong sympathy for those who had to cope with us irregulars. We must have been very trying, and to a man buried to the neck in a tangle of real hard work I realize now, better than then, how nearly I must have been figuring as the victim of an unpremeditated murder.

" I wonder Sir Arthur didn't murder you. I should have if I had been in his place, if only to obtain a brief respite from the advice of those who were jealous of your good work and not particular about your good name.

" I am afraid you were born into the world destined for turbulence. You ought to have been a man, for in my experience women like you have not a dog's hope of doing good without arousing a whirlwind of chatter. I believe you rather like the whirlwind part. You like a fight, and even now I grin when I recollect that you did not always lose.

" Still, it is over, and I hope there is peace. I dare not do more than hope, since no one would describe you as a peaceful person. Yes, you ought to have been born a man. It would have been much better, if less amusing for those of us whose paths lead us from time to time across your track."

Colonel Barron ends his letter by hoping that I do not intend to accuse him of taking refuge under a great name. I have nothing of which to accuse him, unless it is an accusation to ask why on earth he has given up doctoring to go in for improving the stage. I wish him luck, and I would not like to bet that he will not succeed.

Directly I got back to Boulogne I went to the Hôtel Derveaux to see Sir Arthur Sloggett. He was just finishing his dinner and did not in the least desire an interview with me, but I was sweetly persistent, and said I would wait in the car for him. When he came out to speak to me he was perfectly charming, patted my hand most amicably and gave me his word that I should be left in peace. Perhaps if there had not been so much fuss about my pouring out a few cups of tea I should have gone home when my stores had run out, but the opposition made me determined to stay.

*   ᴛ   ᴛ   *   *

Work now began in earnest ; there seemed hardly time to breathe, and when I was sometimes assailed with regrets at not having kept a diary. I wonder if I should have had time to even chronicle the bare events.

The time of the arrival of the trains was more or less a matter of conjecture, and as I had only one assistant

Warwick on the **Nig** t o the Fancy Dress **Ball**, 1805.

[*Facin | p.* 180

during those first strenuous days it meant spending the greater part of the night as well as the day on the station, and also being there at about 5 a.m. to supply the queue of orderlies from the trains who were waiting for hot drinks to give the men before they were moved. About four hours' sleep in the twenty-four was as much as we could allow ourselves during the first fortnight.

I got a room at the Louvre, as it was handy to the buffet. The discomfort was appalling, for the whole town was packed to overflowing and the water supply had gone wrong, which did not tend to the gaiety of nations, but as I spent most of my time on the quay and had my meals at the buffet it did not so much matter. The buffet used to be quite deserted in the evening, the proprietor and his wife, a French Capitaine de Marine and the M.L.O. on duty were generally the only diners.

Sometimes a few Frenchmen would come in bringing news from the outside world. I remember so well one of them predicting a great future for Petain, who was then only commanding a brigade. Petain originally came from the Pas de Calais. Unhappy over his father's second marriage, he left home and was adopted by the famous Dominicains d'Arcueil, at the time one of the best educational centres. Petain was naturally a very strict Catholic, and he soon proved his intelligence and got his scholarship for St. Cyr. Later he paid the monks back all his education had cost them.

At mid-day it was different, as the mail-boat passengers crowded in for luncheon. Meeting the mail-boat and seeing who came off her was for a long time our chief excitement, and even this was an excitement we could rarely indulge in, as it was probably our busiest moment in the canteen.

The King's Messengers were much more obliging in those days than they became later on, when regulations were more stringent, regarding the conveying of messages backwards and forwards ; but even if there was no correspondence to be smuggled through, they generally brought some news either from home or G.H.Q. The King's Messengers were rather unfairly supposed to have a " cushy " job. I suppose one or two were young enough to have been in the trenches, but probably few people appreciated the bravery of Sunny Marlborough, unless they realized what an appalling sailor he was. In any case, that incessant crossing must have been desperately trying, and even the journeys to the more distant theatres of war cannot have been particularly exhilarating.

They were all very good to me, and I found sanctuary often in their cabin on the crowded boat on my many journeys to and fro. Charlie Hindlip was one of the most cheerful, with a fund of good, though not always proper, stories, Colonel Burn the best looking, Lancelot Lowther the most fussy—he took his duties most seriously—and Evan Charteris the most detached.

Things were gradually shaking down, and almost everyone who had been wandering aimlessly about had found a job somewhere or other. It was a case of finding your own niche—no one had time to eject you, though, later on, of course, officials had nothing else to do ! One of the outstanding features of the war was the way people were moved from their jobs as soon as they were efficient—I suppose it would not have done for anyone to have been too efficient.

Eden Paget, who had been pushed over to France by a patriotic wife, with only a grip sack and the prospect of driving an ambulance, had appointed him-

self Director of Transport to the Red Cross, but when
he returned after a few days' rest in England he found
his place usurped by Frank Daniel, who, till then,
had been controlling the traffic on the station !

Paget accepted the position like a true sportsman,
and they worked together most amicably, and when
F. D. eventually left, Paget became once more the
official director.

There were, however, some free-lances still left ;
Tony Drexel, I remember, was one of the wanderers.
I don't know what he was doing, but he was certainly
in khaki ; his car seemed at everyone's disposal, and
you could rely on it being amply provisioned. Poor
Bertie Stopford, who spent his time doing kindnesses
for everyone, and Philip Wodehouse, could generally
be reckoned on to be on the quay to meet the mail
boat.

How glad I was to see Ruby Peto. She and Mrs.
Murray, her sister-in-law, at once offered me their help,
which I promptly accepted, and they were both of them
splendid, as they did not mind at what hour of the
day or night they were called upon to work. They
had come over to meet Ralph Peto, who arrived on
the same evening with some of the 10th Hussars. That
delightful Julian Grenfell—sunshine personified—and
Lord Chesham, looking a perfect baby, were two of
those, I remember, dashing home on leave. We met
them on their way back, and had a festive high tea
in the station buffet. There was something almost
tragic in their hilariously good spirits, as we played
Chemin de Fer in the deserted restaurant on the marble
tables for Belgian coins before they started for the line.

The appearance of Lady Drogheda, who turned up

one day with Miss Maxime Elliott, was our next excitement. Lady Drogheda was only able to stay two days, but she was very kind during that short time, and brought me a whole collection of pots and pans, which we badly needed, to supplement our more than primitive cooking arrangements. Miss Elliott was one of those people busy looking for a job, but for some reason or other even her ambulance—or was it a kitchen car—was not accepted by the Red Cross or any other institution, so, *faute de mieux*, she asked if she might come and work for me.

At that time help was most precious. Mrs. Brown, who was the sister of the Red Cross Director of Transport, and Frank Daniel's daughter, had settled themselves down as more or less permanent staff. Mrs. Brown was really wonderful, and became my most efficient second in command, but, apart from these two, I was more or less dependent for assistance on the casual visitor.

In view of the strenuous red tape of later days people came and went to France in the most slipshod fashion ; the length of their stay was variable, and the reason for their appearance was indefinite.

Lady Juliet Duff was out for a time, so were Mrs. Horlick and Gladys Yorke ; they were trying to establish some scheme of comforts, which was eventually, definitely done under the guise of Cox and Co. Lady Cavan turned up to meet Lord Cavan, and gave us a lot of her time. She was a most charming woman. Lord Cavan's name was, of course, on everyone's lips as one of, if not the best, of our generals. He was most humble about his success, declaring that anyone else could have done the same with men such as he had to command. He had the Guards' Brigade.

"Cavan's House" was the name given to his head-quarters. It was a little farm house, and situated much nearer the line than most generals cared to establish themselves, but every man in the Ypres salient had heard of "Cavan's House."

Though a little sceptical of Miss Elliott's suitability, her insistence and her generosity over-rode my probably unreasonable prejudice. She went over to England for clothes and came back to me a few days later. I rather brutally put her straight on to night duty—as a rule a test of endurance. We did it together, and I must say she did not grumble, but as there were no trains that night she wiled the weary hours away by giving me her views, which were distinctly advanced, on the question of woman's suffrage. I think I was in too sleepy a state of mind and body to digest them fully, and I was certainly not much in sympathy with them ; I have an idea she was horrified at my telling her that I thought votes for women were most un-necessary.

Miss Elliott evidently had every intention of being comfortable, as she had brought a butler and a maid with her, and the suggestion was made that they might wash up. This I keenly resented. I didn't mind doing it myself, but I anticipated a smug smile from the professional at my methods and incompetence. This was, no doubt, very silly of me, as I daresay neither the butler nor the maid had ever washed up in their lives. What I resented even more was the fact that Miss Elliott suspiciously tasted the tea and cocoa made by myself, before it was taken out to the trains ! The culminating point came when she left a tin jug in the middle of the floor for me to fall over ; unintentionally, of course ! Her ideas were grandiose and she wanted an army of workmen to decorate the canteen, and I saw the poor old waiting-room being turned into a Futurist drawing-room or something equally grotesque ! Dirty and dingy as it may have been, there was a certain cachet about it, and I would not have altered it for worlds. Even the old tables which served as counter, and which only later on blossomed forth into oilcloth covers, had their own place in my affections. I am afraid her visit was a bit of a fiasco, and that she thought me horribly ungrateful. I expect I was, but the work in those days was so strenuous that my temper was not always too even. After she left me she went on to the Belgians, where, not only did she do very good work, but probably enjoyed herself much more than she ever would have done with me.

Lord Roberts' death came on the 14th of November, and it brought real sorrow to the whole Army. No general will ever hold so high a place in their affections as he did : the contrast between the joy of his arrival and the sadness of his tragic departure proved this. A day or two after we had witnessed the wonderful ovation he received on landing, his Aide-de-Camp, Colonel Browning, came down to the buffet and asked us if we could help him to find something light and warm for him to wear. He had been reviewing troops, and had discarded his coat, with the result that he had caught a severe chill. The lightest and warmest thing we could think of was the Shetland sweater I happened to have on me. Colonel Browning took this immediately back to G. H. Q. with him, and I always hoped

Lord Roberts was wearing it when he died. Colonel Barron was Lord Roberts' doctor, and he was hurriedly summoned from Paris to G.H.Q. to attend the great little man—the neglected prophet—only to arrive too late.

We have all our own heroes, ranging from Julius Caesar to Mr. Bottomley, and I confess that " Bobs " was mine. I have no compunction, therefore, in quoting, without apology, Colonel Barron's tribute to him :

" Bobs was, without doubt, one of England's great men, and as he honoured me with his friendship, I take a pride in paying tribute to his memory whenever I can. Perhaps his keynote was simplicity. He was, I think, the most transparently clear man I ever met. He had a crystal nature, pure like a saint, hard like a soldier.

" He exercised a rare influence. I used to talk to Hugh Dawnay about it, about, I mean, the love of the Tommy for Lord Roberts, and the love, for such indeed it was, which seemed to irradiate his little body until one lost sight of everything save the spiritual magnitude of the wonderful soldier."

Perhaps something I wrote of him in our camp journal will do well enough to close these remarks.

" He was the most perfect gentleman of us all. Small of frame, fearless of character, loving the good, hating the bad, ambitious always for England, he strove to prevent that by which we are now run : think you he strove in vain ? No man ever did that, much less this man. His work will live through the ages ; his name will be honoured by every patriot to come, but when our own path is trod and we reach at last our St. Omer, the good we have done may well be more than the evil because of him.

" That we do, we do not of ourselves ; we are shaped and moulded by our friends and leaders to honour or dishonour . .

" For the last time I touched his hand.

" The dawn was breaking in the East when I set out for his old home in England to speak there the few and final words in the book of a soldier's life."—*The Return* . *April 28th,* 1916.

His funeral procession was as simple and unostentations as the man himself had been. The French gave him a Guard of Honour, and their bands were playing as the Great General was carried to the destroyer which brought him back to England. The pelting downpour was entirely in harmony with the feelings of the people, and I am sure that every soldier, as he stood bareheaded in the pouring rain, watching the ship that bore him home, felt that he had lost a personal friend.

THE King paid his first visit to France at the end of 1914, and had a splendid welcome from his troops. All the other crowned heads had been so tremendously in the limelight—the Czar was dashing around in remote wastes, the Grand Duke Nicholas, stern and picturesque, was at the head of those huge forces that were supposed to shortly end the war, while the War Lord and his sons were advertising themselves on every possible occasion—that the King's visit was almost doubly appreciated.

He was indefatigable in his efforts to see everything —almost as indefatigable as the people who put themselves in the way of receiving honours, notice and decorations.

It was just after the King's visit that the first official *potin* occurred. I do not remember much about the details, but I know it was connected with hospital arrangements and the Indians, and in whatever way it began, it all ended in peerages and promotions.

Major Lynden-Bell returned to us and was entirely exonerated, whilst Sir Courtauld Thomson arrived as the new Commissioner to the Red Cross.

Seeing the Indians shivering in the wet and cold was a truly pathetic sight. They suffered terribly from the climatic change, and their whole appearance gave one an impression of uncomplaining, dejected wretchedness. They created in the minds of the French population a sort of inquisitive wonderment, but one heard no ecstatic eulogies such as are sometimes voiced in this country over the coloured troops that form part of the pageants and processions over here. They were kept considerably isolated, and they did not seem to want anything out of the canteen except "char" and cigarettes.

Stories of their barbarity were, probably, grossly exaggerated. They were generally attributed to the Ghurkas. Three badly wounded cases were not too badly wounded to polish off three Germans who were in the same carriage with them—and one man could not be persuaded to part with an evil-smelling bag, which was afterwards found to contain the head of a German. Their amazing religious faith could not fail to impress even a sceptic. No matter where they found themselves their religious ceremonial was duly observed and aroused no ridicule. Once, as my train passed through Abbeville at sundown, out came their prayer-carpets and they knelt upon the platform, their faces turned to the west in prayer.

The *potins* that were going on did not in the least affect us. Trains still came in, men were attended to with just the same first fine, careless rapture, I am glad to say, and just the same gratitude and spontaneity was given to us by them. My "official staff" had increased, thanks to Mrs. Brown's efforts, and all the people she collected were splendidly efficient, and I do wish that they had been able to stay on till the end, but, as most of them belonged to Red Cross detachments, they were recalled to their units, when the demand for women became so urgent. Miss Batten, who was with me for some time, eventually had charge of the first women's convoy of ambulance drivers at Etaples.

I had transferred my headquarters from the squalor of the Louvre Hotel, and went out every day to my villa at Le Touquet. Sleeping in the country was infinitely more refreshing, and the extra labour entailed, motoring backwards and forwards, was compensated for by escaping, if only for a few hours, the abominable smells of Boulogne.

I was hoping to have the children out soon, but for the moment one could make no definite plans. The inside knowledge of how very thinly the Ypres salient was held made one err on the side of caution. The Channel ports seemed such a very obvious objective for the Germans that the feeling of safety one had at Boulogne was at times almost unnatural. For the enemy to have almost reached the very gates of Paris, and to have been within range of Boulogne and Calais without consummating a victory seemed an insoluble mystery.

Countess Blücher, in her " Journal," describes the quarrel between the Kaiser and Von Moltke over the strategy to be adopted. She tells us how definitely Von Moltke insisted on the importance of *first* seizing the ports, but how determined the Kaiser was to first make his triumphal entry into Paris. This seems to have been an obsession with him, and I know when I was in Paris he was supposed to have even gone so far as to order a suite of rooms and his dinner there for a certain date—I forgot where it was to be eaten.

This divergence of opinion between the War Lord

and his general led not only to Von Moltke's dismissal, but it also probably saved the situation for the Allies.

In spite of the nearness of the enemy—and I had been in Paris and Boulogne on both the most critical occasions—I never saw the slightest sign of panic. Yet it was neither the courage of ignorance, nor the courage of despair.

*

One took very little notice of time, and Christmas was upon us before we had realized how the weeks had raced away. The mail boat still remained our great excitement, but odds and ends from the outer world would casually stroll into the buffet and relieve the monotony of our days. Maurice Rothschild was a frequent visitor, generally on his way to the fish-market, to buy fish for Sir Arthur Sloggett's dinner. Lord Dalmeny used to look in occasionally. There was a very strong feeling about Monty Parker and Lord D. not being with their regiments, and they were supposed to have had a white hen sent to them periodically. In the latter's case I cannot believe that it had anything to do with " nerves." He was one of the bravest men I have ever seen out hunting, and I am quite sure that courage is certainly not a virtue of which he is deficient. It is far more likely to have been, as is supposed, a question of dignity, and that he would have gone back as a captain, but not as a second lieutenant.

In France such a thing could not possibly happen, for mere rank and social position counted for nothing. I wonder how many people realize—I for one certainly didn't—that in the French army dukes' sons and cooks'

My brother Harry.

[*Facing p* 192

sons are treated on identically the same basis—that no matter to what class a Frenchman belongs he has to start in the army as a private and go through the same hardships as if he had been born a simple *paysan*.

No influence can ensure his promotion ; he has to pass through the various stages of army ranks before he can become an officer. It is curious to think of the well-dressed gentlemen we used to see in peace time in Paris, going through all the discomforts, and roughing it as an ordinary *poilu* as a matter of course.

A French friend of mine, who at the time was a sergeant, was sent one day *en liaison* to one of our brigades whose headquarters happened to be in a dug-out at the time. His mission accomplished, he was just going to eat his sardine, when the General's A.D.C. asked him in a rather patronizing voice why he didn't join the sergeants. My friend replied he'd rather eat his own food by himself, and when the A.D.C. heard his good English, he began to take notice of him. My friend, not being a fool, and really wanting a good dinner, promptly began talking about London and his aristocratic friends. This at once had the desired effect, and after a few names had been rattled off, he was invited with enthusiasm to the General's mess !

English generals at the beginning of the war were not always happy over the position they gave their foreign visitors. On one occasion Maurice Rothschild was driving a French staff major, and when they arrived at official headquarters (the English general had of course heard of the Rothschild family) he gave " the driver " the seat of honour, much to the horror of the French major !

Lord Anglesey and his brother looked in on us one

13

morning at an early hour on their way home from Egypt, and were quite complimentary over the coffee we gave them, and Hubert Hartigan arrived one day with a pack of hounds he was taking up to the front, and which he asked us to temporarily lodge in the canteen, whilst he went off to lunch at Mony's.

Mony's was the fashionable restaurant in Boulogne, and one could be sure of finding someone or other one knew there at luncheon or dinner. Staff cars lined the narrow street, and officers who had snatched a few hours leave from the grim realities of war, strolled in as if there were no such things as Boche shells. The reputation of Mony's was considered to have been sealed when the Prince of Wales went there !

There was nothing, however, about the outward appearance of Mony's to indicate the quality of its viands and wines. Marble-topped tables and a sanded floor were the primitive outward signs of inward luxury. Madame Mony was the *cordon bleu* of the establishment, and her *moules Marinières*, her lobster *Américaine*, and her *sole meunière* would have put many a similar dish at the restaurants de luxe in Paris to shame. The daughter of the house was a universal favourite. She ministered to your wants behind the bar, and seemed quaintly out of place there, with her rather pale, refined looks.

It was about Christmastime that I first made the acquaintance of General Asser ; he was then a Colonel and the Commandant of Boulogne. He had been a big man in Egypt under Kitchener, A.-G. of the Egyptian army, and I don't know what else.

One of the officers at the base was trying to organize a concert, and a lot of artists had promised to come out and sing. Unfortunately when all the arrangements were well *en train*, word came that the concert would not be allowed by the Military Authorities, and I was requested to go and intercede with the Commandant. I didn't know him and I demurred considerably, but I was eventually pushed off on my mission. When I arrived at the Base Headquarters, which were then at the Bassin Loubet, I saw the staff captain (Colonel Herbert), who said he thought Colonel Asser would see me.

I found myself in a small inner office confronting the most alarming person I had ever seen in my life. His brown eyes looked you through and through. He was quite firm, and said the French wouldn't allow the concert to take place, and when I suggested that *I* might persuade the French Gouverneur, he told me that I couldn't do such a thing as he had already had the last word about it.

Out of sheer naughtiness, I drove straight off from his office to the Château, and found no difficulty in seeing Colonel Daru. He was a most delightful old gentleman of the old school, but equally firm about not allowing the concert. He told me, very politely, that this was not a time for music and that if we had danced at Waterloo and still won, it was not a habit to be repeated. As I was saying good-bye, my nerve rather gave way at having flatly disobeyed Colonel Asser's order, so I asked him not to mention my visit. A few days afterwards, however, I got a letter from Colonel Asser. It ran like this :

" DEAR LADY ANGELA,

" I hear that, in spite of my telling you not

13*

to go and see the Gouverneur, you did so. Would you, in future, leave me to manage the Military affairs of Boulogne by myself."

After this I saw myself under arrest, and on the next boat for home, so I went down to try and make my peace. I then discovered that there was a twinkle behind those piercing eyes.

I was forgiven, and the episode led to my making two friends, for both Colonel Asser and Colonel Daru were, to the end of the war, kindness itself to me. I saw a good deal of Colonel Daru afterwards, and a place was always laid for me to go to luncheon with him and his staff whenever I liked. I used to like those luncheons, in a funny little dark room in the Hôtel Bourgogne in the old part of the town.

Our luncheons were perfectly simple ; there was an old world military atmosphere about the place, and when I lunched there I almost felt I was attending a *Conseil de guerre.* The Colonel could talk no English, and his staff were also rather lacking in linguistic accomplishments. He had quite a small staff—a noticeable contrast to the English—all through the war ! The numbers employed in French official offices were really trifling, whilst those in the English departments increased like mushrooms in the night.

Colonel Daru had fought in '70, and was a storehouse of interesting reminiscences. He was a great gentleman, full of sentiment and patriotism. " If England had only come into the war in '70 there would have been no war in 1914," was one of his maxims.

The subject of the treatment of prisoners cropped up frequently, and I don't think they much liked the leniency, with which, they thought, we were treating the Germans in England. I told them it was our idea of English chivalry, to which they replied that we had not always had those same chivalrous ideas, when the French were our prisoners in days gone by. My knowledge of history was rather too indefinite for me to refute this statement in detail, but I have always thought the cases of Napoleon and Jeanne d'Arc were certainly two glaring proofs of our inconsistency which they might most reasonably have held up to me !

* * * *

As arrangements were becoming more organized, there was some alteration in the detraining of the wounded, and most of the trains no longer came into the Gare Maritime, but were diverted to the Central Station.

Here the Red Cross had taken on my work. They had converted three railway carriages most cleverly into a small dressing station ; all the work had been done by the V.A.D.'s themselves under the supervision of Miss Rachel Crowdy. I can never say enough in her praise. Dame Katherine Furze had to go over to take over the rather chaotic administration of the V.A.D.'s in England, and Rachel Crowdy succeeded her in France. Everyone knows what a capable woman Mrs. Furze is, but I think that probably the cleverest thing she ever did was when she passed her mantle of authority in France to Miss Crowdy. She looked no more than twenty-four, but she held the important reins of management as Commandant of all the V.A.D.'s abroad until the end of the war. When one thinks of the enormous organization, of the difficulties which there must, of necessity, have been in a body of women as large, and as socially varied as

the V.A.D.'s were, no one can do otherwise than admire
the way in which she carried out her job, with the
maximum of efficiency and the minimum of fuss.

I thought that these new arrangements for the
wounded would most probably mean the end of my work,
and I had no ambition to be one of the many square
pegs in a round hole ; but just as I was beginning to think
that my job was over, leave started, and from that day,
far from it being over, I found myself with much more
to do than I had had since the very early days, when
the trains of wounded were literally pouring in.

Our service was still rough and ready, and our *clientèle*
included post-office men just off duty, orderlies from
the hospital ships, and motor drivers waiting for their
officers, who were returning to Poperinghe or other
places up the line.

It was not often that a night passed without stray
visitors, and about 2 a.m. (the hour generally devoted
to cleaning the canteen) a brawny fisherman or two, or
the French military policemen with their fixed bayonets
and queer cloaks would slip in, and with irresistible good
manners, politely request a " cup of chocolate." Sometimes the silence of the night would be broken by a wild
shout of joy, and three or four officers, who had found
themselves dumped into Boulogne by a *ramassage* train,
every hotel closely barred, and ours the only friendly light,
would come in half starved and very dirty, and ready
for a bowl of porridge and chunks of cake, to say nothing
of innumerable cups of coffee—our coffee was very good
indeed—and, best of all, a jug of hot water for a wash.
I remember on one occasion four such officers came in ;
one of them had been suddenly told he might go on
leave—" If he could leave in the *ramassage* train in ten

minutes." He had been twelve hours on the journey and had had one glass of beer and half a loaf, which he shared with one or two others, and I think he sampled everything we had twice over. I know he insisted on leaving a substantial payment for benefits received, and came back the next day with a large box of chocolates as a souvenir.

But apart from our occasional visitors, leave was becoming an institution, which meant a steady flow of regular customers.

The men were brought down from the front in buses —our London friends, painted grey. They would often arrive in the evening, and there would be no boat to take them across till the morning ; this meant the men hanging about the quay all night, and the buffet was really a godsend to them, for they had had long train journeys and were proportionately hungry.

We still used occasionally to get some wounded, and one night we were literally besieged by the London Scottish. I had not seen them since I had had tea with them at Aubervilliers, when I was in Paris. They had been badly cut about, and one saw at once the terrible ordeal that they had been through. It would be difficult, even in the Guards, to have found a body of men with a finer physique ; most of them could have got commissions in the early days, but they preferred to stay as they were.

As Christmas-time approached the plum puddings began to arrive. Having failed entirely over the concert, we were having a dinner at Pont de Briques for the men in the Remount Camp there. The clubs in London had sent us out hampers full of turkeys and the buffet was blocked with cases of provisions.

The conditions of these men at Pont de Briques were really dreadful, and it was equally bad for the horses. The mud was knee-deep everywhere, and the wretched animals had often to be dug out if they lay down. The men had been over to see me one day, soon after they arrived, and I found a lot of hunting friends among them. Lord Lonsdale's old groom, James Lowther, who was now a sergeant, and Sam Hames' second horse-man, who reminded me of a day when he had picked me out of a ditch, when I was trying a horse of Hames', and many more. They were short of shirts, and their boots had worn out, and, what was even worse, they had to go to Boulogne for all their cigarettes!

As soon as I had got over our Christmas festivities at Boulogne I hurried back to England to see the children, who were at Stanway. It was delightful to go to bed when one wanted, and to get up when one liked, to eat one's breakfast in bed, and not to have to bother one's head over an obstreperous car—in short, to be thoroughly lazy!

I found a family party, including George Vernon, who was ill in bed with laryngitis. This, however, did not damp his enthusiasm, and, like all the others, he was clamouring to be off. Alas!—out of that party only Guy Charteris is still here. They went in their spring-time, but they have been spared the Autumn and long Winter days!

Yvo,* then at Eton, was the first to be killed, although he did not go out until the following September. I was

* Hon. Yvo Charteris.

at Gosford when he came to say good-bye. He arrived late, having missed his train, thanks to a Zep raid—the first in London, I think. He, Diana Manners and some others, had all been to a play and were caught in it. I asked him if it was very alarming. He replied: "Not a bit; after all, why should one be presumptuous enough to imagine one would be killed?" This remark was very typical of him—he was born with that rare gift of seeing things in perspective. It did seem so unnecessary that he should go; he was so young—just nineteen when he was killed.

It seems to me that the courage of the mothers and fathers, who did nothing to thwart the enthusiasm of their boys, was almost Spartan. The few isolated cases where staff appointments were wangled for eldest sons, were mercifully so few and far between as to be negligible.

Recruiting was the vital point, at home as well as abroad. Coming from France, I knew only too well how really vital it was, how badly men and shells were needed. How often had I heard that heartrending story, reiterated, and reiterated—how every effort was stopped, every advance checked, and every advantage lost through lack of reinforcements and ammunition. Our tragic loss of life owing to general unpreparedness is not pleasant to recall.

Fortunately for us, in view of the shortage of munitions, the mud of Flanders made it impossible to carry on operations on a large scale, and while the armies watched each other, our spirits were buoyed up with the hope of a well-equipped Spring offensive due to begin in May.

Joffre's policy was not spectacular enough to be appreciated by the multitude, yet his "nibbling" was probably one of the most important factors that won the war. It exhausted the Germans and gave the British time to bring sufficient forces into the field to strengthen their line.

The public in France and in England were not able to realize the nature of the conflict: they were as impatient to hear of an attack as the Germans were anxious that one should be delivered. To be able to sit still is far harder than to take action, and Joffre's patient attitude was too subtle to be understood.

I found things rather quiet when I returned to Boulogne, but as I was motoring back to Le Touquet, I saw a rather desolate-looking row of tents, a few horses and some men in khaki just outside Etaples. Up to this period no sign of war had been visible in Etaples, and though there had been rumours that it might be turned into a camp, it had managed to preserve its air of serenity.

These men turned out to be a battalion of the London Fusiliers who had arrived the day before; but no one quite knew what they were doing there, least of all themselves.

It appeared they had been in Malta and thought they were going back to England when they got on the boat. Imagine their feelings on finding themselves at a loose end in France! It was their dejected appearance that gave me the idea of opening a club for them.

Etaples itself was a mere fishing village, abounding in temptations, but affording no recreation of any kind ; so I at once set about finding a suitable house, and a funny old Frenchwoman, who lived almost on the edge of their camp, consented to let me have hers— " but only for the brave soldiers." I am afraid I suspected her of being glad to make a little money.

The Westminster Hospital was just then very slack, and Mrs. Whitburn came and helped me. She was one of the people who disliked being idle. Thanks to her assistance and contributions of pots, pans, and other kitchen utensils the club became a *fait accompli* in about twenty-four hours, and as soon as the men got to know of it, we did brisk business. One of the first to come in was an R.A. artist, Harold Harvey by name. He declared we were a godsend—to him at any rate—and every afternoon he installed himself in the club window overlooking the sea, where he did some delightful black and white sketches of the fishing-boats on the Canche. I have never seen him since, though for some time we kept up a correspondence. He had been badly gassed at Loos and almost lost his sight. His little book of " Sketches from the Firing Line," which he dedicated to me, contains a very pretty tribute to the club.

Some of the officers used to come in during the evenings. They were quite nice, and helped us with the supper rush, but some of them had rather German sounding names, which had led to their being nicknamed by the men " The Kaiser's Own."

Joe Laycock turned up to see us one night, as full of life and energy as ever, but distinctly older, and the Westminster Hospital staff used to look in on us when they could, but most of their leisure time was taken up sand-yachting.

It was some time in January when the children and their governess, Miss Marsters, joined me. They were delightfully enthusiastic over everything, and, curious to relate, they retained this enthusiasm to the end. I confess I was sceptical as to its duration, so many people were full of energy during the first weeks, but got gradually weary of the monotonous routine of canteen work. There is very little glamour attached to pouring out tea and cutting sandwiches—there is nothing of the possible romance about it, attached to hospital work. It is strenuous as well as kaleidoscopic, people come and go in such rapid succession, that there is no time to think of them as individuals. There is no time for gossip ; only occasionally during a slack moment a small party of men or a despatch rider would look in bringing news from the front, but I must confess that their military information was usually hopelessly incorrect.

If they had seen the Prince of Wales they could talk of nothing else. His youth, his simplicity and his courage had instantly secured his popularity ; everyone respected his determination to get to the front, which had carried the day against Lord Kitchener's objection, that it was an unfair additional responsibility to place on the Commander-in-Chief.

I used to get numerous letters of thanks from the men, and one of my most treasured souvenirs is a piece of glass from the cathedral of Ypres, which a despatch rider asked his mother to send to me.

It was difficult to gratify the children's wish to be in the canteen as much as they wanted. My own hours were so uncertain, and depended on the arrival of trains, and I used, perhaps, to motor into Boulogne in the morning and not get back until the next day, so that I

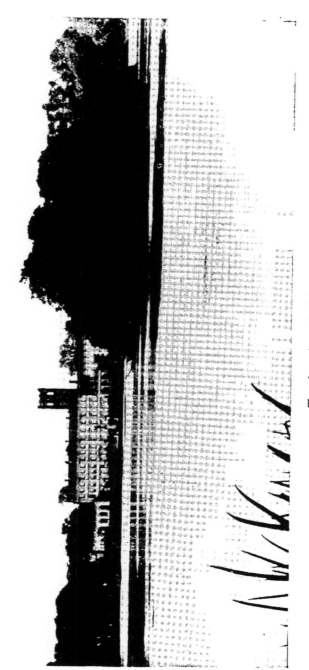

Trentham from the lake.

Facing p. 204

very often had to turn a deaf ear to their entreaties!
They solved the difficulty by finding a job for themselves.

The club at Etaples had been shut up since the
London Fusiliers went away, but I was asked to re-open
it for the use of the " Base Details " who had just
arrived. The children took over the management of this,
and ran it exceedingly well, keeping the strictest
accounts. In those days we had no tiresome accounts
to grapple with at Boulogne, as all our refreshments were
free. However, in January I received a message from the
Commandant, through Major Watson, suggesting that I
should now institute a small tariff, as the Y.M.C.A. had
just opened a hut and *they* were not giving anything
away. At the suggestion of the 'bus-man, who used to
bring the men going on leave, down from the front, we
had placed a money box on the counter. The men were
absurdly diffident about having their meals free, and
assured us they would rather go up to the town, even
though they had to pay through the nose, than be indefinitely " treated," so we compromised to this extent,
and the box was often full of half-crowns at night;
with a very occasional dud Belgian coin; so rarely did
this happen that it need hardly be mentioned.

I was on the whole glad to put things on a more
business-like basis, by charging a small fee. It seemed
fairer and we started with a penny tariff. It is to the
lasting credit of British soldiers that they ate six times
as much when they paid for their meals as when they
were given gratis.

    *   *   *   *   *   *

Boulogne was growing rapidly, developing into the
gigantic hub of the war machine it eventually became.

Hospitals and canteens were springing up everywhere. Lady Hadfield and Lady Norman were both at Wimereux. Monica Grenfell and Venetia Stanley, now Mrs. Montague, were doing their V.A.D. work at Lady Norman's hospital. We all occasionally met on the quay—Lady Hadfield generally dressed in white from head to foot, which proclaimed her identity from a long distance   Hugo lunched with M.G. and V.S. at Boulogne one day—the latter was just on her way home to buy her trousseau and incidentally to change her religion ! Mrs. Hoare, Lord Tredegar's sister, had equipped and brought out a motor kitchen. We used to chaff her a good deal as she was going to work under the auspices of the " Young Christians." The Duchess of Rutland was trying to get to Hardelot with her hospital, but met with opposition on every side, and she complained bitterly of the treatment she received at the hands of the Red Cross in London. Mrs. Clayton Swan had a small hut in the Bassin Loubet. Unlike me, she had gone straight to headquarters for *her* permission and had written to Lord Kitchener for it without even knowing him !

The Bassin Loubet was the most interesting spot in Boulogne, with its endless movement. It was from here that the British Army was provisioned. Seeing the ships loaded and unloaded and the huge hangars filled with fodder was, at any rate to me, always fresh and stimulating. It suggested a something always being done—a getting on with things in a most inspiring manner.

I used to go down to this department at least twice a week to get my stores and petrol, and each time I wondered afresh at the absence of unnecessary officialdom, and the amount of efficiency. It was a perpetual testimony to the superiority of Sir John Cowan's department over all the others of the War Office.

᛭ ᛭ ᛭ ᛭

There had been a rumour since January that there was to be a permanent camp at Etaples. It was at first supposed to be limited to the hospital section, but in a very few months this idea had developed into one of much greater magnitude. The excellence of the water supply made it an ideal site, but the wisdom of combining a large hospital centre with one of the biggest reinforcement camps in France was severely questioned. Those who were sceptical were justified in their criticism at the time of the big air raid in 1918.

The inauguration of a camp at Etaples meant the arrival of a staff. The first temporary commandant was Major Steele, of the Coldstreams, but he was soon afterwards transferred to the line as a brigadier-general. His successor, Col. Huskisson, during his rather brief reign made things delightfully easy for us, and it was due to him and to a very human Padre called Williams, that the idea for the big hut in the camp originated. They used often to find their way to tea with the children in the little club, and they were most insistent that I should apply at once for a site. This I accordingly did, and the necessary permission was obtained—really, I am sure, through the good offices of Col. H., for the Commandant who eventually replaced him would have been far less amenable and enterprising on my behalf! General Graham Thompson was a very nice old gentleman, but I think stood in deadly fear of the higher authorities.

I must put in a word, too, about Col. Jones, the

" Camp Engineer " (of course he became a general immediately), he took such endless trouble in fixing the spot for the hut.   At first I felt that I was being poked out of the way and was faintly jealous of Lady Greenall, who had appeared as a full blown " Young Christian " to run the Walton Hut, which seemed to me situated in the very best part of the camp.   Colonel Jones laughed at me and told me to be patient.   I was, and the site he had chosen was undoubtedly the best, and as the camp developed we found ourselves in the very heart of things.

The New Base Headquarters' Staff established themselves at the Hôtel des Anglais, where a few civilians still lingered, but these were gradually ousted—to their openly expressed discomfiture.

What went on in Paris Plage in those early days was a matter of conjecture to me, or rather, of halving most of the gossip which occasionally reached me in the seclusion of the forest.

The A.P.M. at that time was the centre of numerous scandals, and joy rides, if one was to believe what one was told, seemed to be an habitual occurrence.   Alas ! I never had time, nor any particular inclination to indulge in these.   I think the only time I went off the beaten track was in 1916, when the children and I dined with Alastair in his billet on his birthday.   Some months afterwards G.H.Q. questioned Lord Tweedmouth on the subject and they received an answer very much to the point !

How to raise the money to build the new hut was our next problem, but one which I was sure would be easily overcome.   The generosity of people in those days appeared to know no limits, so I started with the eye of faith. The question of subscriptions was, however, almost unnecessary, for since we had charged for our provisions, even though we still retained our penny tariff, we were making profits, and I could conceive no better method of using these than on our new building.

I confess that these profits surprised me, more especially as every time I opened the newspaper I saw an appeal for the Y.M.C.A. asking for money for the *upkeep* of their huts. Their appeal appeared unnecessary, as the huts were generally given and their staff was an entirely voluntary one. I do not think that the Y.M.C.A. cared for my publishing, as I did later, a balance sheet, and a clergyman who was helping to raise funds for the British Soldiers' Buffets, as we called ourselves, was rung up by one of the Y.M.C.A. heads and informed that he ought not to support me. When he inquired " Why ? " he was told that I did not stand for what they did and was guilty of the enormity of smoking cigarettes at the Folkestone Hotel ! To work for the Y.M.C.A. you had to sign a formidable document and apparently promise not to smoke. Amongst their fashionable lady inspectors was Lady Rodney, one of the most inveterate smokers I know ; but I suppose the fact of her social influence secured for her absolution.

It was really amusing, though, to see the people who came out under the auspices of the Y.M.C.A.—as inspectors nominally, but really to get to France. It was becoming more and more difficult to do this, and the casual visitor who had been of the greatest assistance to me in our busy times, was no longer allowed.

What the Y.M.C.A. lacked in business capacity they did not even possess in Christian charity; and further proof of their antagonism—I put it down to jealousy—

14

was shown, when a baker in the town told me, that they had threatened to withdraw their patronage, if he continued to supply me with bread !

A very different spirit, however, was displayed by the Salvation Army, who from first to last gave me the greatest support and assistance. A word here cannot be out of place in praise of their work for the men in France ; they laid themselves out to cater, not only for their spiritual but their bodily welfare. There was no humbug about them, and the happiest rivalry existed between them and myself, and we mutually assisted each other over stores and transport. The food they gave the men was far better and cheaper than that supplied by any other hut (always excepting my own !) and their labours were not in vain, for they were by far the most popular institution abroad. Their officers showed a delightfully human side, which, until one knew them, was unexpected. When Colonel Haines bade me good-bye, he said he would like to have a photograph of me. I had two, one with my maligned cigarette in my mouth, the other in a slightly more orthodox attitude ; he at once chose the one with the cigarette, but on second thoughts said that perhaps the other would be more appropriate to his office table !

The building of the big hut was going on rapidly, but the large boxing hall which the Padre was very anxious for us to have (he possessed considerable knowledge of the men and their probable tastes) was taboo. Lord Wemyss was to get us our permission for this, but as we were all a little sketchy in those days about the various departments, Lord Wemyss unfortunately wrote to G.H.Q. instead of to the I.G.C. In those days G.H.Q. did not trouble itself about the affairs on the Lines of Communication, and the Inspector-General did not like this request having gone to G.H.Q. first.

Eventually we had an out-door ring, and no spot in the camp was more popular. The men simply flocked to the weekly competitions, and the roof of the hut was treated by them as if it was the Grand Stand. I had never seen any boxing before, but I confess to have developed a distinct taste for it. Another thing which the men appreciated almost as much as the boxing ring was the bath house, which we established in connection with the canteen, and Mr. Kemp most kindly gave me the necessary boiler and other equipment, which included twelve baths.

Just as the big hut was completed I developed an attack of measles. Why on earth at my age I should have had a second attack of this tiresome illness, goodness only knows, and at such an inconvenient moment ! I dodged the camp doctor and avoided complete quarantine, and as soon as my rash had subsided I departed for England and combined the ordering of stores with convalescence.

Thank Heaven, the night sailings had been abolished ; even if one had been torpedoed in the day-time one would not have had much of a chance, but the ghastly possibility of being drowned at night made the crossings seem more fearsome than they really were. Seventeen hundred was supposed to be the maximum number of people that the boats would carry in safety, but I think there were never less than double that number on board. Later on they were well escorted, but in those very early days it was

14*

a case of taking pot luck. I was talking to a captain about it only the other day, and we marvelled that no accident had happened to the mail boat. Her pace saved her, I suppose, but on one occasion two torpedoes only just missed her, about nine miles from the harbour. The wreck of one cargo ship is still outside Boulogne, for, instead of coming straight in she had waited for a more favourable tide, which for her was indefinitely delayed. A submarine caught her during the night, and when they tried to tow her in she broke in two and completely blocked the entrance to the harbour. Some people suggested that it had been done intentionally—an undress rehearsal for Zeebrugge, but I should rather doubt it, as the inconvenience of having to fetch stores from Calais while they were dislodging her seemed a little too strenuous for even a successful naval manœuvre.

The night sailings while they lasted were not only shattering to the nerves of the passengers, but were equally disliked by the captain of the boat. The combination of the night sailings and the attack on the other mail boat proved too much for Captain Walker, and he quite frankly resigned. I had done so many successful journeys with him that his departure seemed like the passing of a friend.

These night journeys owed their inception to " Winston," who had an idea that the boats would make a less easy mark for the Germans than in the daylight. But he had forgotten to reckon for the " weak inconstant " moon, not so weak, unfortunately, as we should have liked. Winston forgot, too, that if the night happened to be dark the enemy's periscope would be even more obscured.

Rosslyn

My Father.

[*Facing p.* 212

It would be difficult to imagine an easier mark than the boat actually presented, as it left Boulogne Harbour. With its twinkling lights it looked like a miniature floating White City. One thing I always marvelled at was the enormous amount of unnecessary hooting that took place, just before starting, for no ostensible reason, unless it was to warn the Germans of our approach!

The First Lord's ideas were not exactly popular at the moment. The services he had rendered, by having the Fleet mobilized at the critical moment, had been partially forgotten when he indulged in his " legitimate gamble." It was a most unfortunate phrase, if possible more unfortunate than the expedition it described. The English people, who refuse to envisage a casino, even for the purpose of reducing their taxes, were not likely to tolerate a gamble in lives! Peter Wright tells us in his very frank book that Sir Henry Wilson complained that the French did not seem to know where Mesopotamia was ; I am sure the Englishmen in France most profoundly wished that Churchill had never heard of the Dardanelles!

No one in the West could have been blamed for being anti-East. To see the shells and men being removed from the Western Front just when the Spring offensive, of which we had heard so much, was to be launched, was heartbreaking. How anyone kept their spirits up under existing conditions was a wonder.

The first gas attack had brought home more forcibly than anything the complete barbarism of the enemy. They had been working at this devilish invention long before the war started—it was a carefully thought-out plan, not a sudden inspiration induced by desperation.

The French were the first to suffer. For some time previously French patrols knew that something unusual was going on in the Forest of Houthulst, in the Ypres salient. The 20th Corps—one of the crack corps— who had been holding the line in front of Langemarck had just been relieved by a Colonial division. Two days later these men saw those first ominous clouds of unearthly smoke. One of the few survivors told me that the men were convinced that this was some supernatural manifestation, and they remained crouching in their trenches, where the full force of the gas was felt. Hardly a man escaped this suffocating death, and the Germans, walking quietly behind their devilish barrage, were able to advance some miles. The Canadians were the next to suffer, and the agonies they went through were far more awful to witness than the worst amputation dressing.

From out of the blue came Repington's telegram. The feeling in France of utter hopelessness over the Government in England had been accentuated by Mr. Asquith's speech at Newcastle. The information on which that speech was based has been attributed to so many different sources that until the inner history of the episode has been revealed it would be foolish to comment on it.

The wildest rumours were in circulation. Sir John French was supposed to be in political intrigue with Lord Northcliffe; Kitchener was supposed to be involved in another direction, and so on, *ad lib*. The *Daily Mail* was burnt on the Stock Exchange, but read with avidity on the quay at Boulogne ; and its pile of ashes in the City was as good an advertisement for Lord Northcliffe as the banning by the libraries to an ambitious author.

And out of all these rumours and happenings there emerged a Coalition Government. But the days of a great man in Israel had already been numbered.

IV

WE may have had a Coalition Government, but they did not appear to have a co-ordinated policy. Diplomacy and strategy were continually at loggerheads. People who ought to have known better were even quarrelling as to who had been the first to expose the shell shortage. In this way the shell scandal differed from most. As a rule the originator of a scandal prefers to lie low, but on this occasion everyone was boasting of their share in the transaction. Great things were anticipated from Lloyd George's appointment to the Ministry of Munitions, and it was hoped that a reduced War Committee would do more and talk less.

The soldier has very little use for the politician. They look upon Politics as a dirty game, so that on the whole the men one saw in France were not too sanguine or over enthusiastic. I think, without a doubt, that Lord Milner was the most popular and the most respected statesman, and he was looked upon as almost the only one who was entirely disinterested.

I heard the news in Boulogne that Alastair was wounded—no one seemed to know if badly or slightly—but Millie got him over to England immediately. He had apparently done awfully well, and eventually got the M.C. He was delightfully modest about it afterwards. He found himself practically alone in a trench

216

with some Germans and he captured the lot. His version of the incident was : " I told them to put up their hands and they did it—if they'd told me to put up mine I should naturally have done so!" Lord Chesham was wounded the same day, and there was a horribly long list of casualties amongst one's friends.

*   *   *   *   *   ⊤

The maggot of intrigue was burrowing into every department, and infecting everyone with jealousy, hatred and malice. Lord Kitchener was apparently the most disliked man in England, but not by the great British public. To them he represented a bulwark of security, and no gossip or abuse succeeded in shaking their complete faith in him. He was absolutely un-shiftable. The Cabinet realized this, and they knew his power over the country.

The evacuation of Gallipoli was causing differences of opinion between the War Council and the Cabinet, and this necessitated Lord Kitchener going to the East to decide on our policy. The fact that an opportunity had arisen for him to leave England, even for a short while, was apparently welcomed by our politicians— and the War Office.

But to return to the base, Colonel Asser was being transferred to Havre, which was now developing into a more important port, and his capacity as a capable organizer was well-known, and, strange to say, was being duly taken advantage of.

I was dining with Claude Levita, then Provost Marshal at Boulogne, when we heard the news. We all hated his going—he had made himself universally popular—and Colonel Daru told me that the relations

between the French and the English would not have
been so good if anyone else had occupied his position.

We were in the middle of one of our night rushes,
when Colonel A. came in with Prince Arthur of Connaught to say good-bye, and with characteristic thought-
fulness he told me he had made all the final arrangements for the hut I was to occupy, instead of the existing
waiting-room. I was to move out of my old quarters
as the room was wanted by the Post Office. They had
outgrown their old quarters, and when the temporary
hospital in the Douane had been moved, the P. O.
had been transferred there, but apparently they still
wanted more space. They had been trying to get me
out for some time, but I had clung tenaciously to the old
spot until a new site could be found for me. Irate
officials from the Post Office visited me at regular
intervals, and I flew as regularly to the Commandant's
office to be protected against eviction—I think he
really felt that we were a necessity, as long as leave
continued.

Colonel Wilberforce, who succeeded Colonel Asser
as Commandant, did not, I fear, share his predecessor's
views as to our usefulness, or rather, he wanted the
E. F. C. to supersede us and at one time our feeding of
the leave men was seriously threatened.

I was rather curtly informed one day that in future
the men would go straight to the Central Station, where
the E. F. C. had established a canteen. To prevent
the men straying into the buffet, we were ordered to
close down, during the times that the men were em-
barking and disembarking. This was tantamount to
telling me I was not wanted, but the very day the
order came through the leave boats were detained

owing to submarines in the Channel, and about 1,200 men who were already on board were clamouring for food.

The E. F. C. were closed, so the poor **B**ritish Soldiers' Buffets were appealed to—and not in vain ! To be equipped for every emergency was my motto. The staff sometimes grumbled at being kept hanging about with nothing to do, but at Boulogne the unexpected invariably happened, and I felt justified for my tyranny on occasions, when such disasters as the torpedoing of the *Sussex* occurred, and we were the only place open in Boulogne.

In spite of our having come to the rescue, and receiving a charming letter of thanks from the Commandant, the order for the closing of the buffet still held good, so I wrote to Sir John Cowans and asked whether it could not be arranged for us to still go on feeding the leave men. Thanks to his intervention the order was not only rescinded, but I was given another hut on the quay and the men were given time as they were marching past to get tea and sandwiches.

One could hardly repress a smile at the military discipline which had been arrived at, when one remembered the early scrimmages in the old buffet, but the men still retained the same good-humoured attitude as they tramped through the sloshy streets, humming "It's a long, long way to Tipperary," the Boulonnais pressing their wares of oranges and chocolates upon them, with the children, trotting alongside calling "Souvenir—souvenir," and it was really sweet to see the men dive into their pockets for a coin or a button to give these little *gamins*.

Sir John's help was of the most disinterested kind

—as I hardly knew him, and when I thanked him, he said he could do no less, as he knew the real good the buffet had been to the men in the early days of the war. This was a tribute I valued highly. Sir John was a human being, not one of those skin and bone automatons who never forgot the dignity of their position or lost their grip on the red tape that bound them to their office chairs.

While the alterations were being carried out, he wrote me several letters which he sent to the Red Cross c/o Eden Paget, who used to forward them to me. The M.L.O. came to see Paget one day, and reprimanded him severely for receiving letters on my behalf, which had not been through the Censor's office. He added that he would not deliver any more, and that he would have to report the matter if it occurred again. " Do," said Paget, " but I am afraid I shall have to report you for refusing to deliver the Quartermaster-General's letters." Tableau !

Winston Churchill, having doffed his Admiral's uniform, appeared in khaki in November. One of the most amusing legends was when F. E. Smith came out to see him. We were quite solemnly informed that he had been marched on board, a prisoner under military escort. The real facts were something like this. He had gone to see Winston in the trenches without a proper pass, and through some blunder in the A.-G.'s office he had actually been put under arrest at G.H.Q. I am sure there was no great discomfort attached to this adventure, and there must have been a certain amount of satisfaction in making Macready apologize !

The same fantastic tales were spread about the

most harmless Generals who were merely going home on leave. So-and-so had been unstuck. In a few days the unconscious victim of this gossip would return, and the originator of the scandal would almost regretfully watch him vanish out of sight in an Army motor car.

* * * * * *

So little use had been made of the cavalry that it had been decided that a certain number should be turned into infantry, and that in future they would take their turn in the trenches. The Scots Greys were billeted not very far from us, and I had promised to pick some of them up in the car, and take them to luncheon at Boulogne. My car was *hors de combat*, so we had to go in the Ford store van. We had started out full of zeal, but a punctured tyre and a wrong turning made it rather a dismal drive. I had hoped that we might see some grey horses which would prove a guide to their whereabouts, but I had forgotten that they had been camouflaged to look like bays (they really resembled a pale pink). We eventually found their headquarters, and hoped that we should be able to have our luncheon there, as it was already late, but they had just demolished their last slice of cold ham, so we had to wend our weary way to Boulogne. We were already fairly tightly packed in the car, but regardless of the possible damage to the springs, we managed to fit two or three of them in. I hadn't seen Eddie Compton or Francis Hill since they were small boys.

We saw a good deal of the Greys later. They used to come over and help us in the canteen. Lord St. Germans was a most proficient barman. We lent him a white apron and he poured out tea and ladled out porridge in the most professional manner. He and Eddie were a most amusing couple. Eddie was the Pelissier of the regiment, and had written a revue called " Wash your Kneck," which had a huge success at the Front. The " Company " came and gave us a performance at Boulogne and Lord St. Germans as a lady was quite inimitable.

It was only very rarely that I could get a whole holiday, for our work at Boulogne was not diminishing, whilst at Etaples it was growing in leaps and bounds. Without flattering myself unduly I think I can say that the British Soldiers' Buffet was by far the most popular restaurant in the camp. Not to know " Angelina's," as the hut was familiarly called, was not to know anything about Etaples, from the Tommy's point of view. A King's Messenger, asking his way to the station, was told to go to " Angelina's and straight on." Naturally, the King's Messenger was as wise after this information as before he received it !

Day by day the camp was growing, and was rapidly becoming a large wooden town whose buildings, though composed of timber, presented such an appearance of permanence, that even the educated French citizens began to question our intentions, and to suspect us of a definite sojourn on their shores. The Quay at Boulogne was crowded, and the traffic congested, with men going on leave, and with the batches of reinforcements that were arriving daily from England. This new army, fresh, and enthusiastic, in their brand new khaki, presented an enormous contrast to the mud-caked, worn, war-weary soldiers returning from the front for their all too short leave.

They numbered in their ranks members of every conceivable trade and profession. The meat-salesman from Smithfield, and the waiter from the " Berkeley " rubbed shoulders amicably with the artist and the actor. This seems quite natural when one reflects that their callings, under normal conditions, were completely ignored.

At one moment one was talking to a gentleman with a diction as clear as Mr. Balfour's, and the next to a bookie, who was bemoaning his loss of income on the racecourse ; but, I suppose making the most of his time in the camp out of his pals at Crown and Anchor, or that historic game " Housie Housie." No one who has been in France will not know that game, but for the uninitiated I may as well explain that it was only another name for Loto ! At every corner of the camp a group of engrossed men sat waiting, in rapt attention, for a number to be called in a monotonous, raucous voice. To see them, such things as guns and trenches might have been on another continent. One man was a really amusing crook. He showed me the three card trick and let me into the secret of his loaded dice and double-faced penny. He must have made a nice income at home, as he thought the hundred or two he had netted in the camp a very paltry sum ! The British Tommy preserved his sense of humour in the most trying circumstances. On one occasion I was looking at a new motor hearse, built by the Red Cross to carry four coffins. Two men were passing at the time, and one of them turned to his pal with the very àpropos remark : " Look, Bill, they are going to make us form fours to the very end ! "

The exigencies of the canteen had seriously interfered with the children's education. Their governess had turned out a most splendid worker and was my right hand, but she could not be in two places at once, and lessons went sadly to the wall. Marigold was practically grown up, so it did not matter for her, and I tried to console myself that what Flavia lost on the swings she gained on the roundabouts, for she now talked French like a native, but instead of relishing the absence of copybooks she expressed a wish to go home to school ! This laudable desire I felt ought to be encouraged, but I was rather doubtful of its ultimate success, and I was right in my surmise, for after three weeks of school life she prayed so hard to be taken away that I rather weakly acquiesced, and compromised by leaving her with a governess in London and bringing her back to France in the summer.

The Eshers were going over and had promised to look after her on the journey, as it was impossible for me to get away until after Christmas. We all dined together at the " Folkestone " the night before ; the Maurice Bretts were there too, and I thought Mrs. B. as nice as she was pretty. King Manoel was also there, none the worse for what might have been a really bad motor accident. His car had collided with a horse and cart on the Etaples road, and had very nearly gone over the precipice on to the railway line, but by some extraordinary good fortune it had remained poised on the brink.

I saw Millie at the Folkestone Hotel, and thought she looked rather tired. No wonder ! They had been bombing all round her hospital, and even if one doesn't lose one's nerve in a raid, one certainly loses one's beauty sleep. Though we were so close we had hardly seen each other, she did not come into Boulogne oftener than she could help, and somehow I never managed to get out to her hospital, but when I did I thought it too delightful and comfortable, and was filled with a longing to live permanently in a wooden hut, it all looked so clean and homelike !

Millie did not take long to get over her experiences at Namur, as a German prisoner. Directly she got back to England she began to raise a hospital unit which she brought back to Dunkirk, to the Hôtel Bellevue, Malo. Here she had a hundred beds and also was instrumental in getting the huge goods sheds on the station converted into a clearing hospital.

She was cosmopolitan in her ministrations, and French and German wounded were received, and welcomed into her hospital. Her expeditions to recover some of the worst cases, from places further up the line, did not meet with wholesale approbation from the British officials. Dunkirk was the German airman's favourite hunting ground along the coast, and the bombing became so desperate that she was obliged to move fifteen kilomètres out of the town. Here Millie established herself and her unit in tents pitched in a corn field, and it was not till 1916 that she was finally settled at Calais. Rosemary* was with her all the time, and was, I believe, a most efficient nurse, whilst her very happy, sunny disposition made her a universal favourite. She fondly imagined she was maintaining a perfect incognito in her cap and apron, and was rather embarrassed one day, when a patient, whose wound she was dressing, quietly remarked that the last time they had met was at the Pytchley Hunt

* Viscountess Ednam.

ball ! Rosabelle Bingham, and Diana Wyndham were with Millie for some time. David Bingham and Percy Wyndham had both been killed in those very early days.

Later Rosabelle came and worked for me in Boulogne —but only for a short time, and she broke every rule that was established regarding permits, and turned up in London quite unexpectedly. I had gone over to see about stores, and she came to apologize, with such a radiant face, that I suspected some better reason than boredom had prompted her to leave, and I was right— she had deserted me to marry Gertie Brand, who had unexpectedly got leave.

The curt announcement of Sir John French's departure was not unexpected. No one here was taken in by the rather absurd excuse that he was really wanted in England. During the shell crisis he had acted with the greatest moral courage, and by his own action he had probably ruined his career. Sir John had undoubtedly been subjected to a vast amount of unjust criticism ; he might well now retort by asking if his successor had done any better. The answer would be " not so well," for surely Haig had no retreat of Mons or battle of the Marne to place on the credit side of his balance sheet. The absurd scandals of the happenings at G. H. Q. were most untrue and malignant, and the reports of the ladies and the card parties at St. Omer were without a shred of foundation. Exhausted imaginations were reduced to these pitiable inventions.

French was an optimist in the best sense. It was not a swaggering conviction in his own ability, but a supreme confidence in the men he had handled, and in the justness of the cause. His own firm belief in the ultimate results re-acted on the spirits of the entire army, and kept them steady and hopeful when they might have been legitimately down to zero.

He went away very quietly, and as he stood on the steps of the bridge, one could not but think of another, greater than he, and of his picture looking towards the shore as the ship set sail for St. Helena.

V

LE roi est mort, vive le roi. Sir Douglas Haig had replaced Sir John French. It was a fact that aroused little enthusiasm; his name at that time meant little more to the army than that of any other general, but there was not a man who had not known Sir John's. It was the rank and file who appreciated what he had done! Haig had not been popular amongst the officers at Aldershot, and if all one heard was true, he was not a particular favourite amongst the politicians —which of them was it, by the way, who gave that ex cellent word-picture of him, " all chin and no head " ? That featural indication of obstinacy did not belie him, and it was this characteristic, so often the accompaniment of stupidity, which must have made him refuse, till the game was nearly up, to come under the command of a better man than himself.

Changes in the General Staff included that of Sir William Robertson, who had gone back to the War Office. Everyone regretted that he had gone. " Wallie," as he was familiarly called, inspired confidence. He had no outside influence, no " Maid of Honour " wife to help him in his career ; his rise was due solely to his own indomitable efforts and ability. Many amusing stories are told of the bluntness of his manners " You're for 'ome," was said to be one of his methods of politely intimating to a general that his services in France were to be dispensed with.

Sir Philip Sassoon, who had started the war as General Rawlinson's secretary, had transferred himself into a similar position with the C. in C. He is supposed to have wired to the florist

" Stop flowers to Lady Rawlinson, but send them to Lady Haig," and later :

" Send flowers now to Mrs. Lloyd George."

I cannot vouch for the truth of this, but it is amusing enough to repeat ! And as a sequel, Diana Cooper is supposed to have wired to Sir Philip on Easter Sunday : " Christ is risen, apply for secretaryship ! "

New brooms sweep clean, and great things were predicted for the Spring offensive, but it was one of those interminable hopes destined to disappointment. Instead of being half way to Berlin, our troops were entrenched in the same muddy, bloody line. One felt desperately like the man in the Flanders trenches who was asked in 1914 how long the war would last :

" I don't know," was his reply, " *when* it will end, but I know *where* it will end—and that's here."

The terrific attack on Verdun had begun. To write or even imagine anything of the horrors of this epoch-making conflict would be impossible. Stories of indescribable ghastliness and endurance filtered through. The absence of food and drink nearly drove the men mad. The brother of one of the Red Cross drivers was with the French Army there, and he told me how the men were literally drinking their own blood, and a French priest I had given a lift to, had just come from Douaumont. He had the red ribbon of the Légion d'Honneur and other decorations and was having a two days' permission to see his flock. He told me that on the last occasion that Douaumont had been lost and retaken, the French had refused to move again : the men said they infinitely preferred to die or to fall into the hands of the Germans. They lay in the trenches oblivious of anything but their utter exhaustion. Pétain, however, had said that the fort *was* to be retaken. The officer in command called up the trumpeter, who played the Marseillaise. At the first notes played by the boy the men were instantly roused from their stupor— as one man they rose and charged—Douaumont was retaken and for the last time passed out of German hands.

The Irish Rebellion was looked upon from an entirely selfish point of view at the Base. What right had an Irishman, however great his grievance, to think of it at such a moment when his own flesh and his own blood were at grips in a battle for world freedom ? Ireland seemed almost like a parish quarrelling over its pump, and her sons would have been better employed, at a moment when every man was desperately needed, in rallying to the greater cause. That they did not must be a blot on the race only redeemed by the gallantry of those Irish regiments that we saw in France.

An Irishman wrote to me later a description of the Easter rising, which I am giving.

" You have asked for a history of the Dublin rising of Easter week, 1916, as it appears to an average Irishman. Here is one for you told by several eye-witnesses :

" As you want facts, let me state the most important

one first—it was not a Sinn Fein rebellion. No one can deny that its results have been to throw the weight of three-fourths of the Irish nation into the service of that party; but at the time of the insurrection the Sinn Fein leaders were not in the council of the men who directed it, and most of the latter would have protested against being dubbed Sinn Feiners as violently as would, say, Mr. Chesterton at being labelled a Prohibitionist. The term Sinn Fein has been adopted since then by journalists to describe every man of Irish birth who happens to be discontented with the muddlement or misgovernment in his country, much as till recently those who do not love Mr. George were ticketed with the badge of Bolshevik; but those who professed the creed of Sinn Fein in 1916 were few compared with other political parties in the island. Their objects then—for they have been modified by subsequent happenings—do not concern us more than to state that armed insurrection certainly was not one of them.

" The rising was the result of the fusion of two small organized bodies, the Citizen Army of Dublin, composed of sweated and exploited workmen led by James Connolly, and the Irish Volunteers, men of good social position and intellectual brilliance, whose leader was Patrick Pearse. In this way Socialism joined with Republicanism, dreams of a nation winning its independence, sword in hand, were mingled with schemes to redress evils in the policy of the commonwealth; the result was a protest, terrific in its unexpectedness, ringing in unwilling ears. The Citizen Army bore the existing fabric of the State a grudge for its defeat in one of the most savage industrial wars ever fought in Ireland; the Republicans had lost patience with those leaders whom they thought chameleons, promise-crammed by the hot air of Westminster. The incompetence and stupidity shown in every department of Government control in Ireland seemed to these men to demand a cleansing river, and on Easter Monday, April 24th, 1916, these discontents overflowed so suddenly that the Government got its feet wet.

" The day had been well chosen. The fine weather had driven most thoughts out of the heads of sport loving Dublin save that of the great Irish meeting at Fairyhouse. It is said that at the Castle those responsible for the safe guidance of the country were languidly considering whether, in view of Casement's arrest on the previous Good Friday and rumours of plots in the metropolis, extra precautions should be taken, when a shot at the gates announced that the rebellion had begun. This may or may not be true, but there is no doubt of the fact that a couple of hundred Irish Volunteers, wearing uniform and carrying arms, met no hindrance as they marched through the streets and about noon took possession of the General Post Office in O'Connell Street and proclaimed the Irish Republic. Round these headquarters barricades sprang up at once, built of all sorts of unexpected materials. One in Lower Abbey Street was formed of new bicycles in their crates. Of such defence the British artillery made short work when the time came.

" Simultaneously other strategic posts in the city were seized. Telegraphic wires were cut and railways interrupted. Motors were stopped on all the roads round Dublin, and many a racegoer was left to walk home while his car was driven into the city and parked at St. Stephen's Green to serve as a barricade. But

the insurgents failed to capture Dublin Castle or to cut
the telephone wire which connects it with the Curragh
Camp. The capture of Jacob's biscuit factory, Boland's
Mill, and the Four Courts did not outbalance the failure
to gain the Castle or the Magazine Fort in the Phœnix
Park. At Trinity College and the Bank of Ireland, too,
the insurgents were frustrated by their own countrymen
in the Dublin University O.T.C. During the horrors
of the coming week ' Old Trinity ' was not only a fortress,
but a city of refuge ; its defenders lost neither their
heads nor their humanity, a state of balance sufficiently
rare in Dublin just then to be worth recording.

" The Republic was proclaimed at noon. The people
of the abyss accepted this as an invitation to help
themselves to some of the good things of life whereof
they had never yet had any taste. The slums of Dublin
disgorged their waste products of modern industrial
civilization and enlightenment, who proceeded to loot
the shops in O'Connell and Grafton Streets, the Oxford
and Bond Streets of Ireland. Needless to say, none
of this looting was done by the men of Pearse and
Connolly. What they required was either paid for
on the spot or taken after due lists had been made and
receipts given. The mob, however, with neither money
to pay nor credit to pledge, was not so honest, and in
many cases after having plundered the shelves, it burnt
the shop. You cannot expect people who have lived
since . birth disregarded and disdained in ignorance,
hunger, dirt, disease and a living death, to show the
nicest of behaviour when the chance comes to them of
celebrating a holiday after the manner of the ancient
Saturnalia. Yet during the whole of that week they
committed none of those gross lust outrages whereby

brutalized men often express their hate towards those who seemed responsible for their former misery. This security of women from insult has always been one happy feature of Irish insurrections.

" Already before sunset on the Monday the hopeless nature of the rising was patent. Though few troops were available, and no direction was to be had from the amiable Under-Secretary, Mr. Birrell, being, as is usual with Irish Chief Secretaries, in England at the time of jeopardy, by Tuesday the insurgents had been driven from the Castle area, the South Dublin Union and Stephen's Green. It was merciless fighting, and the main brunt of it was borne by Irish regiments.

" Not till the Wednesday did troops begin to arrive from England. Their coming was accompanied by the shelling and destruction of Liberty Hall near the quays. The gunners did more execution on neighbouring property than might have been expected from good shooting. Anyway, the Mecca of the Dublin trade unionists was blown to bits eventually, and a goodly portion of O'Connell Street went skywards with it.

" I shall never forget my feeling of horror when three years later I looked upon the ruins of what had once been the finest thoroughfare in the city. But sadness gave place to something like rage as I noted the armoured cars and lorries filled with soldiers patrolling up and down, and realized that I had come home to a country occupied by troops who plainly were determined that the natives should not forget their presence. God forgive me, for a moment I could not help feeling like an enemy towards men with whom I had been making common cause against Germany all through the war. Then, after a moment's reflection, I bestowed my damnation where it was properly deserved—the shifty politicians who sent decent men to do bullies' work.

"Apart from the damage done unnecessarily to property, the authorities were careless of the lives of their own soldiers. On Wednesday evening, the Sherwood Foresters were marched into the city from Kingstown by the route where they would be most exposed to hostile sniping. It is on record that their C.O. was warned by a lady to march by another than the direct route, and that she was shot for her pains. But they could not know. In the course of the march they captured by means of bombs and dynamite the houses held by the insurgents, but their casualty list showed the price paid.

"On Thursday morning, the G.P.O., the Four Courts, Jacob's factory and the Royal College of Surgeons were the main positions still held by the insurgents, and these isolated each from the other, but sniping and street fighting were still going on all over the city.

"To the danger of death by bomb or bullet, the horrors of famine were now added. The people of the abyss no longer looted for amusement, but for bread. The authorities invoked the aid of volunteers to distribute such food as was available or was being sent in from across the water. The civilians who answered this call did so at the risk of their lives, having to traverse streets humming with bullets. One friend of mine, in response to the entreaty of a highly-placed official, ran the gauntlet on a bicycle fired at by troops and rebels alike and reached North Wall, where he was obliged to stay several days superintending the distribution of rancid American bacon with no chance of getting home to his family. Later on he received neither recognition nor thanks, and the authorities haggled over paying the expenses of his room at the Station Hotel. *Sic semper !*

" By Thursday ten thousand troops had arrived in Dublin. That night O'Connell Street was in a blaze from end to end. All Friday the fire continued, and the work of immolation was helped on by artillery and bombs. The main object of attack was the G.P.O., where Pearse and Connolly commanded, and in making it untenable for the insurgents, not only O'Connell Street, but the greater parts of Lower Abbey, Middle Abbey and Henry Streets were completely destroyed.

" On Saturday inside the G.P.O. the end was near. James Connolly had been wounded twice and crippled on the Thursday, but lay on a bed in the firing-line still directing his comrades. A Marxian seemed out of place in such a setting. But there was a reason for it. Perhaps it was by way of apology that Connolly said to his daughter during their last parting before his execution :

" ' The Socialists will never understand why I am here. They all forget I am an Irishman.'

" At four o'clock on the Saturday afternoon Pearse surrendered his fortress. Commandant Daly laid down his arms at the Four Courts later on the same day. The garrison of Jacob's factory and the College of Surgeons held out till Sunday. At the latter place the troops, not without admiration, beheld the Countess Markiewicz kissing her revolver before surrendering it to an officer, a tall, graceful woman in a green Volunteer uniform, second in command there, but never second to any in daring. The last fighting of all took place around

Boland's Mill and Merrion Square, with the division commanded by Eamonn de Valera.

" A spectator in the streets of Dublin on the evening of Sunday, the 30th of April, saw curious sights. Long lines of prisoners, men and women in green and white uniforms, marching with heads held high and singing rebel songs, while those who lined the streets were cheering them in defiance of the machine guns and bayonets of the guards.

" ' Sure we cheer them,' a woman remarked to a Canadian officer, who had rebuked her for the demonstration. ' Why shouldn't we ? Aren't they our own flesh and blood ? ' Certainly blood calls to blood in misfortune more than in prosperity.

" The three thousand soldiers who had matched themselves against the strength of the British Empire had lost—and losers must pay. Some had already paid ; how many will never be known. The secret lies in the graves of Glasnevin, where the dead were buried in batches of twelve in one trench, or beneath the wreckage of houses, in cellars or gardens where the toll of civil war was paid to the uttermost. But on those who yet lived, the hundreds of men and prisoners, there was still a tax to be levied. The method whereby England forced the reckoning turned every decent Irishman into a sympathizer with the rebels.

" National feeling in Ireland was alarmed. Had the prisoners been Germans or Turks they would have been well treated ; had they been English or Scotch rebels they would have been assured of a fair trial according to the law of the land ; had they been Boers no more blood atonement would have been exacted ; being only Irish a court-martial was good enough to send them in

batches to the firing-squad. The procedure was illegal
and unconstitutional, the executions as rank murder as
any that had happened during the rising. Ireland began
to shout : ' Are they not our own flesh and blood ? '

" Sympathy was succeeded by admiration, and as the
Government had seen fit to begin a whole-hearted perse-
cution of the leaders of the Sinn Fein party for acts not
of their conceiving, that admiration was rapidly transferred to these and was bestowed on clever men who
well knew how to draw advantage from having a nation
at their back. Hence the subsequent revolution in Ireland which seems now about to end in her practical
independence.

" Perhaps the prime mover of the revolt foresaw this
ultimate result. One who was beside Pearse during
those last hours in the G.P.O. has recorded his leader's
hopes. Let me give them in Desmond Ryan's own words :

" ' I stood beside him as he sat upon a barrel, looking
intently at the flames, very silent, his slightly flushed
face crowned by his turned-up hat. Suddenly he turned
to me with the very last question that I ever expected
to hear from him : " It was the right thing to do, was
it not ? " he asked curiously. " Yes ! " I replied in astonishment. He gazed back at the leaping and fantastic
blaze and turned towards me more intently " And if
we fail, it means the end of everything, Volunteers,
Ireland, all ? " " I suppose so," I replied. He spoke
again. " When we are all wiped out, people will blame
us for everything, condemn us. But for this protest,
the war would have ended and nothing would have been
done. After a few years they will see the meaning of
what we tried to do.' "

When one thinks that at the time of the Rebellion

my correspondent was a Carsonite and that only circum-
stance and conviction converted him to the cause of a
united Ireland, that he is not the slave of a Celtic temperament, but a level-headed lawyer, this gives one hopes
that perhaps now legitimate and illegitimate grievances
may forever be laid to rest.

*　　*　　*　　*　　*

It never rains but it pours. The Easter Rebellion
and Verdun were followed by the Battle of Jutland, the
news of which, in contradistinction to War Office methods,
came to us first clad in the sombre garments of defeat,
and temporarily plunged us into a state of consternation.

The news of Lord Kitchener's death in all its tragic
circumstances seemed to be the culminating point of
our disasters. For him it was probably for the best.
He had learned to mistrust the friendship of his peers,
and great as was his hold on the minds and affections
of the people, he would probably not have escaped from
the political machinery, that ground reputations with
regular, and relentless mechanism.

Unnecessary interference, and an insistence on the
personal supervision of details, appear to have been the
accusations most frequently levelled against him. I have
talked to many men who held important posts under
him in Egypt, and their experience certainly did not
corroborate this view of Lord K. On the contrary,
when he gave a job to a man he left him to it. If he
did it well, he was not interfered with ; if, on the other
hand, he did it badly, K. made short shrift of him. This
was a very different method of procedure to that
employed during the war. A failure was either overlooked, or the offender merely moved to some other

post—probably a more important one. (It depended, of course, to a certain extent, who the offender was !)

There are critics who maintain that Lord K. was incapable of grasping the magnitude of the war we were engaged upon, and that he judged it by the same standard as his Egyptian campaigns. But it seems to me that this criticism does not tally with his assertion in 1914 that it would be at least a three years' war, when most people were saying that it would only be a matter of weeks. Toby Long told me that Lord K. had been against conscription on the grounds that the country that had the largest army at the end of the war would win the war and he wanted England to be that country. This sounds far more probable than the current story, that he wanted the honour and glory to be attributed to " Kitchener's Army "—such petty vanity was, I am quite certain, beneath him.

That Lord K. was interested in spiritualism is not so widely known, but he was undoubtedly not only interested, but a believer in it. Count Hamon, better known as Cheiro, told me a story which to the incredulous may only appear as coincidence, but cannot fail to be interesting.

Count Hamon was a friend of Kitchener's, and in reading his horoscope had, apparently, always told him that his death would be a sudden one, but that he need not anticipate danger in the field of battle. Just before Lord K. went abroad, Count H. went to the War Office, and K. showed him a little blue vase, which he had once given him as a mascot, and told him that he always kept it on his table. He asked Count H. if there was anything he could do for him, before he left the country. The Count replied in the negative, but K. told him there was one thing he would do—if anything happened to him he would give him a sign. At the very hour the *Hampshire* went down, Count Hamon was in the music room of his house in the country, at one end of which was a large hatchment, securely nailed to the wall. For no reason at all it fell with a crash, and might have been cleft in two by an axe. Count Hamon guessed instantly that something had happened to Lord Kitchener, and that this must be the promised sign.

I met Count Hamon dining with the Geoffrey Lubbocks. He appeared to me rather mysterious, and at the time I did not know that he was Cheiro. After dinner he did horoscopes, and I was still under the impression that he was an amateur—not that there was anything in the least amateurish about the horoscopes. I gave him the birth dates of several people who were not there and found him quite amazingly correct in his readings of their characters. He had just come over from Ireland, where he was developing an invention of his own for converting the bog peat into coal. He brought a sample of the new fuel with him, and whilst we were at dinner the fire was left to go down, leaving when we came back only a few dying embers. Almost directly the new coal was added, a beautiful blaze resulted, which gave out far more heat than that from ordinary coal. It appears to be very cheap to produce, and if it were possible to develop it on a large enough scale would make us very independent of coal strikes, but I suppose some technical hitch will arise. The bye-products were also wonderful, and we were shown slabs of material which would replace asbestos for building purposes at an infinitely lower cost.

*   *   *   *

The big events of the war stand out in solid blocks, leaving the lighter side misty and indefinite. Looking back it is difficult to place the trivial events, which made up a great portion of our lives at the Base, in any categorical sequence. They were brief flashes of harmless dissipations, into which we threw ourselves with almost childish enthusiasm.

The war machine had spread itself insinuatingly along the coast. Paris Plage and Le Touquet were swept up by the ever advancing steam roller. It was no longer an isolated and secluded spot, sheltered among the pines. The Canadian Hospital was at the Golf Hotel, and the Claims Commission were ensconced with all the panoply of office tables and orderlies at François de Croisset's villa near by. General Morrison was in command here—such a delightful person, and his death came as the greatest shock. He hàd lent me a motor that day, with an apology for it not being his own Sunbeam, but he was using that to go to Amiens. It was on the way there that the steering broke, and he was instantaneously killed.

The golf links, whose greens had been kept in more or less semi-order since mobilization, were the venue first for a cavalry camp, and followed by the Machine Gun School. The cavalry brought us polo to lighten our afternoons, and the first news of the Tanks reached us through Major Baker-Carr, a constant visitor to our forest. He was very popular with the V.A.D.'s, and I think some of them were distinctly disappointed when they heard that he possessed a wife and several children ! The polo caught on, and players such as " Mouse Tomkinson " made the best of the army horses. Lord Tweedmouth, commanding the Blues, was often about.

The 10th Hussars were not far off, and our old friends, the Greys, had not deserted us. Lady Greenall, Lady Sarah Wilson and Mrs. Keppel had all passed like ships in the night, but the Duchess of Westminster and Mrs. Whitburn still had villas. The Headquarter Staff had left the Hôtel des Anglais and were established in new buildings in the camp, and the Anglais had been turned into a hostel for the relatives of the wounded.

There were *potins* and scandals galore, as in every country community. Some bore the impress of truth, but the majority were imaginative inventions.

The Duchess of W. had left her original villa and migrated to the forest into the one next door to mine, and it was here that she met Captain Lewis and trilled duets with him through the long summer evenings. Her dances were amusing and broke the monotony of the V.A.D.'s lives. But, needless to say, some captious people took exception to them as being unsuitable to the time. I braved public opinion myself on Marigold's birthday and followed suit. A suggestion of giving a dance in my house in peace time would have been thoroughly comic, but in war time all things, apparently, are possible. The floor was composed of the roughest deal boards and the cubic dimensions considerably less than would have been authorized by the sanitary inspector, but everyone throughly enjoyed themselves, or, anyhow, appeared to. We only thought of it at the last moment, but by some happy inspiration everyone one could think of seemed to be in the neighbourhood that day. The Herberts both arrived very cheerful, and one of them inclined to be demonstrative towards a rather attractive little French lady. Eric Ednam and Lord Airlie paid us an unexpected visit and were commandeered for the evening, whilst Mousie St. G. and Eddie Compton contributed to our programme with selections from the revue.

And through these kaleidoscopic memories the figure of Alastair stands out. As I write, he is being laid to rest at Dunrobin. I can see him now, wrapped in a bath towel, greeting me with that ideally sunny smile. He and Michael Wemyss were amongst my most regular visitors—the bath being the magnet that drew them! Alastair had gauged the capabilities of my boiler to a nicety and always got the hottest water! When Michael's motor bike had disappeared from the scene of action, my services were regularly commandeered to motor Alastair back to his billets after dinner. He was so terribly optimistic about the distance, so deliciously uncertain about the road, and the lights on my car so sublimely erratic, that an all night drive was no uncommon occurrence.

Some people will always seem alive—Ali is one of them. Always gay with his inimitable buffoonery, his imperturbable disposition, that smiled at troubles and never failed to see the humorous side of every contretemps—Alastair, who always turned up at the most unexpected moments, either to play polo, or merely to see us *en passant ;* it was always the same Alastair, never bored and always affectionate—God bless him !

Easter, 1917. We had just heard that the cavalry were going into action, but the weather was so impossible that even now it looked as if the " gap," which had become almost a standing joke amongst the officers, would once more not materialize.

Encamped the night before on the racecourse at Arras, horses up to their hocks in mud, conditions could not have appeared worse. The 8th Cavalry Brigade, Essex Yeomanry, 10th Hussars and the Blues were ordered to proceed to Monchy le Preux. The casualties were terribly heavy, but I suppose in the circumstances they might have even been worse. The Greys were left to mourn General Bulkeley-Johnson's apparently unnecessary death, Bertie Wilson was blown up—since the days when he first came to Leicestershire, soon after I married, Bertie had been universally popular and I don't think he had an enemy, or ever said or did an unkind action to anyone. He and his brothers were christened the Three Bears; they were the sleepiest trio I have ever met, and used invariably to arrive half an hour late for the meet. They were quite absurdly kind about mounting their friends, and generally did so on their best horses, an action not usually practised! Lord Gerard was also badly wounded again, and Lady Gerard came out to the Hôtel des Anglais and was there for some time.

VI

MY own work was growing in an almost alarming manner. The success of my two canteens had inspired me with the wish to extend my activities further afield, but, so far, my suggestion had met with no enthusiastic response. The Expeditionary Force Canteens, however, were spreading themselves in every direction, and of course received the support of the authorities—so much so that I used to think the commandants must have had shares in the business! No doubt professional jealousy on my part!

I had a visit one day from Colonel Nasan, who had seen a good deal of service in Egypt, and was the O.C. Reinforcements. He came armed with the idea of my starting a hut on the new siding at Etaples. He pointed out what a blessing it would be, as the Y.M.C.A. arrangements were inadequate to deal with the ever-increasing crowds and they had a habit of closing at an arbitrarily appointed hour, totally regardless of the fact that, during a war, such a thing as a much delayed train might occasionally appear, bringing hundreds of hungry men.

The train services for the Front were notorious for their unpunctuality, which meant that the men had often to wait about for hours or—and this very frequently happened—they would stray back to the town, and manage to lose their train altogether. The Y.M.C.A.

had a sort of soup kitchen, but as they opened it only at their own sweet will the men's patronage was not exactly extensive. It was perfectly amazing, however, to see the way they bucked up and flew round with feverish energy, when we appeared on the scene—but all the same, they never had a real look in with us on the new siding.

Our huts, owing to territorial limitations, had to be of the smallest dimensions, and I had not the slightest idea how strenuous this new work was going to be until I actually started operations there, nor how many men would be passing through daily.

Having completely exhausted the stock of local industries in the direction of boilers and stoves, I made a foraging expedition to Paris with Eden Paget for these very necessary commodities. Paget was terribly agitated, because he was quite sure that my pass was not in order, and, I think, anticipated being arrested *en route !* It was a very skiddy day and we nearly ran into some of the horses belonging to the 11th Hussars, which we passed on our way. We arrived, however, with no more serious mishap than two punctured tyres.

We found Colonel Barry in Paris, and were introduced to the heroine of Loos, who gave us an account of her life there under the most appalling conditions. She had killed three Germans with her own hand, nursed our wounded, looked after her brothers and sisters and made her father's coffin. She was quite a child, only eighteen, and so pretty, and she well deserved her many decorations, and I think she is the only woman who received a Military Medal.

Denys Bailey was also at the Meurice. He had done wonders, raising funds amongst the miners, for the Red

Cross, and if my information is correct he played an important part in the settlement of the coal strike. The men's leaders and the coal owners apparently met quite amicably as his guests !

The food in Paris was quite excellent, and if there was any shortage it was not noticeable. Everybody had plenty of bread tickets, but at the restaurants your dinner was limited to two courses. Eden Paget was thoroughly annoyed by this, as he wanted some delicious *mousse* of duck which I had selected, but he had to go without as he had already consumed a *filet de bœuf* and *langouste !*

We came back by train, a very much delayed one, and we were desperately hungry. We could get nothing to eat on the way but a hard ham sandwich of the pre-war English refreshment-room type, and my sympathies flew to the troops who had to endure this sort of thing as a matter of course.

The work on the new siding appealed to me enormously, its necessity was so real. It brought one back to actualities, back to the primitive reason of oneself being in France at all. I had once again the sensation which had been dominant in those early days of 1914, and which had subsided gradually with the advent of red tape, organization and over civilization.

In the big hut one felt one was in no sense a necessity —merely a luxury. Our menu there had expanded from the ordinary sandwich and porridge, to ice creams, and fruit salad. We were almost an excuse for waste—and we might have been at Aldershot, not at war, but for the convoys of wounded and the creeping ambulances that rumbled by.

Later, when the food scare became acute, and Lord

Derby was at the War Office, I wrote to him and suggested, that if the other organizations were willing to sacrifice their profits, I would gladly lead the way and convert my hut at Etaples from a restaurant to a recreation room. This suggestion of mine, I remember, was in one of my letters to him with reference to the proposed scheme for amalgamating all private enterprises with the E.F.C. or the Y.M.C.A. I refused, point blank, to join either. I had been in France months before they came out, I disapproved of the Y.M.C.A. methods, and I was a little sceptical as to how much of those E.F.C. profits were really going back to the men! I told Lord Derby I did not want to be obstructive and that if the question of affiliation were insisted upon I would gladly attach myself to the Salvation Army, provided I did not have to wear the uniform, and I thought his sense of humour would appreciate the idea of me in a Salvation Army bonnet! The amalgamation only came partly into operation.

The difficulty of obtaining bread to supply the enormous number of huts was increasing, until at last the French bakers were no longer allowed to supply the English in the camp with this commodity, owing to the shortage of flour in France. It had always been difficult to get enough for our needs, and I confess to having done a considerable amount of wangling in the Army bakeries.

I had anticipated the crisis and turned the bath house into a bakery as there were plenty of baths in the camp by this time. An oven had been ordered in England, and I surreptitiously borrowed a lorry from the Transport, to get it from Boulogne to Etaples, but to my horror, when I found it on the quay it was six times as big as

I expected, and the lorry was nearly going back without it. By dint of pleading and a considerable amount of bribery, I got it on to the lorry, but the unloading at Etaples was an equally difficult situation to tackle. Realizing the difficulty there would be, I had begged for a fatigue party to unload, and as I refused to leave the hut until it arrived we all sat in the hut kitchen till the lorry appeared. Some of the road, and the greater part of the fence, was demolished before the oven reached its final destination. I cannot think where we should have been *without* that oven, for we used to turn out thousands of cakes and apple turnovers—to say nothing of loaves per day, and the hut at Boulogne was also kept supplied with bread. In fact, in the way of provisions we were able to crow over our neighbours with pure and undiluted joy !

On July 1st, 1916, the Battle of the Somme was really launched, and we were favoured with the usual optimistic *communiqués*—which, needless to say, became more restrained during each succeeding day. Those who knew, could read between the lines, an aecomplishment which, with us, had by this time become a fine art. The most insignificant skirmish was made to read like a decisive battle—cleverly worded phrases converted failures into the semblance of victories. Disquieting news was generally palliated by the announcement of the number of Germans we had killed, and we suspected our losses were nearly as numerous as the enemy's. Guns and shells were not there to be used with such prodigality.

Our offensive was immediately realized at the new siding by the increased number of men we had to feed. One night I was on duty alone, and I think I established a record in frying some eight hundred eggs between 4 a.m. and 7 a.m. single-handed, with no other assistants but an orderly for stoking, and a little French girl from the town, who spread sandwiches as fast as she possibly could—even then not nearly fast enough to satisfy the clamouring crowds at the window.

The irregularity of the trains gave us some trouble in apportioning the work, and with the rather stupid way in which some things were managed in France, the permission for my new hut had only been given on the understanding that I did not ask for any more workers' permits. The question of permits was a thorn in our sides. No doubt the free and easy style of the early days wanted revision, but a little latitude might well have been given to the local authorities, who were in a position to judge the merits of individual cases.

For a long time the granting of permits was done by L.O.C. Until his summary dismissal, Lines of Communication had been under General Clayton, but with the arrival of Macready at the War Office everything changed, and G.H.Q. took possession of everybody and everything, and became a sort of superior detective force. Before anyone could get to France, an application for a pass had to go through at least four offices ; the workers had to promise to stay four months, and they were only allowed to leave if a doctor's certificate of ill health was given. An excellent rule in theory, as any number of people merely applied for permission to work in France, with the intention of getting out to see a friend, or get a glimpse of what was going on. Some people were singularly unscrupulous, and if they did not find the conditions to their liking, the work uninteresting or hard—it generally was—

a desire for home swiftly came. The plan of campaign was then quite simple. The aid of a doctor friend was sought and obtained, and the necessary medical certificate issued with marvellous despatch. In this way the rule defeated its own ends, and reacted on the heads of institutions, as they were not allowed to replace helpers until the four months for which they came out had expired. Though some of my workers were excellent, there were several glaring exceptions.

One woman, I remember, sent me a photograph and gave her age as thirty-eight. When she arrived she told me she was nearly stopped in London, as she was forty-five, but had given her age as thirty-eight to me, because she had been informed that it was difficult for anyone over forty to get out to France at all. *She* went to the doctor in about a fortnight !

Another woman brought her car out to me to drive the staff home at night, and finding this did not amuse her, she retired to bed and said she was ill. One of the doctors at the Westminster Hospital saw her, and then came to me. He said she was not seriously ill at all, but that he could, if I liked, give a certificate to say she would be better at home. I interviewed her, and she calmly told me that if I did not get the certificate for her she would stay in bed, so that she would still be no good to me or the workers. In despair I went to the Commandant's office, and he telephoned to Colonel Herbert, at Abbeville, to see if he could arrange it. He said she might go home if there were a certificate, but on no account could her car go, as strict orders had been given by G.H.Q. on this matter. It was a quite reasonable and understandable order, as every inch of space was needed on the boats for the troops.

I went off once more to interview the lady. She refused to leave her car, and brandished a letter she had written to Haig, telling me she'd bet me that she would get home within two days. I am glad I did not take the bet, though I might easily have done so—sure enough, in as short a time as possible, a message came that her car was to be sent home. As the letter was a personal one, Haig must have given the order himself, and one could not help feeling that he might have been better employed—to say nothing of making the various departments under him, who had already refused permission, look ridiculous.

*   *   *   *

Changes in the official personnel were every day occurrences, and they were for the most part ignored, but the treatment of General Clayton aroused a general feeling of indignation. In a difficult post he had won admiration and respect, and an act of chivalry was converted by the prurient minds of G.H.Q. into a scandal of unworthy dimensions.

There were speculations as to who would succeed him, and everyone was delighted when the rumour that it was to be General Asser was substantiated. I had not seen him since he left Boulogne, but I was on the quay the evening he arrived to take up his new duties, and we had tea together. I think he liked the idea of his new appointment, as it would mean a good deal of travelling about the country.

One of his first inspections was to the camp at Etaples, and when he came to the " Bull Ring " he asked where the men were fed in the middle of the day. He was told, nowhere. Being a man of few words, he merely told the Commandant that this must be arranged for before his next visit.

The next morning when I arrived at my hut I found the Etaples' staff in possession of my kitchen. They had come to consult me over the feeding arrangements !

Having so often asked to be allowed to give the men tea in the " Bull Ring," and always been so definitely refused, I could not prevent myself from feeling considerably elated at being so promptly consulted. There were, or might be, ten thousand men to supply with tea, and only half-an-hour to do it in, and after looking at all my cooking arrangements, it was decided that ten huts should be erected on the ground, and an equal number of men marched up to each hut. The huts were to be on the same principle as the one I had on the new siding. I arranged to present these huts and the necessary boilers to the camp, and was very glad of an opportunity to employ some of my profits immediately for the benefit of the men. The Army was to supply all the rations, as well as orderlies to attend to the boilers, but I was to superintend the arrangements, and when we started I think the Quartermaster was surprised at my frugality over the tea and sugar !

There was no time to be lost, for General Asser might make another inspection any day, so I started for Paris that afternoon to order equipment, and before leaving the order for the huts was given. In a fortnight all the boilers had arrived from Paris, and the feeding arrangements completed and blessings showered on my head by the men who spent their days on the " Bull Ring ! "

The political situation in England seemed, from all one heard, in a most thoroughly unsatisfactory condition. It was said that Mr. Walter Long had already threatened to tender his resignation. Even the pro-Asquiths and the anti-Georges were beginning to doubt in the existing policy. That Lloyd George was working to supplant Asquith, few people had any doubts. As for us on the other side, we had waited too long, and seen too much in France to be tolerant of the " Wait and see " policy at home. Lloyd George had for some time been coquetting with the Tory Party ; and he possessed galvanic qualities, which he had been longing to force forward. In his effort to obtain the reins of office, he was being gallantly helped by Lord North-cliffe, who, in season and out of season, never ceased to throw journalistic brickbats at Asquith, attacking in turn his family, his friends and his policy ; whilst at the same time asserting vehemently that untold blessings would accrue to the nation if once Lloyd George were at the hehm.

Asquith's well-known indifference to public opinion probably contributed to his downfall.

Lloyd George's many successful short cuts to the Premiership were looked on as a good omen, and now that he had reached the goal of his ambitions, we were inspired with an optimistic feeling that he would be as lucky in his short cuts to terminate the war.

England was not the only country in a state of political and military intrigues. France was suffering in the same manner. The war was lasting too long— patience was beginning to flag. There was perpetual friction between the Grand Quartier General and the Ministère de la Guerre. The former were inclined to

act without sufficiently consulting the War Office.
Every general had his political supporters. There was
a pro and anti-Joffre party in official circles, but the
anti-Joffres gained the day, and he was replaced by
General Nivelle. General Nivelle's rise to fame was
even more rapid than Pétain's ; he had been only a
Colonel at the beginning of the war. His reign was,
however, short, and his spring offensive disastrous.

The tremendous losses had inspired the War Office
to forbid all further attempts to advance. There was a
divergence of opinion as to the wisdom of this order
—Nivelle declared that a further loss of 50,000 men might
have secured a definite success, but the *morale* of some
regiments was not good at that moment. The Germans
were not satisfied with the result of the war, and
they were conducting a second campaign, endeavouring
to undermine the discipline of the army and to shatter
the patriotism of the nation. French revolutionary
papers such as the *Bonnet Rouge, La Tranchée Républi-
caine* arrived anonymously with the troops' rations, and
were scattered broadcast at the stations amongst the
men who came on leave.

Drastic measures had to be taken and confidence
was once more restored when Pétain took over the Command of the French armies.

Clemenceau was doing his best to clear the political
atmosphere and to convince the population that their
leaders were at last to be trusted. Mata Hari's execution
was one of the sensations of the year. People of every
class flocked to Vincennes to see the once famous dancer
die. The *demi-mondaine* was one of the Germans'
principal channels for obtaining useful information.
Frenchmen did not imagine that a *femme de plaisir*

Dysart House, Fife.

could be also a *femme politique*. Courage was not lacking in Mata Hari—there was no cringing shame for her crime—not even repentance. Dressed in her dancer's clothes and decked with all her jewels, symbols of her sins, she stood, refusing to be blindfolded whilst the shot was fired. Her last words were : " Vous avez bien fait de me fusiller, mais vous feriez mieux de fusiller Malvy."

I once remember seeing Malvy at the Ambassadeurs he looked like a walking skeleton, his yellow face sinister and repulsive. His dinner consisted of a potage, the only thing he was apparently allowed to eat. His private life was well known as one of the worst. He was surrounded by a gang of crooks, both male and female, and of course he owed his position entirely to Caillaux—as the French describe it, he was his *homme de paille*. France owes Clemenceau a double debt for having freed her from the Malvy clique.

*　　*　　*　　*　　⊤　　⊤

I saw the New Year (1917) in at Boulogne with General Asser and Colonel Herbert. We had foregathered by chance at the " Meurice," and had a merry evening. A little Base gossip, but we allowed ourselves the luxury of no real war conversation. The General and Colonel Herbert reminisced over Egypt. I told them that their life there sounded like all play and no work. The General was a great admirer of Lord Kitchener's.

We drank the Old Year out, and the New one in, in a deserted dining-room, save for the French charwoman, who polished the floor in solemn silence. She was an old friend of the General's and Colonel Herbert's, as their Headquarters had been at the " Meurice " in the days when the former was Commandant, and she had

apparently polished it nightly since 1914, if not before
—what a life! If one were condemned to it, one would
inevitably turn Bolshevist.

It was an amusing evening, and we all talked a lot
of harmless nonsense.

The General was much amused when I told him of
the appearance of the Etaples staff in the canteen *re*
the huts on the training ground. As long as the men
were fed, *he* didn't mind who did it! I told him that
if he postponed his visit for a week the whole thing
would be in working order. We had a good laugh over
our first and second meeting in 1914, and he told me
I ought to have been locked up for disobedience. I
agreed, but at the same time pointed out to him that
no one with a sense of humour enough to write me the
letter he did, could have contemplated such a course.
We also agreed that a sense of humour was singularly
lacking in most officials, but I confess I didn't know to
what extent until I interviewed the A.G.

I had moved my headquarters from my old villa in
the woods and had taken Mon Rosier in Paris Plage. I
was glad of the change in some ways, as we were rather
isolated in the forest, and the question of getting our
provisions out there was tiresome. The tradespeople
were from force of circumstances independent, and
very often the butcher and the baker forgot our existence,
or, anyhow, had no means to bring us meat and bread.
I had got a very nice villa, and though it had two bath-
rooms, both the geysers went wrong, and the only man
who understood them in Paris Plage was mobilized, so
that we had to wait till he came back on " permission "
to have them put in order. I used to have my bath
at the " Folkestone " when I went in to Boulogne,

which was not at all the same thing as having one at home ! It was so bitterly cold, I used to go to bed in my fur coat, and even then my teeth chattered ; the water was frozen in the jugs, and I think the cold was by far the worst trial we ever had to endure.

Eddie Compton and Scot Robson were our first visitors. They had come down to Boulogne for twenty-four hours' leave, and I found them lunching at Monys, with no very definite plans, so I motored them back to Paris Plage for the night. Eddie told me of Toby Long's death. They adored him in the Greys, and they had all been miserable when he had left them to command a battalion of the New Army. He himself would sooner have stayed with the regiment, but he had a great sense of his duty, and at that time he knew how badly regular officers were wanted. He had come down to Etaples only a few days before to make a report on the various depots. He had been very full of the shortage of men at the Front, and had come down to see for himself what men there were in the camp, and he was also of opinion that considerable economy could be effected by doing away with the old I.B.D. Colonels and substituting men of lower rank. This was one of our many extravagances that the French could never understand. They themselves would have employed a captain, where we should have placed a general.

Marigold and I dined with T. L., and he had interesting news of political affairs in England. It appears Ll. G. went to his father and asked him if he could rely on his support in the forming of a Ministry ; without his support he said he would be unable to do so. W. L. hesitated, as I fancy that in spite of believing that Lloyd George was the best man to win the war, he did not approve of his methods any more than he did of Mr. Asquith's dilatory policy. This hesitation on Walter Long's part accounted for the delay between Mr. Asquith's resignation and Mr. Lloyd George actually taking office. I know Mr. Long is almost the only perfectly disinterested and honest politician, but I don't think I had realized before how much power and influence he had in the country. I believe he was the only Member of the Cabinet who didn't know Lord Northcliffe by sight. At one of the first Cabinet meetings Lord N., most unorthodoxly, interrupted it by wanting to see L. G. As the Ministers went out they passed Lord N., and most of them spoke to him, but Mr. Long asked who he was !

The arrival of the Geddes family on the political stage had marked a new era. No one was sure if their meteoric rise to notoriety was due to personal friendship with Lloyd George, or to their cousinship with Macready, who still ruled the roost in Whitehall. Sir Auckland as Minister of National Service was quickly followed by the appearance of Sir Eric in an entirely new office created for him—Inspector-General of Transportation. Certainly the railways were not beyond reproach, but I don't think that Geddes was a necessity in order to render them efficient, and if an Army officer had been endowed with the same powers of incurring the same unlimited expense, he would probably have done as well. The civilian could order a thousand miles of railway line, but the soldier had to make the best of the material at his disposal ; the civilian could order motor-boats for the transport of wounded, but an application from the officer responsible would meet with a curt refusal. This actually happened. General Strick, when he was G.O.C. of the Mediterranean Lines of Communication, was told when he wanted them that there were no motor-boats available. Geddes' representative visited his headquarters, and Strick mentioned this to him and said he only wanted two, but Geddes' man ordered twelve for him by wire, and they promptly arrived.

Squandermania was born in Geddesburg !

Geddesburg was the name bestowed on the elaborate and expensive headquarters of the Director General of Transportation ! On every side symptoms of this most malignant and contagious disease were apparent. The small staff which had sufficed General Asser at Havre to deal with both railways and docks was instantly quadrupled to grapple with the railways only. Contented captains were made into even more contented majors by Sir Eric, as the higher rank meant higher pay.

E. G.'s extravagance caused a certain amount of amusement at the time, but no one saw where it was going to lead us, or had the least idea that in a few weeks he would appear in an admiral's uniform and ride roughshod over England's seamen—and certainly no one could see what special qualities he possessed for this particular post.

The female portion of the Geddes family was not overlooked. Mrs. Chalmers Watson appeared in an officer's uniform as Controller General of the W.A.A.C.'s. She was very conscious of her military rank. One day Colonel Wilberforce took her out to luncheon, and with the customary courtesy of a gentleman towards a lady, he opened the door for her ; but instead of going through it, she waved to him with the delicious remark " I think you are senior to me, sir ! "

Whatever I can say about the Geddes family fades before the felicitous picture of Scott Moncrieff's, which appeared in *The New Witness*, and which I have been allowed to reprint for the benefit of those who have not seen it ·

THE CHILD'S GUIDE

TO AN UNDERSTANDING OF THE BRITISH CONSTITUTION

THIRD LESSON

There are no stars in all the sky
Outshine the blest Dioscuri ;
Castor and Pollux, sons of Zeus
Immortal, and by common use—
   Called patrons of seafaring men,
   Who lamp their radiance back again.

As none in heaven can match their worth
So is it with two men here on earth
Still two great brethren we implore
To guide our helm in peace or war :
   For there is none alive whose bread is
   More buttered than the brothers Geddes.

Not very long ago they came
To wealth, emolument and fame ;
While the sea rolls o'er British ships,
And all our sun is in eclipse,
   And England hardly seems alive,
   Quite suddenly the pair arrive.

Five years since, men who know aver,
One was a Railway Manager
The other an Anatomist,
Till in a trice, ere any wist,
   They outstripped all their fighting pals
   As generals or admirals.

" Or," say I, for alternately
They've governed us by land and sea,
And ever dressed themselves anew
In khaki and in navy blue,
   Enrolled recruits—laid railway tracks.
   (Meanwhile their sister ran the Waacs.)

Now Whitehall, very sore afraid,
Sees Auckland at the Board of Trade ·
Where while he guards his secret box
Canals, roads, rivers, railways, docks,
   Tubes, omnibuses, charabancs,
   Eric accepts with grateful thanks.

The first contingent of the W.A.A.C.'s came into the Canteen at Boulogne for their tea. Their appearance created a certain amount of amusement amongst the French population. I believe there was a good deal of jealousy amongst the various Women's Organizations, but this was mostly in England, and I never fathomed the intricacies of their mechanism, nor the details of their grievances, but I believe the Women's Legion supplied the motor drivers and were attached for purposes of discipline to the W.A.A.C.'s.

The First Aid Nursing Yeomanry, or as they were better known by their nickname " The Fannies," were, I think, the first Women's contingent to come to France. Their services were refused by the British, but gratefully accepted by the Belgians. The time came, however, when their work was sufficiently appreciated for the Red Cross to take them over. They showed themselves full of courage, and of inestimable use during the bombing raids at Calais. The members of all the Women's Organizations presented a most level and dignified appearance in their brown or khaki uniforms ; they were all excessively well shod, and possessed as a rule extraordinarily neat feet and ankles.

Naturally the arrival of a huge body of women gave rise to the most fantastic stories, and their morals were, I believe, most unfairly criticized. They had the most disciplinary rules and it was a most heinous crime for an army officer to be seen talking to a W.A.A.C. Tommy, even if she was his sister, and when the cavalry were at Camiers and their Mess was run by the W.A.A.C.'s, Lord Blandford was seen speaking to one of the prettiest waitresses on the sands. He was only passing the time of day with her out of common politeness, but I was told that he was brought up before the W.A.A.C. Commandant to be severely reprimanded for his behaviour.

*　　*　　*　　*　　*　　*

The summer passed more or less peacefully, and uneventfully for us, though I had an extremely anxious moment when Flavia was taken suddenly ill; her temperature went up to 105°, and we could get no Doctor, as a big convoy had just come in. When eventually he arrived, it was to tell us she had got pneumonia. Luckily I had a trained nurse working in the Canteen, and she at once came to my rescue. " All's well that ends well," and Flavia recovered with almost the same speed with which she had been taken ill.

I was getting busier every week. I had enlarged the big hut and there was plenty of work on the new siding whilst the tea huts on the Bull Ring were working well. Paris Plage was full of life with the various cavalry and Yeomanry regiments in the neighbourhood, whose officers trooped down on Sundays. Tea rooms and cafés had sprung up in every small street to cater for them, and the " Continental " was generally crowded for week-ends.

When the Prince of Wales came down one Sunday

he found his room temporarily occupied by Flavia, who had been fagged by Eddie Compton into packing his clothes, as he was just departing. All the other hotels were already converted into hospitals and hostels. Peggy and Nancy Brockenhurst, old friends from Melton, had arrived to work for the Young Christians—so had Mrs. Toby Long. Our neighbours, the Forestry, the latest official Ministry, under Lord Lovat, kept open house, and we used to peep at their guests over the garden wall, and we made free use of their telephone, as they were not yet so entangled with the red tape that bound more older departments.

A horrible rumour reached us that G. H. Q. were going to move from Montreuil to Paris Plage, but luckily the accommodation was inadequate, and they contented themselves with endless visits, and the C. in C. was rumoured to be a frequent visitor to the golf links. As I had given up golf entirely I never had the pleasure of seeing him.

VII

BARBARA POWELL came out to stay with me in
August. I was naturally delighted, for with the
exception of a few days in England I had been well over
a year without seeing a friend—always excepting one or
two passers-by. There was nothing much going on, but
we were fairly busy in the canteen. Then came the
first real excitement in the camp! Trouble over the
police had been simmering for some time. The saying
" like master like man " was more than true in this case,
for ever since Strachan had been A.P.M. the red caps in
Etaples had become thoroughly offensive individuals,
and no greater contrast could have been found than in
the manners of the police in Boulogne and Abbeville, and
of those in Etaples. The Australians especially resented
their methods and they were most unsuited to them, for
with all their reputation for lack of discipline, I found
them singularly amenable—they were extraordinarily
like naughty children and far more mischievous than
wicked.

The trouble began in this way. Just outside my hut
there was a bridge which marked the out-of-bounds
limit for the camp. An Australian was talking to a
girl at a few minutes past the hour when all men were to
be in camp. The policeman started hectoring the
Australian, whose contention was that as he was on the

bridge he was breaking no rule. The policeman con-
tinned his bullying attitude, with the net result that
the Australian was locked-up—a tactful word and the
finale would have been very different. As it was, the
next day a party of Australians decided to raid the police
station. It was about four in the afternoon. My hut
was full to overflowing when a shot was heard. The
hut was suddenly emptied. I ran out to see what had
happened, and found myself being swept down the hill
to the new siding in the midst of an angry mob. It
was nothing less than a man hunt that I was indulging
in ! When the Australians attacked the police hut
the policeman had fired—quite unwarrantably. His
shot had gone home, and a gallant Scotsman lay dead.
The effect on an angry mob can be imagined. The
policeman had meanwhile escaped through the back of
the hut and was making his way to shelter and the
station. With quite amazing promptitude Colonel
Nasan and Major Skirrow reached the station by a short
cut from the Reinforcement Office. These two held
the station-master's office, where the policeman had found
sanctuary, against a crowd of some thousands. The
natural respect for an officer held that mob at bay. They
were unarmed, and if the men had not paused voluntarily,
they would have been powerless. It was really an impressive sight and a personal triumph.

After a few words from Colonel Nasan in almost as
short a time as it takes me to write, the mob were wending
their way back to the camp. But the spirit of the men
was not altered, and it was obvious that there would
be rioting. Not a red-cap dared show his face To his
credit, be it said, the Commandant rode through the
camp, capless in the scrimmage, but otherwise unhurt.

That night the workers refused to do night duty on
the new siding, so Barbara and I, though we had had
a long day of it, had to remain alone. We had a perfectly peaceful night, and I think next morning some of
the others were a little ashamed of their attack of nerves !
The following day the rioting continued, and it was
rumoured that the Australians had got some of their
own back. I was advised to shut the canteen, but this I
refused to do, and I did not regret it. Most of the other
huts were closed, and came in for some of the rioting,
but though we were crowded out there was not a pane
of glass broken. The men did not want us to close at
the regulation hour, but were perfectly reasonable when
I told them that I had had thirty-six hours without
sleep, and a self-constituted bodyguard of Australians
insisted on escorting me out of the camp, and I drove my
car through the town at a snail's pace with thousands of
men all giving three cheers for Angelina !

General Asser had meanwhile arrived on the scene.
He made a tour of all the depots, and investigated the
men's grievances. Some of the disciplinary rules were
relaxed, and various harmless concessions granted. The
Etaples riots marked the death of the red-caps, and their
disappearance did much to clear the atmosphere, for
they had always been the soldiers' bugbear. Incidentally,
the A. P. M. Strachan had been removed, and things
soon simmered down—though at one moment they had
assumed an ugly appearance, and a regiment had been
sent from the Front, in case the riot developed into anything more serious.

G.H.Q. were very anxious later on to reinstate the
A.P.M., but on that point General Asser was adamant.
No one quite knew why Horwood was so anxious for his

return, but later events pointed to the fact that he was one of the tools being used to collect evidence against me, and presumably it was not so complete as they might have wished. He and I were mutually antagonistic. I had come up against him soon after his arrival, and I disliked him at once on account of his abominable manners. I suppose I ought to have ignored them, as he obviously knew no better, and should have remembered the silk purse and sow's ear adage. But I was not wise. When, however, he called Marigold by her Christian name and told her to shut his office door, and started paring his nails with a penknife while he was talking to me, I complained about him to Colonel Plumer, the A.A.Q.M.G., and asked to be allowed to use him as an intermediary for any business I had to transact.

As a precautionary measure all the men in the camp were to be moved up the line. This meant a busy day for me. To produce tea and sandwiches for 10,000 men was no joke! From five in the morning all hands were kept busy. Cases and cases of eggs were fried, and backwards and forwards went the car to our bake-house, and the bread and cakes came down to the siding still steaming hot. We had borrowed an extra baker from the camp, and they had been working all night in the old bath-house, turning out thousands of *petits pains*. The Salvation Army also came to our rescue and gave me all the cakes and biscuits they had, and we positively cleared out the *pâtissiers* of Etaples.

Without ceasing, the men poured down, and as one train moved out another moved in—and it was in the middle of this that General Asser's car came down to the new siding. He wanted to speak to me, he said. I pointed to the crowd of men besieging my sandwiches and cakes, and told him I was too busy. But he insisted, and I saw he looked unnaturally grave and worried.

What could have happened ?

" I have just come from the A.G.," he said, " with a message for you."

I jokingly retorted · " To order me out of France ? "

" Exactly," was his reply.

I burst out laughing, I remember, and not very politely told him " not to talk rot." Then I saw he was really serious and I was dumbfounded. What on earth had happened ? I had broken no rules or regulations—I had not the smallest sin on my conscience to give me any clue to his extraordinary message.

When I had partially recovered from my astonishment I asked him " Why ? "

But to this he only shook his head, and told me he had less idea than I had.

It was impossible to discuss the subject in these circumstances. " Sandwiches, miss ? "   " Couple of Woodbines " " Six cakes " were being called at me from all sides, so I arranged to motor with Barbara to Abbeville to dinner, after the last trainload of men had been despatched. As Barbara and I had been working since daylight we were in rather an exhausted condition. We found Colonel Herbert and the A.P.M. at dinner. No light could be thrown by anyone on the affair, which in itself was extraordinary, as the merest tyro in military law and discipline would know that any complaint must go first through local channels, and through the A.P.M. of Lines and Communciations—and that G.H.Q., however autocratic, should receive secret reports and act on them over General Asser's head was unthinkable.

Various lines of action were suggested, but the simplest was to write to Lord Derby direct. This I did, and I also wrote to Lord Wemyss. Lord Derby replied that he had " heard something of the matter and would investigate," and Lord Wemyss' reply came simultaneously that he had seen Lord D., who had been very nice, but " had made some rather veiled accusations." When tackled by Lord W. on these, they were hurriedly withdrawn. The first thing to do was to get to London. I wanted to see Lord Derby, but he declined to grant me an interview, saying that he ought not to see me *until* the matter had been settled, and that he had given instructions for my " case " to be " fully investigated," and that he should " believe nothing unless convinced of the truth of it." I had meanwhile ascertained that no one in authority at the Base knew anything. All sorts of conjectures and surmises carried us no further.

I had only been given a pass to England for two days, and I had obtained this with some difficulty so I could not postpone my return. I had been back at Paris Plage a few days when I got a rather belated message that I could go and see the A.G. I went to Montreuil with a pencil and notebook—I had had it rammed into me by all the officials to be sure and *say* nothing, or the authorities would try and pretend they had done what Lord Derby had ordered them, that is, " investigated my case."

The memory of that interview with the A.G. is one

of the most amusing incidents in my life. To begin
with, I drove my car up the street reserved exclusively
for the C. in C.'s car. Then came a quite unnecessary
wait in an office. (I'm sure the A.G. was much more
alarmed at my visit than I was. He had dodged me
already once or twice.) At last I was shown into his
office and felt really rather sorry for him. We both
stood looking at each other (I remembered my instructions not to speak). General Fowke (the A.G.) was
a rather stupid-looking, benign man, with a comfortable
middle-aged spread on him. In a sense his looks belied
him, as I believe he was not really stupid, merely lazy,
and in the hands of Macready he was surrounded by
unscrupulous cads, and was probably blamed for things
he knew nothing about. I am told that he was quite
nice about me afterwards and sorry that he had let
things drift so far, but having once done so, he adopted
the line of least resistance. In the room was another
man—I cannot remember his name. He was the A.A.G.
I discovered. He had a most unprepossessing appearance, and wore an eyeglass.

The A.G. cleared his throat several times and then
got out his first sentence.

" I believe you wish to see me," was his opening
remark for the prosecution. As I looked at those two
men the thing that flashed through my mind was how
on earth had such people got to such high estate !

I meekly replied, " Yes." Monosyllables could not
be called talking ! He then had the effrontery to ask,
" Why ? "

How was I still to be silent after that ?

I suggested blandly that as he wished me to leave
France I was anxious to know the reason.

More coughing, much unsettling of paper, and he began appealing mutely to the unpleasant gentleman in the corner, who was toying with his monocle.

" This is most unpleasant."

I whipped out my notebook (what a bore if I had suddenly broken the point of my pencil !) and started writing.

" Please don't mind me."

And he continued :

" Your influence is not a good one with the troops— and the C. in C. wishes you to leave."

I was feeling I wanted to giggle.

Another pause, more clearing of the throat.

" We have very fully investigated this case and are satisfied that our evidence is correct."

Seeing me writing every word down must have been disconcerting for them.

" A clergyman has heard you say ' damn.' Really this is most unpleasant," he went on. I assured him I did not mind.

" You washed your head in the canteen."

This was the *comble !* I longed to ask him whether he would prefer me to go dirty, and if he would have kept smiling if he had spent the winter, as I had, without any hot water. It so happened, however, that this was fiction founded on fact. I had washed my head in the canteen kitchen ! As Marigold and I were the cooks it does not sound such a very improper proceeding.

This comic interview drew to its close, after more grotesque and inaccurate accusations as to the awfulness of my behaviour had been read to me and duly inscribed in my notebook. As I was leaving the A.G. asked me if it was true that we were making profits out of the canteen, and if so, how I did it. I told him it was impossible to do otherwise. The last word was the reiteration of the first—that there was no more to be said, Sir Douglas Haig wished me to leave France.

I wrote to Sir Douglas through Sir Philip Sassoon, who told me he had delivered my letter, but I never received an answer. Later, General Asser told me that when he protested on the way the whole affair had been conducted over his head, Sir Douglas assured him that he knew nothing about the case at all.

A fresh development awaited me at home, and threw some light on the methods of truth and justice employed at G.H.Q. Some time back I had been obliged summarily to dismiss one of my workers. It was a letter from her to another worker that was brought to me. In it the writer stated that efforts were being made to get me out of France, but that so far this was impossible. A high official had actually been to see her. Between them they had concocted a scheme to accomplish this. Signed evidence was absolutely necessary, but the signatures, according to the writer, would not go further than official headquarters so that the stories need not be truthful! "In fact," the letter continued, "it doesn't matter what you say, as they have promised to keep our names out" The fellow worker to whom this strange communication was addressed, sent it to me directly she heard what was going on, together with her reply, which was to the effect that she had been very happy in the canteen, and had seen nothing wrong to report. If the originals of these letters were not in safe keeping and available for inspection by the incredulous, I should expect my account to be treated as a fairy tale.

The R.T.O. on the new siding received a visit from

Colonel Mellor, who in the most unconcerned fashion insinuated that at 5 a.m. everyone was likely to say " damn," and that I cannot have been a beautiful example to the contrary. But the R.T.O. was not to be drawn—even if his admission that I had been guilty of such a crime might have been rewarded by a transfer from the dreariness of Etaples to a more important and interesting railhead. The loyalty displayed by all the local officials, from the highest to the humblest, has more than compensated for the malice of the jealous !

The letter from the discharged worker, to which I have referred, I sent on to Lord Derby, in the confident expectation that he would need no further evidence of the methods being employed against me. He made no comment upon it, and concealed the awkward position he was in by changing his attitude of friendly justice to one of official aloofness.

Interest in my own affairs was suddenly disturbed by my having to take Flavia post haste to Paris for the Pasteur treatment. One of the Alsatian puppies we were trying to cure of distemper had bitten her, and the doctor said that we must take no risks.

Three weeks at the Hôtel Meurice was a most pleasant rest and change. Colonel Barry was round and about, and the Kemps most hospitable. The Eshers were in Paris, as nice as usual, and Lord Esher did what he could to help me by writing to Lord Derby. He made me realize that I was only one of the many who were suffering from the ruthless injustice which was meted out so recklessly at Headquarters. As he quoted instances my resentment lessened, remembering how small my grievance was in comparison with careers absolutely finished.

18*

The most absurd *potin* had been started in Paris about Mr. Jeff Cohen (Lord Michelham's agent). It began, I believe, by his having written at the commencement of hostilities to the Kaiser about his racehorses, which were in Germany. From this small beginning a Cohen and an anti-Cohen faction arose. The Embassy was anti (I believe inspired by a lady out of jealousy over the Michelham Convalescent Home), and Cohen was denounced as a spy. (His house, meanwhile, was the unofficial headquarters of any generals who came to Paris.) Lord Bertie, in spite of all the important things he had to attend to, became obsessed with this idea, and once, when a celebrated general went to see him, he had taken up half the interview discoursing on the subject, so much so, that as he went out, the general told one of the Embassy's secretaries, that his time was too valuable to waste! The secretary smiled, and quoted an instance of another ambassador, whose obsession was a new garden pump! Among the pro-Cohens was Lord Esher, who showed throughout the whole affair—which lasted a very long time—what excellent qualities of loyalty and fairness he possessed.

Lord Esher, I should think, was the only man in England who could have successfully performed the rôle he did during the war. From the first he was regarded with suspicion and jealousy by the busybodies of the war. He had no official appointment, and the freedom of his movements and actions caused many hypothetical conjectures over his business. He was, I believe, an unofficial liaison officer between G.H.Q., Grand Quartier General and the War Office at Home. Could any job have required tact more than that? But, all the same, he was Lord Kitchener's friend, a staunch supporter of French, and retained his friendly relations with Haig, whilst he was immensely popular with the French authorities.

Hugo came over to discuss the case. He had seen Sir John Cowans, who was of the opinion that Macready was at the bottom of the trouble, and that it paid the others to obey his instructions. I know he was supposed to run the A.G.'s department in France, and to have staffed it with not too scrupulous people to carry out his instructions—" one of Macready's tools " was a common enough expression in France during the war.

As soon as Flavia's treatment was over I took her back to Paris Plage and made arrangements to go over to England myself to see Sir Charles Russell, who was to act for me in the event of my succeeding in getting an inquiry. I cannot speak in sufficient gratitude of the kindness which Sir Charles showed me. He interviewed every sort of official at the War Office, and he helped me to draft a letter to Haig. I think at first he had been inclined to be prejudiced against me, his prejudice went no further than the colour schemes he had seen me in at Boulogne! I confess that in these days of uniforms, that coloured jerseys were inclined to give an impression of frivolity. However, he satisfied himself over my credentials and subjected me to a rigid cross-examination. He had had enough experience during the war to realize the immense difficulty of obtaining justice at the hands of existing officials, so that he gave me little encouragement to hope that we should ever get the inquiry. The better my case, the less likely I was to get satisfaction in that direction. He told me something of how badly Claud Levita had been treated. It had been necessary for Sir Charles to get to Calais, in order to obtain evidence which was to completely exonerate an officer who had been summarily cashiered. Claud Levita's sympathies had been on the side of justice and humanity—two sentiments not appreciated at G.H.Q. The officer was exonerated, but Claud Levita paid the penalty. I must say I should like to have been present at the Levita-Child interview afterwards!

The first of our tactical moves was for Arnold Ward to ask a question in the House of Commons. Mr. Macpherson's reply was to read out a wire from G.H.Q. saying that I had had my inquiry. The local authorities, who had advised me to say nothing at my famous interview with the A.G., were pretty shrewd judges of the methods likely to be employed, as in spite of my precautions, that one-sided interview had, nevertheless, been interpreted into an inquiry. I chaffed Mr. Macpherson about it afterwards, but I realized that he had really no alternative. This lie shattered my last illusion. After all the paraphernalia of prayers, which is the preliminary to the day's business in the House of Commons, I had imagined that lies were not told as glibly there as in the Law Courts. The result of this travesty of truth and justice was to enlist many friends on my side. If there was any truth in the information they had surreptitiously collected, the authorities had nothing to lose by granting the inquiry I was pressing for, and their emphatic refusal was tantamount to admitting that they had no reliable evidence with which to substantiate their accusations.

Undeterred by the failure of our efforts in the House of Commons, the subject was to be brought up in the

Shooting Party at Easton in 1895   [meet King Edward, then Prince of Wales.

House of Lords, and Lord Ribblesdale came to see me about it. He gave all the papers to Lord Buckmaster to read, including Lord Derby's letters, and as I did not know Lord B. his interest in the matter could not be attributed to personal friendship, and the fact that he was willing to support Lord Ribblesdale and Lord Wemyss in the House of Lords was in itself a triumph.

The peaceful tactics which were eventually adopted resulted from an eleventh-hour suggestion from Lord Buckmaster. After carefully considering the matter he came to the conclusion that my accusers would probably be my judges in an inquiry, and his opinion of certain people's sense of justice was not exaggerated ; also the question of finance entered largely into our final decision. Lord B.'s idea was to negotiate with Lord Derby himself, and the result of his intervention was a compromise. Lord Derby was to make a speech, drafted by ourselves, in reply to Lord R. and Lord W., provided that " the noble lords " would in their speeches refrain from attacking the War Office or G.H.Q., either in the House of Lords or in the Press.

What a comic situation for the Secretary of State for War to find himself in !

Lord Derby was in an unenviable position—I had his letters, promising a full investigation into my case, but his subordinates refused me the facilities of even answering the charges !

I have always marvelled at Lord Derby's attitude. Having known him all my life, I should have said unhesitatingly that he stood for a certain type of Englishman, not, perhaps, overburdened with brains, but essentially just. I may have attributed this quality to him, judging too much by his appearance. Bucolic John

Bullness is an excellent shop-window dressing, and is inclined to inspire confidence not usually bestowed on a less rotund figure . . . the goods are not always hall-marked !

Annoyed as I was at not seeing the A. G.'s department exposed in its true colours to the world at large, the two people most disappointed at the peaceful climax were Lord Ribbledsale and Lord Wemyss, who had prepared acrimonious speeches, by which their names were to be handed down to posterity, and to have to change these at the last moment to eulogies of myself was, to say the least, very trying for them !

The disclosures, if there had been an inquiry, would have meant a huge upheaval in the A. G.'s department, and I heard afterwards that a most regrettable individual, whose name I forget but who was one of the pets in the Provost Marshal's office at G.H.Q., had rung up one of the staff at Boulogne to ascertain if there was any chance of my getting the inquiry—" because," he added, " if I did, their jobs were all gone, as they had no evidence against me."

Nothing could have been more flattering or consoling than the crowds of letters which literally poured in on me, both from known and unknown individuals. Indignation at my treatment and thanks for what I had done for them was the keynote of their contents.

The case had been going on from September, 1917, to February, 1918, yet the canteens were still in operation. The workers were like the ten little nigger boys, and they dropped off one by one, and I was, of course, not allowed to replace them. They were not even permitted to go home on leave ; if they went they were not to be allowed to return.

I think this method of retaliating on me was one of the worst, as it reacted directly on the soldiers. The workers behaved heroically in sticking to me, but they were human beings, and they could not work indefinitely without a rest or entirely abandon their home ties. Urgent private affairs compelled some of them to leave ; my manageress at Boulogne was to be married, Miss Marsters had to come home to a dying sister, and so on. As the staff diminished, they were more or less replaced by French girls and orderlies. and at the finish the Big Hut had to go to the wall as the station work could not be neglected.

Having got over this episode of my life, I began to contemplate working for the French. Our own men were, or should have been, amply provided for by this time, and the French *poilu* had none of the luxuries which fell to the lot of the British soldier, so that I looked forward to doing something for them. My two cars were at their disposition, and I received various suggestions and offers of work. Colonel Daru was very anxious that I should go to St. Quentin and help with the *Ravitaillement* of the *Pays Devastés ;* but at that moment, owing to the extension of our line, St. Quentin was under the British régime, so that my appearance there was barred. One rather amusing thing happened directly after my return. I received a visit from our new A.P.M., telling me that he had been instructed to give me a motor pass, apparently from one end of France to the other, for a month. I have never understood why this generous offer was made, but perhaps on the

grounds that, given enough rope, I should hang myself,
and that Satan would surely find some mischief for my
idle self, which would really give the authorities the
right to evict me.   Unfortunately, *homme propose et Dieu
dispose*.   A severe attack of jaundice knocked any hope
I may have entertained of joy rides on the head ; but,
even so, my movements were evidently being watched,
and my maid was stopped in the street to answer inquiries
as to who was staying in my house.   I really might
have been the A.G.'s wife he was trying to get rid of !

After settling up my canteen business, I motored to
Paris to see Colonel Daru, and to find out what he would
like me to do, as the St. Quentin idea could not materialize.
I felt so desperately ill on arriving in Paris, that Vera
Bate insisted on my going to bed and sent a doctor to
see me.   He was Clemenceau's doctor and most interesting to talk to, but I should have enjoyed his conversation
more if I had not been so completely *souffrante*.   He was
very full of King Edward's wisdom and foresight, and
looked on him as a great diplomat and as the saviour of
France, owing to the Entente ; but, he added, " il a
sauvé l'Angleterre aussi."   Without the Entente, he
insisted, the Germans would have destroyed first France,
then England.   I did not like his tisanes, or his medi-
cines, and as I felt no better I determined to struggle back
to Le Touquet to English doctors.

Colonel Barry arrived to see me one morning, full of
a suggestion that I should organize a convoy of cars like
Miss Lowther's for the French Army.   The idea smiled
on me tremendously, as I had had a surfeit of canteen
work.   I wrote to someone I knew in England to see if
any drivers could be collected, and got an answer in the
affirmative, and meanwhile Colonel Barry went on with

the arrangements with the *Service de Santé* in Paris, but for the moment I was helplessly tied to my bed.

Colonel Barry was one of the great personalities at the Base, surrounded by a halo of mystery. He had gone out with Mr. Kemp in the first week of the war, and between them they had organized the Anglo-American Ambulance Section. He was attached, according to how it suited him, in turn, to the British or French Army, and on occasions to the Red Cross, but, generally speaking, he was his own master. He was a colossal opportunist, and his life was led according to his own rules and regulations. One minute he was in the trenches, the next at G.H.Q. Another day found him dining at the French G.Q.G., and the following evening he would be entertaining an important magnate in Paris. He led Denys Baily by a string, twisted Paget round his little finger, and spoilt my children with presents in the intervals! He was incessantly on the road, and he would call on us at the most unexpected hours.

I had plenty of other visitors in those days, having abandoned any vanity I may have had, and quite ignoring my orange face, I welcomed them gladly

Vi de Trafford had just arrived and joined the V.A.D.'s who were working at the Westminster Hospital. I was very surprised that the Frenchmen didn't rave about her looks, for she is so very lovely. But they didn't, and they thought Olivia Wyndham, who was another new arrival, better looking.

I was just beginning to feel alive again (never more will I laugh at anyone with jaundice), when the Household Cavalry arrived at Camiers, to be trained as machine-gunners. They were all old friends, and, much to the delight of the children, spent most of their spare time at Paris Plage. Archie Carlton was just going back to be married, but of Ali, alas ! we saw next to nothing, as he was " courting," and his marriage to Mrs. Leischmann took place about this time at Boulogne.   They were all very good about coming to see me and bringing me the news.   Count d'Aramon, who was interpreter to the 2nd Life Guards, was a particularly regular visitor. He was always entertaining, talked English perfectly, and had a surprising fund of good stories.   He took a gloomy view of the situation, and told me that though they had been for months up at St. Quentin digging, the trenches they had dug were useless.   He had taken Colonel Stanley over to the adjoining French lines and pointed out to him the difference in their preparations ; but, after all, it was General Gough's look-out, or someone above him.   They seemed to have had plenty of horse-shows up there, anyhow.   Count d'Aramon's anticipation of the Germans attacking there, and the result, was justified by the events that followed.

*   ᵣ   ✦   ✦

The news of the great German attack burst with surprising suddenness, in spite of the fact that it happened on the very day that it had been prognosticated.

The cavalry were hurried back to the line at a moment's notice.   I groaned at my forced inactivity and looked impatiently for the news that used to be brought to me in the evening by one or another.

For the first time there was real consternation amongst the inhabitants of Paris Plage.   A great number of the population were refugees from Belgium. They had seen the Boche once, and that had been enough for them,

so they packed their *baluchons* and were prepared to
" trek " once more. I was left with only my maid in
the way of servants. Her husband, an Alsatian, was
missing since 1914, but she had a fixed idea that he was
still alive, and nothing would have moved her from Paris
Plage, as she expected him to turn up there one day.

The wildest rumours came through the postman and
the baker, and still the Germans seemed coming on.
The camp, they told me, was literally thick with men
who had lost their units in the wild retreat. Would the
Germans reach Amiens ? The worst was anticipated
by the inhabitants when the tocsin sounded for all the
boys of the next year's class to report at Boulogne.
And there was I, still in bed ! It was some comfort to
hear of the German losses being so severe that they
lay in heaps against the wire entanglements, so that the
men had to climb on these masses of dead bodies to cut
their way through the wire.

As the refugees left Paris Plage, others who had
fled from Amiens came in. Our French mademoiselle
and Flavia were in Etaples when mademoiselle fell
into the arms of her sister, who at first she failed to
recognize. Her three children were with her. The
bombardment of Amiens had been too much for them.
They had been living in a cellar and their house was
the only one in the street that had remained untouched.
Having been unable to stand the strain any longer,
they had joined in the general exodus. They were
clotheless and penniless and in an altogether pitiable
condition, having walked the entire distance, sleeping
by the roadside, and their description of their journey
was pathetic. They had been swept along by the crowd
on the road, and one of the boys, who had brought a

change of shoes and slung them on his back, had had them cut off, without even detecting the robbery. The things some of these wretched people had tried to save was too quaint. Imagine fleeing from the Germans and insisting on carrying a canary with you! An extra panic had been created in Amiens by crowds of unarmed men in khaki rushing back into the town. The inhabitants thought that the whole British army had run away—whilst really they were Lord Portsmouth's land army, who had been peacefully tilling the fields, but who had hurriedly thrown down their spades when the shells came too near to them!

The confusion that reigned in the camp at Etaples after the practical annihilation of the Fifth Army was stupendous. Thousands poured in, trying to get news of their units ; all traces of them had disappeared amidst the chaos. The huge accommodation resources of the camp were taxed almost beyond their limit, even though the reinforcements were being poured out daily.

The hospitals were crowded, but only the worst cases were kept, and the rest hurried over to England to make room for fresh casualties.

Two days after the Fifth Army retreat, General Gough appeared, to visit the patients at the Westminster. Contrary to expectations he seemed to be in the most cheerful frame of mind, and it did not tend to soften the criticisms levelled at him by those who had been in the Fifth Army when they heard him announcing that Haig had given him another job. The general feeling was that he should have gone home after Passchendaele, and there was also a feeling, right or wrong, that he owed his later command to his old friendship with Haig.

The historical meeting at Abbeville, six days after the Germans had broken through, altered the destiny of the world. The quick appointment of Foch as Generalissimo of the Allied Armies was the best news that we could have hoped for. It meant concentration of power and responsibility, the one thing which had been so sadly lacking and which had not been arrived at during the deliberations of the Supreme Council. The tangled web of affairs was hurled at Foch only when its unravelling appeared quite impracticable. The generals in the field welcomed the change of régime unanimously, and it was only the G.H.Q. staff officers who had anything to say against it, as they automatically lost some of their prestige and importance.

Would Haig be sent home now ? The question was on every lip, but Colonel Repington's description of him : " Haig has become a Post Office," obviously made his return unnecessary. There had been enough accusations and scandals, so he was left to enjoy his peerage and pension, from a grateful but impoverished country.

But this was not the only change. Lord Derby was our new Ambassador in Paris. The *Morning Post* was not altogether polite in its comments on the appointment, but though I had no reason to love Lord Derby I confess that no one could have made a greater success, than he apparently did, of his ambassadorial duties. That bluff good temper and apparent honesty carried him far. His popularity was in some measure due to the great desire on the part of the French for a still firmer alliance with England. By making a social pet of Lord D., they relied on his carrying a pleasant, and flattering recollection of his sojourn among them, and thus securing his good offices, should the Entente be ever on the brink of a crisis.

The appointment of Lord Milner as Lord D.'s successor to the War Office received universal approbation.

＊　　　．　　　＊　　　ı　　　＊　　　－

Amiens was saved ! The news seemed almost too good to be true. " Le rétablissement de Foch " is now an historical phrase. The chaos and disorder of the retreat must surely pass imagination. Whole depots of stores and war materials were profligately abandoned. A few venturesome individuals did some good salvage work, and one man took a lorry into Albert, which was quite deserted, and rescued thousands of pounds worth of supplies. Rather than allow the Germans to enjoy the luxury of the canteens, pathetic destruction was the order of the day. Whisky and champagne flowed like water, and Corona cigars were to be had for the mere picking up !

With the check of the Boche advance the Household Cavalry returned to us once more. They were to be hurried through their course of machine gunnery at Camiers as quickly as possible. I was slowly recovering from my jaundice, but still felt horribly weak, and it was even an effort to stroll down to the tennis courts.

That tennis went on in those critical times was a source of surprise, and, I think, considerable annoyance to the French ; they had always looked rather askance at the golfers, and tennis players. The number of men employed at the base by us seemed to the French almost preposterous. They ran their offices with the barest minimum, and were inclined to think that a few of our men at the base could quite well have been spared to go

Lady Angela Forbes and her daughter Flavia.

up the line. And when they saw them indulging freely in *le sport* they redoubled their criticism !

The behaviour of the French nation during the war has been a distinct contradiction of what the Englishman has been led to expect from the excitable French temperament. Their misfortunes were accepted in a perfectly heroic spirit and one can have nothing but admiration for their calmness in the face of every danger and trouble. In the bigger love for their country, the pleasure-loving side of their nature seemed to vanish. One thing that shocked them tremendously was the number of our war widows who had remarried so quickly. A Frenchwoman told me that she did not know a single French war widow, however unhappy her married life had been, who had remarried. If they had, she said, they would be looked on askance and their social ostracism would be greater than if they had been through the divorce court. This feeling, I think, is inspired by respect for the dead and especially for the death they died.

Marigold's engagement to Sir Archibald Sinclair distracted our attention for the moment from the military situation. We had only known him a few weeks, but I liked him immensely, and thought him decidedly clever, but I had my doubts as to whether he was as Socialistic as he was supposed to be. Anyhow, he talked of his vast possessions in Caithness with real pride and affection.

He was going in for politics after the war, and I was particularly pleased that Marigold should marry a man with a probable career ahead of him. I think she will be interested in the serious side of life by and by.

She is thoroughly industrious, so he ought to find her the right sort of wife, and, as far as one dare predict, their future should be rosy.

The engagement meant another visit for me to England, as, Marigold being a ward in Chancery, and not yet twenty-one, there were various formalities to be hurried through, if they were to be married immediately. I returned with the ring in my pocket and a wedding frock for M. the night before the wedding. The children and Archie met me in Boulogne and we all dined at Mony's with Eden Paget.

The civil service at the Consulate had to take place at 8 a.m. and I motored " the family " back to Le Touquet, and dropped Archie on the way at Camiers, as he was to do a day's duty before the Church service, which was to be in the afternoon at Le Touquet. It was really a most charming wedding, and a great relief from the usual London set-out. Much of its success was due to Lord De Vesci, who had taken infinite pains over the flowers, and the hymns, during my absence in England, and whether he or Marigold remembered the champagne I don't know, but I found it there awaiting us !

The little church was packed with V.A.D.'s, and all our local celebrities, and afterwards the happy couple departed for Hardelot for their honeymoon.

It was the following day that we had the big raid on Etaples. We had just come back from dining at Camiers, and were in the drawing-room when it started. Our original idea had been to dine at the Pré Catalan at Hardelot, but General Mullins had been to tea, and we were so late starting that we had altered our plan and stopped half-way, otherwise we should still have been on the road, in the middle of our own gun-fire, and in the very thick of the bombs.

At first we did not realize it was a raid. We knew that an attack was due to begin the next morning, and when we heard the first boom of the guns, Lord De Vesci, who was with us, thought it was beginning earlier than expected. We could often hear the guns quite plainly at Paris Plage.

It was not long, however, before we realized what was happening, and we all rushed out to see what we could. Whrr! Whrr! Bang! Boom! the areoplanes, our defence guns and the bursting bombs kept up a crashing noise, with a moment of silence, as the evil bird got out of gunshot. Another, then another; there seemed to be a never-ending procession passing over us. There was a mound behind our house, and on to this Major Dormer and I climbed and watched the bursting bombs. It was the first raid I had ever seen, not counting two in London, which seemed to me very dull. The enemy's objective was the Bridge of Etaples, about three miles from our house. We had always wondered why they had not attempted to get it before now, as every day we had an enemy plane over our village, evidently taking photographs.

The night was perfectly clear, and we could almost have spoken to the pilot as he flew almost directly over my house. I was really enjoying the sight from a spectacular point of view, so that any idea of danger did not cross my mind, until I suddenly remembered that Flavia was in the garden.

I then lost my nerve entirely and could not make up my mind where to deposit her in safety. Really I think we were just as safe outside, if not safer. My opinion may have been the result of a guilty conscience, for I knew that in the basement there were stored gallons of petrol acquired by a perfectly illegitimate method !

For hours the aeroplanes seemed whirling and whizzing with their relentless noise, the whole sky lit up as the bombs burst, which to our minds appeared almost within a stone's throw. The houses shook, the pictures came off the walls in my house, whilst our anti-aircraft guns responded with their deafening barrage. Then suddenly the noise was redoubled. It appeared that one of the invaders had lost his way and was ridding himself of his bombs as quickly as possible, regardless of their destination.

The fact that they were dropping in sand made the damage less formidable than it might have been. As it was the Duchess of Westminster was nearly thrown out of bed with the bombs falling near her chalet. A splinter from one of our own shells landed in a V.A.D.'s room at the Hôtel des Anglais, and a few bombs fell round the Atlantic Hotel, but otherwise the damage was more or less confined to Etaples. Here the inhabitants were having a taste of war to its full, shattered houses, broken windows, and shell holes testified to the night's work. Some of the 2nd Life Guards who had only arrived the night before and were encamped on the Camiers road were badly knocked about, and the Base Details whose camp was on the outskirts of the town unfortunately took to their heels for safety. The Boche could see them quite plainly by the light of the moon, and his bombs were, alas ! dropped with such accuracy as to make a big gap in the ranks of these poor wretches.

Outside the little café where I had many meals there

was a huge shell hole. The windows had been smashed to smithers, but the undaunted *patronne* announced " business as usual," and supplied us with out-of-season strawberries and asparagus. *Il faut être chic sous un bombardement,* was her contention. Her attitude was superb. She could not sleep in Etaples as was her wont, as the ceiling of her house had given way, so when she had finished her evening's work she either drove or tramped to Paris Plage to sleep.

The entire population of Etaples took to sleeping on the sands in these days, as the cellar for safety had been proved bad advice. Nearly all the casualties happened through taking cover in this way. My housemaid's entire family had been done in, the only survivor was the grandmother, who had temporarily left the cellar to fetch a shawl. At Boulogne Colonel Wilberforce and the staff had had a narrow squeak, and old Marie, who had supplied me with the tons of fruit and vegetables we used in the canteen, had lost her grandchild. The poor old thing was distraught with her grief. She shook the body to and fro, not believing that the child was dead. We had lived in such serene security in our little backwater that the possibility of these horrors happening under our eyes had not been contemplated.

The V.A.D.'s of the Etaples Convoy were out all night gallantly doing rescue work, one of them having to go to Trepied to pick up the pilot of a machine which had been brought down there. They deserve the highest credit for their calmness, and there was not a case of panic amongst them.

The questions in the House of Commons, and the comments in the papers, about the " outrageous and barbarous attacks on the hospitals " showed the

profound ignorance of the questioners, and the corre-
spondents. If anyone is to blame it is our own authorities, who had mingled hospitals, ammunition dumps,
and stores with one of the biggest reinforcement camps
in France, in close proximity to a main line bridge, which
was of strategical importance to the enemy. Practically
the whole road from Boulogne to Etaples was by that
time a long succession of buildings, connected in some
way or another with the active fighting forces, and our
ammunition dump at Camiers is still not disintegrated !

Everyone knows that an airman cannot drop his bomb
on a definite spot, so how can he be blamed for doing
damage even some miles from his objective ? Added
to that the German airmen had previously dropped
leaflets advising us to remove our wounded and giving
us adequate warning of the intended raid.

These unfounded allegations of barbarity did a lot
of harm. The German crimes were so atrocious that
they needed no fictitious additions to arouse further
indignation, but the large population at Etaples, who
read these inaccurate indictments, were inclined to
wonder if German brutality had not been exaggerated
on other occasions.

Colonel Barry had made all the necessary arrangements with the authorities in Paris for the convoy of
ambulances, and a very nice French officer came to my
villa to explain my duties to me. I was to be under the
orders of a French Capitaine, and the convoy was to work
in sections conveying the wounded to the various
hospitals. The district extended over a pretty large
area between Paris, and Rouen.

I was not sorry to get Flavia away from Etaples. In
spite of the damage done in the air-raid, the main line

bridge was still untouched, and till they had succeeded in getting it, further visits from the enemy might be looked forward to with some certainty.

My drivers were due in Paris any day, so Flavia and I started off in the car to meet them. We lunched at Beauvais and all along the road traces of the recent activity of the German airmen were apparent Abbeville had been badly knocked about, and General Asser's headquarters looked in a most battered condition and wanton damage confronted one in almost every village.

We inspected the convoy and I rather liked my proposed headquarters, and the French authorities all seemed very pleasant people.

The military situation was as grave as it ever had been. The Government did not go to Bordeaux, but all the gold reserves at the banks were sent to the South of France and the pictures from the Louvre were equally removed to safety. Profiteering in packing-cases was at its height, and unless you were a friend of a railway official trucks for private use were quite unobtainable. Places on the train were not to be thought of. No one admitted that the military situation had anything to do with the general exodus, but everyone seemed to be taking their holiday very early.

The German onslaught was being redoubled in intensity and attacks were being launched all along the line. The task given to Foch seemed almost impossible of accomplishment and the anti-allied command party were almost in a position to say : " I told you so." It was only on August 8th that the result of Foch's strategy produced definite results. On that day the French and English forces attacked with a new and brilliant vigour on the Amiens front and set the seal on Foch's reputa-

tion.   From Amiens to Montdidier all the troops were
engaged.   General Mullins' division was the first to go
through the famous gap of which we had heard so much,
and which we had begun to regard as a complete myth.
The 5th D. G.'s had an amusing experience with a
German train that was bringing their men back from
Lille.   The unsuspecting Germans were all in their
compartments, expecting to find their comrades where
they had last left them.   To their horror the English
were in occupation and the whole trainload were taken
prisoners.

The 8th of August may truly be looked on as the
definite turning-point in the fortunes of our armies.
If anyone had been in doubt of the ultimate result óf the
war their scepticism had no longer any foundation to
rest on.   From that moment the Boche was on the run,
and Foch was not the man to lose the advantage he had
secured.

                *   ⊤   ⊤   ⊤   *

Instead of finding my drivers in Paris I received a
wire that their permits had been refused by the
authorities in London.

This was an extraordinary *impasse* to be in ! Some
objections had been previously raised on the grounds
that no more women could be spared out of England as
they were all needed by the Government organizations,
but I knew that this objection had been overruled by
Lord Milner who had himself signed a letter asking that
permits should be given to them.

Now it appeared that it was the French Red Cross in
London who refused to deliver them.   On the face of it

this was absurd as they were coming on to work for the
French.   I felt instinctively that there was something
at the back of all this, but it seemed difficult to fathom,
more especially as I had seen all the officials in Paris,
and that I knew the cars were ready and waiting and
were urgently needed.   My suspicions were confirmed
after a visit to the French War Office.   I saw an important person there and I was given a *sauf conduit*
to England with a request that *I might return with my
drivers as quickly as possible*.   All this took several days,
during which time we had a raid every night, though
nothing like so bad as the one at Etaples.   The Meurice
was a very nice safe place to be in.   The first night Flavia
and I joined the rest of the visitors on the first floor
and found ourselves in the middle of what resembled a
fancy dress gathering, so varied were the costumes,
which included Signor Orlando, the Italian Prime
Minister.   Even in these safe quarters some of the people
were terrified.   I went into the Rue de Rivoli to see the
barrage—a really pretty sight, but after that night we
refused to be roused.

What did make us rather jumpy was Big Bertha,
who had made her first appearance about then.   Suddenly her big boom would be heard, with no indication
of where it had come from or where she had landed
her deadly missile.   The damage she did was trifling,
but she made me jump as I was driving into Paris, and
again when we were dining at Henry's and she hit one
of the figures on the Madeleine, and shook the restaurant
like a cardboard house.

There were several Americans in the Hôtel Meurice.
The American troops had been in action for the first
time, and everyone spoke highly of their courage.   They

were as keen as the Australians, and resented every moment that kept them from attacking. They would, no doubt, be sobered by experience. Paris itself was full. All the politicians were over there, Lloyd George, Lord Milner, Rosie Wemyss and " Sir Eric," enjoying themselves, when the business of the day was over

Armed with my letter from the French War Office, Flavia and I returned to Boulogne. I had decided to take her back to England, as it seemed a wiser course to adopt with these air raids going on nightly.

I imagined that I should meet with no difficulty in getting across, having the *sauf conduit* from the French War Office, but this was not so. The A.P.M. did all he could, but he was not allowed to help me. I could go to England, but I could not get back ! Meanwhile the French were waiting for me in Paris.

I went to Montreuil myself, and saw the French Head of the Permit Department, and then I found out how this latest impertinence had been worked. The official I saw, and the official who gave the visas in London were brothers. I think their names were Weiss, or something like it, and they were working obviously in conjunction—I wonder under whose orders ! This was entirely against Lord Derby's word, and his speech in the House of Lords, but it was easy for the English officials now to put the blame on the French. I could not move Mr. W. at Montreuil, who was rather non-plussed as to how I got to see him at all !

My next step was to write to Mr. Macpherson, then Under Secretary at the War Office. I was really anxious now about Flavia, and wanted to get her on to the other side, but I could not agree to the visa offered me, as I had a house in France and all my belongings were

in it. I found Lancelot Lowther was King's Messenger
that day, and I asked him to take the letter. He took
himself and his duties very seriously, and was very
pompous about the rule that did not allow King's
Messengers to take private individual's letters. I explained that I thought he would not get into trouble
over mine as it was to the War Office. As he still demurred I took it up to General Wilberforce, who most
kindly had it specially despatched.

There was nothing more to be done, but to sit still
and wait. Flavia and I were sharing a room at the
" Meurice " at Boulogne when we were woken by
tramping male footsteps, and a knocking at the door.
This was a visit from the Intelligence Officer, the A.P.M.
and Eden Paget.

Mr. Macpherson with the greatest promptitude had
wired to Major Comber to let me return at once. He
had come to see me to say that to save time he would
arrange for us to go back on the leave boat in the morning. His own office would be open extra early, and he
would have my passport stamped, and in order for me.
This was most awfully kind of him, as, in the ordinary
way, it would have taken some time. They were as
pleased as I was at G.H.Q. having been scored off, and
that I should be in England before G.H.Q. even heard of
my having left Boulogne. This is testimony of the feeling
that existed regarding G.H.Q. at the Base. All went well
according to schedule—the boat was held up for ten
minutes whilst we got on board. We exploded a mine
on our way over, and it made such a noise and shook
the boat so much that I thought we had actually struck
one, and I couldn't help thinking at the time that it
would have been a queer fate if, after all the trouble

that Major Comber had taken over my journey, it had
proved to be my last.

I went round to the War Office and saw Mr. Macpherson ; Macready came into the room and hurried
out. · I suppose he knew me, but I had never seen him
before to my knowledge. Mr. Macpherson assured me
that Macready had given his sanction at the Army
Council Meeting for my drivers to be given permits.
I suggested he had done it with his tongue in his cheek,
and told him about the Brothers Weiss. There was,
of course, nothing left for anyone to do as long as the
onus for the refusal of the permits was laid on the French.
G.H.Q. had certainly scored off me this time !

The drivers were, meanwhile, thoroughly exasperated
by the numerous delays, and one by one they were
dropping off into other jobs, so regretfully I abandoned
the whole scheme. I did not feel in a fighting humour,
and it was really not the moment to dwell on one's own
personal grievances.

I liked Mr. Macpherson immensely, and behind the
big, horn-rimmed spectacles he wore, there lurked a
humorous twinkle. I felt thoroughly ashamed of taking
up his time—I had taken up the time of so many important people when there were so many far more
important matters for them to attend to, that I felt it
incumbent upon me to apologize ! I did not know until
later that Mr. Macpherson had offered to go to Boulogne
to inquire into my case, but, of course, this was not
allowed as it would not have suited the A.G.'s book
at all !

I had no very definite plans at this moment, but
I had left my house on the other side in such disorder
when I made my hurried departure, that I felt it was

necessary at all events to go over and see what was happening. When I arrived at the permit office for my passport to be viséd, I found that G.H.Q. had just telephoned, giving an order that I was not to return to France. This was one of the most stupid things they could have done, as they had no jurisdiction over my movements as a civilian, and could not enforce their order.

Once more I had to make myself an official nuisance ; this time Mr. Balfour was brought in, with perfectly satisfactory results. What idiots those officials at G.H.Q. must have felt as I made another triumphant entry into Boulogne !

Life *en civile* in France was inconceivably dull, so that I quickly made up my mind to go home for good, and escape for ever from the red tape that was tying everyone up in knots.

VIII

BY the time I was settled again in England the end of
the war was in sight, and the prospect of another
winter's fighting seemed more than doubtful.

I felt the reaction of inactivity and chafed at the
lack of any definite occupation. All one's old interests
seemed rather futile, and the daily round desperately
boring. Life in England appeared very little changed,
except for the rather irksome restrictions and minor
discomforts imposed by the Food and Coal Controllers,
but even these were negligible, and there was no very
apparent sign of shortage. People had got used to
parlourmaids, and in some cases even preferred them.
Hotels were full, and if the clientèle had changed somewhat the proprietors certainly raised no objection!

The Wilson Commandments—fourteen of them when
God had condensed His into ten—had reached us.
They seemed to the lay mind singularly lenient, and
one wondered if the enemy might not, after all, be too
lightly treated, but one rested safe in the knowledge
that Clemenceau possessed a retentive memory!

In the light of after events there is something
grotesquely humorous in the important part which
America played in dictating the peace terms, when
she herself had no intention of signing the Treaty.
Small wonder that the French are resentful!

War work of one sort or another was still in progress —from nursing the wounded to providing them with recreations, and George Robey was still adding to the thousands he had already collected.

One of the best individual enterprises, the Surgical Requisites, had their depot opposite to me in Mulberry Walk, and Flavia used to go there every day for a time. Whoever started it deserves the greatest praise, not only for its organization, but for the ingenuity of its devices in *papier mâché*. What a relief to the men having an alternative to those desperately heavy limbs provided by the Government.

I was some time debating in my mind how best to employ the profits from my canteens. After a general settlement in France, I had approximately three thousand pounds left, and I was anxious to devise some scheme that I hoped would prove a more or less lasting memorial to the buffets.

The back to the land doctrine was being preached and was catching on among the soldiers. So many had left their office chairs, they hoped for ever. For the first time they had tasted the open-air life, and, in spite of its hardships, they had been able to appreciate its joys. To help those who wanted permanently to establish themselves in a new life, seemed the best channel through which I could employ the Buffet profits.

There was something amusing about the aloofness of my funds. In the early days I had written to the Army Council, suggesting that they should be paid to them as they accrued, but the Council declined my offer on the grounds that they had no machinery to deal with the matter, but they were devising some scheme by which all canteen profits were to be assimilated. I suppose, however, that this scheme never materialized, for I heard nothing more on the subject.

The bulk of my profits had been distributed at different times as need arose. The mine sweepers at Aberdeen, the Red Cross, as well as private individuals, had all benefited, and a very large proportion had been spent on providing huts for the training ground, and all our other buildings and extensions. To spend the balance on practical training for the men who were going to sheathe the sword, and hoped to wield the sickle, seemed a suitable solution. .

I accordingly interviewed Sir Arthur Boscawen, who was then at the Ministry of Pensions, and found him very charming and unexpectedly responsive. The Government, it seems, were already evolving training schemes, but they were apparently quite grateful for individual, auxiliary help. I found what I thought an ideal place at Brentwood, where there was scope for training in the various branches of agriculture. It belonged to Miss Willmott, who when I saw her was full of enthusiasm over the idea.

Putting the scheme into execution was not quite so simple as it first appeared, and there were the usual A.B.C. departments to be consulted; the County Committees and the various directors of training to be interviewed, and it was Christmas before the first man arrived.

The responsibility of paying the men the allowances, which they received during training, rested on my shoulders. It was a burden which I took on lightly, imagining that I should receive the money punctually, and in correct amounts, but I do not think this ever happened

Wemyss Castle.

[*Facing p.* 304

until the last week I was at Brentwood! There was either a credit or a debit balance each week, entailing the most tiresome amount of mathematical calculation, and in many cases I had to advance men their money in order to enable their wives to live whilst officialdom was floundering in centralization!

The local Pensions Office was most kind and helpful. Mr. Dalton, who had given his services voluntarily, all through the war, as secretary, had, more often than not, found himself in similar difficulties, owing to the negligence or pomposity of the County Director, and Sergeant-Major Price, an ex-Guardsman, and Mr Dalton's second in command, was for ever breaking rules to meet the necessitous cases.

I thought the allowances for the men very good, but the channels, through which they received them, singularly dilatory, and it is small wonder that muddles and complaints were multiplied again, and again.

Gradually all local authority was being taken and vested in a county office, supervised by a well-paid official, generally distinguished by an entire lack of any imagination. It seemed the height of absurdity that before a man could be buried or have a tooth out, official sanction had first to be obtained by the local authority, from an office many miles away.

Our curriculum included market-gardening, general farm work, dairy, poultry-keeping and carpentering; and I had from twenty to twenty-five trainees. Most of the men hailed from London and knew nothing of country life and its pursuits. Their disabilities were varied, and in most cases their ideas for their ultimate future were nebulous. I generally tried to discover what they expected to do after their training, and found them

20

in some cases most ambitious, and in complete
ignorance of the qualifications required, to gratify their
aspirations. One man, who had never been in the country
before, told me he wished to be a bailiff when he left!
Most of the men had leanings towards complete independence. "Starting on our own" seemed to them the
simplest thing in the world. It was an idea that had been
fostered by the dream pictures held out in the poultry
papers advertisements—"a thousand pounds a year
from three hens" or some such catch phrase. The
question of capital seemed to them entirely superfluous,
and the grant from the King's Fund was apparently
their ideal.

One boy had turned out so satisfactorily, that, if all
the others had been failures, his success would have
compensated me. He did not come through any official
channel, but arrived one day and asked if I could train
him in poultry-keeping. I told him that all the other
men had Government allowances, but that if he cared to
come, we would board and lodge him free, and help him
to a job. He jumped at the offer and I then suggested
that he might like to take up dairy work. He at once
fell in with the idea and showed so much ability that Mr.
Wilson of the East Anglian Agricultural College took him.
He passed his course most brilliantly and is now on a large
cheese farm, and with an assured future ahead of him.

The men's politics and their opinions on current
events were freely aired. While some of them were
apathetic, the majority held advanced views. Their
belief in Trades Unionism had not yet been shaken,
that was to come later—when they found the unions
barring the doors of their profession to the men who had
fought to preserve their trade.

Some of their views were sound, while some of their opinions, on the other hand, were hopelessly fantastic. Unfortunately, they were convinced that their wildest notions were based on solid foundations. Nearly all the men that first came to me were members of the Soldiers and Sailors Federation, and they at once set about forming a local branch. I went to several of their meetings and entertained some of their leaders to tea. They certainly had some very good speakers among them, and to me they seemed to adhere to an attitude of complete political independence. They were very much against the Comrades of the Great War, whom they declared had the support of the Government for political reasons and were making an attempt to counteract the strength of the Federation.

One of my trainees was an ardent believer in the nationalization of everything and everybody. His father had been secretary to Frank Hodges, whilst Mr. Smillie was a familiar friend, and it was through him that I heard the story of Mr. Smillie's early life.

I had Mr. S.'s views and reasons for nationalization carefully explained to me. I found them difficult to combat, and could only suggest that the Government made a muddle of most things they ran ! They admitted that the advantage would not be felt immediately, but that the next generation would be relieved from the burden of taxation, direct or indirect.

Quite frankly, one cannot help seeing their point of view. Their idea is that their children shall not be brought up under the same conditions as those in which they themselves were reared. The industrial unrest is surely the sins of the fathers. If wage-sweating had not been in existence there might have been no wage war,

20*

and one cannot expect men to rest satisfied under the old-fashioned régime in a world. bristling with new ideas and ambitions.

When one thinks of the agricultural wage paid by our grandfathers, even our fathers, and tries to imagine life for a man and a family brought up on eighteen shillings a week, one wonders, sometimes, that class resentment is not more accentuated.

This is not a dissertation on economics, it may even be that there is no room for a new scheme of things and that the new order will not lead to greater happiness than the old. But what sounds like a revolutionary idea, is often a genuine belief on the part of the men that they are advancing towards a goal which may, after all, only benefit the next generation.

*   *   *

On the 11th of November 1918, the guns had ceased firing. I had gone up to London for the night, so I came in for all the mad mafficking of Armistice Day. The reserved English people have a queer way of expressing themselves on occasions. There was something nauseating about the horseplay; something rather pathetic in the ebullition of joy which found its expression in breaking the windows or the springs of a taxi-cab, and blowing bladders in people's faces! My own impression was one of marvel that anything so awful, that had lasted so long, could end so suddenly at a given moment. It took one back to the Creation.

I went to Paris for the Peace Celebrations. The quatorze Juilliet is the symbol of freedom—even if only fancied—of every Frenchman, and the rejoicings were fixed for that day. I stayed with the Barrys, which was lucky, as the hotels were crammed. I had an excellent view of the procession from the Champs-Elysée and could see the whole route from the Arc de Triomphe to the Place de la Concorde.

The crowds were dense, one solid mass of humanity reaching from the houses to the trees. From every corner of France, widows, bereaved mothers and fiancées, had gathered together to pay tribute to the allies. The President and Clemenceau drove up to the Arc in closed carriages, but they were recognized by the waiting crowd and a loud cheer broke the tense silence all along the line. Then all was still until a fresh outburst of enthusiasm, like rumbling thunder, announced that the first troops had passed under the famous arch. The chains which protect the majesty of the Arc had never been removed since 1860, when the troops, fresh from victory after the Italian campaign, passed through. The Germans had walked on either side of it in 1871, but to-day, which is to signalize the freedom of the world, there is no obstacle to hinder the direct progress of the conquerors. Every allied nation was represented, every regiment of France sent its detachment, from the little Chasseurs Alpins to the grim and romantic Légion Etrangère— picked men, who walked proudly behind the tattered flag they had so gallantly defended.

As each man passed through the Arc he reverently saluted the monument to the dead.

The procession was led by the Americans in their immaculate uniforms and with their brand new colours in striking contrast to the faded flags which followed in their wake.

The Guards and the Highlanders met with a deafening

welcome. It seemed impossible that there could be another cheer left—but as the French troops appeared slowly and majestically in their war worn tunics, these sons of France, marching along the Champs-Elysée, evoked a fresh burst of enthusiasm.

The crowd seemed to know every general by name. Le Petit Mangin, severe, alert and energetic, Gouraud, with the empty sleeve, still saluting gravely, Le Père Fayolle, as he was familiarly known by his men, Castelnau, a veteran of 1870, who had lost three sons in the war, were all acclaimed by name. As Pétain passed, cries of Verdun and *on les aura* were literally yelled. In spite of the enthusiasm it was no light-hearted rejoicing—the spirit of the day seemed embodied in that waiting multitude. They were imbued, one felt, with reverence and gratitude, sorrow mingled with rejoicing.

The masters of victory were there with one exception. Where was Lord French ? It was a question one heard on all sides, for the French people have good memories. Foch was a dignified example to some, as he passed on his favourite white charger, and with only two generals on his staff. He looked neither to the right nor to the left as he saluted. One felt a little sadly about Joffre riding behind, but his heart must have rejoiced at the special ovation he received—and after all it is never Moses who enters triumphantly into the Promised Land.

The Peace rejoicings were carried on at night—and the same spirit, that one admired in the morning, held the crowd that thronged Paris. I was lost for an hour in that surging mass that marched, in self-arrayed order, up and down the Champs-Elysée. Once with them one was swept by them, but with no sense of discomfort, no sign of panic or of rowdiness.

The fireworks were quite wonderful. All the monuments, private houses and buildings were lit up, and the bridges spanning the Seine made Paris, old and new, into a glowing fairyland. For the first time since the war the restaurants were kept open all night. At Montmartre the fun was stupendous, but even here no sign of rowdiness or drunkenness was to be seen. Sir John Cowans was one of the many who found their way there in the small hours of the morning, and rode gaily on a wooden pig, and spent many sous on the switchback railway. For one day at all events class distinction—even family quarrels—were forgotten. A Frenchman so well described it to me " *Nous sommes tous sur le même bateau, et nos cœurs ne fond qu'un.*" They were all brothers that day who had fought for the same cause, with the same courage.

The best laid schemes go wrong. I had, very stupidly, taken possession of Miss Willmott's house before the lease was signed, at her urgent request, and backed by her promises of assistance. I had, unfortunately, not been warned of her idiosyncrasies until I was established there, and no sooner was I installed than fresh clauses were drafted, and impossible stipulations laid down. As a result the negotiations completely broke down, and at the end of a year I moved.

The Government scheme of training had been trans ferred from the Ministry of Pensions, and was in future to be under the Ministry of Labour and the Board of Agriculture. A representative from the Board came and inspected me, and apparently approved of the Centre,

so, in the circumstances, it seemed worth while looking
out for another place where I could carry on.   There was
nothing to be found at the time in the neighbourhood,
but a representative from the Ministry saw and " passed "
a place I had selected in Sussex.   Most of the men had
finished their training, but the few left were to be transferred as soon as possible.

The Railway strike developed as soon as I was in
the throes of moving.   Some of my goods were already
on the train, but the date of their arrival seemed more
than problematical.   I spent my own time during this
short upheaval by driving my car for the Great Eastern
Railway.   I felt full of importance carrying despatches
between Liverpool Street and Cambridge, and various
other stations.   I met with no untoward mishap, but
with the cussedness of Fate my lighting set was in a
rather dicky condition, and on one of my trips, struck
work altogether.   Luckily, the last faint glimmer subsided in a village where I was able to buy a bicycle lamp,
but I finished my journey, illuminated by imagination,
rather than by the light it shed !   The motor lorries
with the food supplies kept to their own side of the
road, which made things much easier for me.

Sir Henry Thornton, the managing director, asked to
see me when it was all over.   He was a very charming
man and seemed to know all about my work in France,
and I was much touched later at receiving a gold pencil
case from him, as a souvenir of my despatch drives !   I
don't think that he anticipated that the Railway strike
settlement was going to be conducive to a permanent
industrial peace.

The move from Essex to Sussex entailed more than the mere uprooting of my possessions. My funds were more or less depleted and a year's farming wasted. The only way to solve the financial difficulty was to sell my house in London and make my permanent home at the training centre. The Board of Agriculture had promised me huts for the accommodation of the men, but when it came to getting these it was a most complicated matter, and once more I found eternal officialdom across my path. The huts, though already promised by the Board, had to be applied for through the County Agricultural Executive Committee, and the Board forgot to tell me this until very late in the day! Meanwhile the A.E.C., irate at not having been previously consulted, were most obstructive, and but for the tactful and firm intervention of the Board, would most probably have left me planted with the Training Centre, but with no men, for automatically they were responsible for sending the trainees.

The Board were in a predicament. I had Lord Goschen's letter before he retired from the Board, agreeing to the scheme, and at the same time they were anxious to avoid issuing a direct order to the County Committee. Eventually things simmered down, but the A.E.C. looked on me from first to last with antagonism. As soon as they sent an inspector—who inspected nothing, except in the most casual manner—fault was found and I had to appeal to the Board, who at once sent *their* inspector, who reported favourably! It was the most absurd game, and one felt one was dealing with thwarted children instead of a responsible body of men.

Meanwhile, I put myself in communication with the

Ministry of Labour. Ever since the inception of the scheme, the making of poultry appliances had been one of the subjects taught, as it was one from which I had had the most satisfactory results. With the sub-division of the training I was not permitted by the Board of Agriculture to allow a man to specialize in this, even if he possessed a heaven-born gift in that direction and showed no taste whatever for the land, as carpentry came under the jurisdiction of the M. of D. The *allowances* came from the common pot !

Of the various Government departments with which I have come into contact, I have found the Ministry of Labour the most prompt, practical and considerate, and the least hidebound. I had to draw up a scheme for the Divisional Director, who obtained for it the approval of the Ministry. My great hope had been eventually to establish a business on co-operative lines, so that the most badly wounded cases might automatically pass from their training into employment, where their disabilities would not handicap them in the same way as in the open market. Before co-operation is appreciated, or even its advantages understood, much propaganda work will have to be done. The men are suspicious of it, a bird in the hand, they consider, being worth a great many possible ones in the bush.

I had practically agreed with the Ministry of Labour either to employ, or provide employment for the men after their training, and my first batch of men were all satisfactorily placed—a firm in the North wired me during the coal strike to send them four more. The comparatively easy task of placing men trained in the workshops, and the difficulty of finding any employment for men trained on the land, made me concentrate entirely on the former. The weak spot in the Government training scheme is the future of the men when their training is over. There are hundreds of bootmakers who have been trained and not placed—the same is the case in other trades—but the Ministry of Labour were recognizing this and as far as possible diverting the men from blind alley occupations.

The overlapping of public and private endeavour is one of the regrettable things that strikes one daily. Individual jealousies might so well have been wielded into universal harmony, and the men who fought and won the war, but who lost the only thing that makes life possible—their health—might have found sanctuary and occupation to the everlasting benefit of the State.

The weekly Government allowance given to the men while training is, to my mind, very generous, but one feels it is money thrown away if the man is not to be employed afterwards, and it is a pity that something practical on the lines of the German scheme, of which I recently saw a report, cannot be adopted here. The Report was made by a man who has had considerable experience amongst the disabled men, and their workshops, in this country. In Germany unemployment is practically unknown and it is punishable for a disabled man to beg in the streets. The German Government have established training schemes and factories, and the grants, which they give for this purpose, are allocated to the mayors in the respective towns. Able and disabled men work side by side, and the result of this system is that the factories are self-supporting. Apart from this, every employer of labour is compelled to employ one disabled man to every five able-bodied ones in his service. Every tradesman has to reserve some portion of

his counter to display the goods which are turned out
in the factories by the disabled.

To have adopted a similar scheme in this country
would not have exceeded the amount of money which
has been expended on that most pernicious measure—
the Out of Work Dole. There is not a decent-minded
man who does not resent its existence, and who stoutly
avers that its institution has been the cause of half our
post-war troubles. The blame of its inception has
been laid, rightly or wrongly, on the shoulders of one of
our most dangerous Ministers. Whoever did invent it
is cursed from many a home to-day. It is the root of
our unemployment and the main reason why wages have
remained at so high a level. Common-sense will tell
you that if anyone can get a pound a week for *not* working, only a full-fledged idealist will labour for an additional ten shillings.

The existing scheme of training was evolved, without sufficiently careful consideration, as a palliative
thrown to the men who were calling out for the redemp-
tion of some of the Government promises made in 1915.
Every man was to return to his occupation, or his business, which in some manner was to be guarded for him,
and with the passing of the Military Service Acts and
the enrolling of practically every able-bodied man in the
Crown forces, fresh promises, of an even more alluring
nature, were held out. The men, to do them justice, had
not made any stipulations for their future welfare, but
the gaudy prospects that were dangled before their
eyes, naturally made them inclined either to force the
Government to redeem their obligations, or thoroughly
to mistrust a Government which had broken them.

What a queer thing loyalty is ! The Coalition, which, like the poor, is apparently to be always with us, has made an even more complex problem of the word. Politicians have apparently decided that loyalty to their chief is preferable to loyalty to their convictions.

" Kill that fly," a familiar catchword not so very long ago, was hardly more absurd than the " Kill the Kaiser " cry at the last election.

To insist on this point was the stupidest thing Lloyd George ever did. He had the entire confidence of the country without it. The general relief at the war being over was the main feeling at that time. L. G. and Clemenceau had deservedly, or undeservedly, received the full credit of winning it, and were consequently secure in their respective positions, without having recourse to any election cries. The Kaiser's annihilation made good paragraphs for the Yellow Press, but really the public were not thirsting for his head on a salver to the extent that might have been imagined. On the other hand, because the head is still on Wilhelm's shoulders, the non-fulfilment of that promise is constantly raked up by his opponents as proof positive of the Prime Minister possessing an elastic memory.

If I were a Prime Minister I should promise nothing, but I should spend my time in devising means to reduce this strangling taxation and unemployment, and if I succeeded even a little in that direction my tenure of office would be secure. I should reduce Government staffs to a practical minimum, and I should order other people about—not be twisted round other people's fingers. I think I should know that Kharkow was not a general, even though I could not put my finger exactly on its situation on the map. I should bind our colonies to us with bars of steel; I should make the firmest alliance possible with France; I should fight alien labour to the death; I should squash the Jewish invasion by every means in my power, even if it meant having fewer new frocks.

But then I never *shall* be Prime Minister.

I found it difficult to remember incidents accurately that occurred when I was a child, but the important events since the war are even harder to sort and transcribe. The last two years seem to represent at first a period of reckless spending, followed by groaning retrenchments. People are looking for shillings where they scattered pounds; weak whiskies-and-sodas are replacing magnums of champagne, and soon the whisky will be entirely omitted. We have passed through the coal strike period, a barren victory. We are now dealing with the ever-present Irish problem. Voices are raised loudly for and against the Government, but they soon sink to whispers, and one realizes the real apathy that exists among the majority. They are drifting anywhere the tide carries them, stirring themselves only to very temporary anger, as they are called upon at regular intervals to pay their income tax and rates!

Unemployment increases and wild schemes, Utopian in their conception, are breaking the monotony of the daily cry of want. The days of war were better than the days of peace. Yet war was to purify and cleanse, to lighten the world and deliver mankind from bondage to freedom!

Le Touquet—Summer, 1921. Three weeks here, and I am already regretting the misguided sentiment which has kept me away from France so long. One sometimes dreads to revisit places; one is sometimes frightened of recommencing friendships, lest one is disappointed in the result of either. But the love of France had me too firmly in its grip, apparently, and I am not disillusioned.

There is a desolate and decadent atmosphere along the line from Boulogne to Etaples; the débris of the camp is still lying about. At one portion quite a number of the huts are still intact, and have been turned into a holiday home for hundreds of small children, who are revelling among the pine woods. Further along, with the sun's rays full upon it, I can see the cemetery where thousands of our men lie peacefully sleeping in that oasis by the river surrounded by fields of corn.

In the town of Etaples itself the havoc made by the German airmen is being steadily repaired, but except for these signs of destruction the little place is once again pre-war. When I last saw it, the streets were blocked with military traffic, regulated by a military policeman. To-day the only vehicles are market carts and hotel omnibuses. At Paris Plage there is still less sign of war, and the place is crowded. I feel a little like Rip Van Winkle as I watch the crowds on the tennis courts and the golf links, and the years that have intervened since I was here last seem a hundred instead of three! Most of the villas have changed hands, and amongst the new tenants I found Major Langton and Gertie Millar, who has lost little of her charm.

My old villa has been bought by some delightful French people, the de Monti de Reze's. I found him an anti-Jew of the most rabid order. It appears that in France a strong feeling of antipathy is steadily increasing towards the chosen race, and resentment is ripening at the firm grip of Jewry on national affairs. The French nation are gradually realizing that the Jewish pest is a microbe that is multiplying in strength more rapidly than any known bacilli; but there is a grave fear that the significance of their power will only be realized when the disease has spread too far to be curable. Perhaps the *Morning Post needs* to exaggerate to bring this feeling home to Englishmen! It is all very well to pick brains which in many cases are, unfortunately, obviously superior to those of other nationalities; but it is a dangerous experiment to allow Semitic individuals to burrow indiscriminately, until they emerge triumphantly into every important post which should be a Christian heritage.

*

Our relations with France cannot be described at the moment of writing as happy. A summer spent among French neighbours has changed many of my erroneous impressions, and one is regretfully called upon to sympathize where patriotically one yearns to condemn.

I have been sometimes chaffed over my pro-French tendencies, and an instance of Gallic graspingness has invariably been quoted, namely, that we were called upon to pay rent for the trenches that we fought in. Put baldly, like that, it certainly sounds bad, and in a moment of patriotic defence I have raised this fact as an argument in our favour—only to be silenced for ever. The rent so glibly talked about was *compensation* due to the owner of the land, and if we paid the compensation on one part of the line the French paid on the other. And what about the price France was called upon to pay for coal when she was not in a position to refuse to take it ?

If only a great financier would find some means of adjusting our war debts !   Private financial loans generally mean an end to existing friendship ; international indebtedness is bound to be a stumbling block to mutual understanding.

Lloyd George has fallen from his pedestal in France ; he may only be bruised, but if he is to be reinstated on the pinnacle of French esteem and affection, he must definitely prove that he is France's *friend*, and is not merely keeping up a society acquaintance with her.

I am ending these " jotments " at Le Touquet, where I have spent the happiest and the most miserable hours of my life.   The world goes on—the cocottes, the Jews, the *bourgeoisie*, the *noblesse*, are mingling once more in the baccarat rooms.   They have a bond in common— their dead.   The croupier announces the coup—the bank loses or wins—Mlle. Cagnotte alone wins at the finish.

The game is played where the dead have lain, where the wounded have suffered.   As I stake my five louis I turn to look superstitiously over my shoulder, to glance at the heavy curtains, expecting to hear a voice cry out : " Was it worth while ? " and I am ready with my answer : " What is worth while ? "